*All Around the Year*

# ALL AROUND THE YEAR

Holidays and Celebrations
in American Life

JACK SANTINO

UNIVERSITY OF ILLINOIS PRESS
Urbana and Chicago

First paperback edition, 1995

Library of Congress Cataloging-in-Publication Data
Santino, Jack.
All around the year : holidays and celebrations in American life /
Jack Santino.
p.  cm.
Includes bibliographical references and index.
ISBN 0-252-06516-6 (pbk. : alk. paper) / ISBN 978-0-252-06516-3
1. Holidays—United States. 2. Festivals—United States.
3. Seasons—United States—Folklore. 4. United States—Social life
and customs. I. Title.
GT4803.A2S26    1994
394.26973—dc20                                          93-1516
CIP

*Dedicated to the memory of my sister, Joyce Marie Santino*

# Contents

# Acknowledgments

I grew up loving holidays, and for that I have my family to thank. I think of my sisters, Tookie and Joyce, and my parents when I remember my childhood holidays. So, along with my sister Joyce, to whom I have dedicated this book, I would like to thank my mother, Anna J. Kiley Santino; my sister, Anne P. Nykvist (Tookie); my brother-in-law, Russel Nykvist; and my father, the late John F. Santino. The Long family, especially Rufus and Peggy, have always been encouraging and supportive, and I thank them. I also hope that this book will help the next generation enjoy the holidays as much as I have. In my family, the youngest generation includes Kristen Anne and Jonathan Frederick Nykvist, and Ian Alexander, Will Kiley, and Hannah Margaret Santino. I wrote this book with love for them.

My colleagues at the Department of Popular Culture, Bowling Green State University, have been extraordinarily understanding and helpful throughout the writing of this book. Ray B. Browne, formerly chair of the department, and Christopher D. Geist, then assistant chair, have done everything in their power to facilitate my research. The book also reflects many discussions I have had with them, and also with Marilyn Ferris Motz. Michael T. Marsden and John G. Nachbar were always forthcoming with ideas and anxious to help in any way they could. The late Brenda McCallum, formerly head librarian, and Jean Geist, associate librarian of the Popular Culture Library, helped me immeasurably in my research. They generously allowed me access to archival materials, allowed me to work with and photograph holiday-related artifacts such as old greeting cards, and generally made themselves available to help with this project. I would also like to thank Ann Bowers of the Center for Archival Collections at BGSU for allowing me to research the collection of greeting cards in their possession and for aiding me throughout. David Hampshire of the Instructional Media Center at Bowling Green photographed endless illustrations, cards, and other artifacts for me uncomplainingly. I extend my sincerest gratitude to them all.

In 1986, I was awarded a departmental research semester leave in order to work on this manuscript. During this time, I conducted a graduate seminar in ritual, festival, and celebration. The students enrolled in that course contributed ideas and research to this project, and I thank them for their work. They are Karen Binder, Deborah Dawson, Yasue Kuwahara, and Janice Coleman.

Acknowledgment of the specific scholarly inspirations and influences on this study can be found in the source notes at the end of the book. However, here I would like to thank Professor Don Yoder, Department of Folklore and Folklife, University of Pennsylvania, for his early encouragement of my interest in calendrical customs (among other things). I would also like to thank my other professors at Penn, including Dan Ben-Amos, Thomas A. Burns, Tristram P. Coffin, and Kenneth S. Goldstein, both for their own fine work and for the training they gave me. I hope that this book reflects well on them in some way. I would also like to thank Edward D. (Sandy) Ives and his students, who aided me when I conducted research at the Northeast Archives at the University of Maine in Orono.

My work at the Smithsonian Institution's Office of Folklife Programs has also been significant to the development of the ideas contained in this book. My years as a program coordinator for the Festival of American Folklife, and especially the eighteen months during which I coordinated the Living Celebrations series at the Renwick Gallery, contributed to my thinking concerning the nature of celebratory events. My thanks to Ralph Rinzler, formerly assistant secretary and director of the Office of Folklife Programs; Robert H. Byington, formerly deputy director; Peter Seitel, senior folklorist; Jeffrey La-Riche, formerly senior administrator; and Magdalena Gilinsky, who was my assistant coordinator on the Living Celebrations series.

Special recognition and gratitude must go to Wendy Wolf, whose hard work and editorial expertise is reflected on every page of this book.

Throughout all, I relied on the encouragement of my friends. Folklorist Mark Workman's ideas have always influenced my thinking. I'd also like to thank Samuel Brylawski, Recorded Sound Division, Library of Congress; Marsha Maguire, Archive of American Folk Culture, Library of Congress; Gerald E. Parsons, Archive of American Folk Culture, Library of Congress; and Alan C. Gevinson, American Film Institute, Los Angeles. All these people have helped me both personally and professionally. Finally, thanks to my wife Lucy M. Long, folklorist and ethnomusicologist. She has contributed more to this book than I can acknowledge. She conducted field research, took photographs, suggested ideas, and also allowed me time to write and created an atmosphere in which I could write. I have no doubt that I could not have written this book without her.

# Introduction:
# Searching for Holidays

The first October that my wife and I spent in Bowling Green, Ohio, the people at the other end of our block painted some pumpkins a dazzling array of fluorescent colors that glowed in the dark. These were no ordinary jack-o'-lanterns, I thought, and I decided to keep my eye on this household.

I was rewarded. Before Halloween itself arrived, the luminescent pumpkins were joined by a family of Day-Glo orange plaster-of-paris chickens. The winter went by, Memorial Day arrived, and as I passed by my neighbors' house I could not help but notice that a small plastic snowman stood guard in their front yard, clutching an American flag. Paper footprints left a trail from the house two doors down. The next day a small Santa, also holding an American flag, stood at the front door of the home. What was going on?

I learned that a group of my neighbors celebrate and decorate for the holidays in a unique way. A network of friends make elaborate and amusing holiday decorations, usually a small scene of some sort, which they deposit under cover of night on each other's porches, or in each other's yards, for the many holidays of the year. The chickens I mentioned above are central components in these holiday assemblages.

In the years since I first saw the Halloween chickens, I have gotten to know the people involved, some of them professors at the local university. Rex Lowe, a biology professor, explained to me the beginnings of this unique holiday tradition:

> We noticed that over our neighbors' fence they moved a little stone Buddha into their garden. Bill takes great pride in his garden. He has a big compost heap and he spends a lot of time out there. So my wife and I were coming from somewhere and saw at a garage sale these chickens. A hen and three chicks. We stopped, and they were kind of attractive. I decided to buy them to stick in their backyard, to stick out

in their garden, as little ornaments. They stayed there a long time, and we had a good laugh over it. And then the following Christmas we went out on our porch. I don't remember exactly the date but it was just before Christmas, and they had a scene on our back porch with the three little chicks, who all had antlers made out of pipe cleaners—elaborate pipe cleaners and little half-walnut shells glued to their heads. And the chicks were pulling a sleigh with the big chicken in the sleigh, with a bag of toys over his back, a beard, and a long red stocking cap. Just generally a Christmas scene. So once they did that, that sort of started us searching for holidays to pass this whole menagerie back and forth.

And as we did that, it got increasingly elaborate with each holiday, trying to outdo each other, and trying to find *new* holidays that no one else had found before. Strange holidays. For example, not even a holiday, when we got home from Douglas Lake, where I had a summer appointment at the University of Michigan, we pulled into the driveway and there was this big sign pointing toward the attraction in the backyard. It was a display of the Harmonic Convergence. There was the Great Mound effigy [the Great Mound is a nearby site of Indian remains that was used for Harmonic Convergence gatherings] in the backyard, all of the chickens standing around the snowman with lots of glitter, headbands à la the Sixties; the snowman, which I picked up at another garage sale and entered into this whole thing, was holding a sign for parking at the Harmonic Convergence, and the whole business.

The Harmonic Convergence is not a holiday, strictly speaking. Author José Argülles predicted, based on his interpretation of ancient Mayan and Aztec calendars, that August 16, 1987, would begin a twenty-five-year period that would be crucial to the future of the earth. People would need to collectively marshal their spiritual energy to create a "harmonic convergence" that would prevent the earth from literally falling apart. As a result of widespread media coverage, thousands of people gathered together at ancient religious sites or in places of great natural beauty. What ensued were festive events similar in many ways to the "happenings" and "be-ins" of the 1960s. So, while not a recurring calendrical holiday, the Harmonic Convergence was certainly a special celebratory event.

But Bill put up the display not only to mark the Harmonic Convergence but additionally to note the Lowes' return from their summer away. Rex explains that the snowman is often used for what he calls "welcoming celebrations": "If it is somebody's birthday or anniversary, or somebody's been away and is coming back—the snowman was up in May one year, holding flowers, as a welcome back to Bill's wife, Mary. She was in Pennsylvania, and was due to arrive

On Memorial Day weekend, Bowling Green, Ohio, 1986, a snowman greets summer with a flag in hand. Photo by Jack Santino.

back." So rites of passage and family celebrations are also noted, as are all the calendrical holidays. One Easter the chickens were given rabbit ears and cottontails; on Saint Patrick's Day they were dressed in green, looking into a pot of gold at the end of a big cardboard rainbow. "One Columbus Day," says Rex, "the chickens were dressed in Viking outfits, laying claim to being the first Caucasians to set foot in North America, and sort of pushing Christopher Columbus off to the side."

My interest in these activities was rewarded one February when my wife and I heard some thumping on our front porch. We went out to investigate and found a small Styrofoam building, a chicken dressed as Cupid with a bow and arrow and Styrofoam wings, assorted Styrofoam hearts lying on the porch, and several chickens with arrows through their heads. They appeared to be bleeding. Paper money was scattered about. A little calendar inside the Styrofoam building indicated that the date was February 14, 1929, the date of the Saint Valentine's Day Massacre in Chicago. With this scene, we had been initiated into the network.

A snowman decorating a house in May is startling. One cannot help but notice it. How much of this has to do with sarcasm? "A lot," says Rex. "I guess I think that people take holidays too seriously. They don't enjoy them enough. I see people, especially at Christmastime, competing with each other on how elaborately they can decorate their houses, and they just take it entirely too seriously. I like to have a good time with holidays and with those kinds of symbols." So he and his friends invert and subvert the symbols in order to restore playfulness to the holidays. Rex says he knows something is up when he notices his neighbor Bill emerge from his basement covered in Styrofoam dust. What they do may not be to everyone's taste, but it is always clever and generally adds an amusing and colorful note of originality to the neighborhood.

Rex Lowe and his family and friends play with the symbols of the holidays as a way of celebrating. It has been my experience that the more people know about the origins, histories, and meanings of the holidays and their symbols, the more fun the holidays are for them. That is one reason for this book: to increase our knowledge about holidays and celebrations, and thereby to increase the rewards they offer us.

People often ask me how I got interested in the study of holidays. The question surprises me, because holidays seem to me so obviously and compellingly interesting, from historical as well as contemporary perspectives. Each of the customs and symbols found in holidays, and related rituals, festivals, and celebrations, has its own story, its own folklore. Furthermore, although we have a tendency to view these customs as quaint, people celebrate holidays very vigorously today. In that sense, they are very much a part of contemporary life. To investigate holidays fully and correctly, I believe, we need to think of them as dynamic processes of human behavior and look at the ways people create them by regularly recreating traditional symbols and actions.

One reason I have spent so much time looking at holidays is that I have always enjoyed them. I began my scholarly research with a study of Halloween. I remembered vividly my childhood love of the day, and as an adult I saw that, despite the widely held and often-voiced opinions to the contrary, Halloween was not dying out; rather, more people than ever before were out in costume on that special evening. However, I recognized that Halloween was changing: adults participated in large urban parades, while children were being cautioned against trick-or-treating. The holiday reflected recent concerns such as the fear of murderers or candy poisoners, and other threats, real or imagined, of the ever-changing urban neighborhoods and rural landscapes. The same can be said, in one way or another, of the other contemporary celebrations of our calendars and our lives, and so my work expanded to a consideration of all the holidays of the calendar, and other festivals and celebrations as well. This book is the result of that research and of my lifelong love of holidays.

Much of the material in this book comes from my own observations and fieldwork, along with my personal experiences. I was born in Boston, Massachusetts, and lived there for twenty-five years. I spent three years in Philadelphia, at the Graduate Department of Folklore and Folklife at the University of Pennsylvania. I then moved to Washington, D.C., where I worked at the Smithsonian Institution for eight years. Since 1984, I have been a faculty member in the Department of Popular Culture at Bowling Green State University, in Bowling Green, a small town in northwest Ohio, twenty miles south of Toledo and seventy-five miles south of Detroit. As a result, many of the examples in *All Around the Year* were found in the New England, Middle Atlantic, and Midwest areas of the United States.

Many other materials were drawn from the work of other scholars, especially folklorists, ethnomusicologists, and anthropologists, many of whom are my colleagues. The source notes contain full references and suggestions for further reading in specific areas. I also relied on archival resources such as diaries, greeting card scrapbooks, and old, small-town newspapers, along with current newspapers and periodicals. Holidays permeate our culture: their symbols and their influences are found on candy wrappers, magazine covers, and television; on buildings; and in kitchens, churches, and town squares. I collected as much of the ephemera of holidays as I could, and I tried to make some sense of it all.

If they did not continue to be meaningful, holidays would die. However, far from ignoring them, people today are celebrating holidays more than ever, still finding much value and meaning in them. The old holidays, those tied to the seasons of the year, with long histories and well-established symbols, are increasingly popular. The extent to which whole communities now partake publicly in holiday symbols and decorations demonstrates this resurgence of interest. For instance, whereas many people once decorated their homes only for the Christmas season, now it is quite common to see elaborate decorations adorning homes all around the year. Halloween dummies on porches, illuminated plastic ghosts in windows, and devil masks on trees have become common features of the contemporary holiday landscape in October. Along with the wreaths, handmade dummies accompany not only Halloween and the harvest period, but other holidays too. Likewise, plastic eggs and stuffed bunny rabbits hang next to outdoor statues of Jesus at Easter. Heart-shaped wreaths announce February's arrival (sometimes hung next to images of Presidents Washington and Lincoln); construction paper shamrocks are posted on doors and windows in March. In short, people hang decorations throughout the year, changing them according to the months and the holidays.

People also decorate their houses for important days of the life cycle in ways they did not in the past: balloons and paper wedding bells may be hung from the light post in the front yard on the occasion of a marriage in the family; a large, homemade sign in gold and white, also accompanied by balloons, announces a fiftieth wedding anniversary. Even in the elevator of a city apartment building, balloons and a WELCOME HOME sign may greet a newborn baby, as well as telling other residents that this building is special, for it contains a new life. These decorations for births, weddings and anniversaries (and graduations, retirements, significant birthdays, such as the fortieth), along with the year-round decoration of houses for holidays, point to the renewal of old customs and the rise of new ones as ways of marking our passage through life and through the year. They also indicate that the holidays of the calendar, the rituals of the life cycle, and other festivals and celebrations of all kinds are more elaborate and more important than ever. Even the increased commercialization of our holidays (principally Christmas, but others as well), despite frequent crassness, is really an economic indication of the ongoing importance of holidays.

Festivals are periods of communal celebration, often centered around holidays. By "holiday" I mean a socially recognized day or period of days set aside to celebrate an important person or event of the past, such as saints' days, Thanksgiving, Christmas, or Washington's birthday, or to mark a transition of some kind, such as the beginning of the new year or the turning of the season. I am interested primarily in holidays of the oldest sort: those that are ancient in origin and whose customs and traditions can be traced to the Middle Ages or earlier. Some of these are national holidays, such as Christmas, which was established in the first few centuries after the life of Christ but whose precedents are far more ancient, and Thanksgiving, which, although as an official national holiday is little over a century old, is derived in part from British, European, and even Middle Eastern harvest feasts that lead back to the dawn of humanity. Others, like

Easter and Passover, are specifically religious holidays and holy days that are also descendants of very old celebrations of the spring and rebirth.

Many of the holidays discussed in this book are folk holidays: although widely celebrated, they are not officially recognized by the government. We are not given time off from work or school to observe them. These include Saint Valentine's Day, Halloween, and April Fools' Day. Civic and patriotic holidays such as Memorial Day, Labor Day, and especially the Fourth of July also have their meaningful places on the calendar and their own precedents. Some saints' days, like Saint Patrick's Day, have become both ethnic festivals and national celebrations; others, like Saint Joseph's Day, are exclusively emblematic of a particular group, in this case Italian Americans. Times change, and celebrations change with them, but holidays continue. New ones, such as Martin Luther King's birthday, are added to the calendar as older celebrations, such as the Feast of Fools, have disappeared. Rituals of the life cycle (birthdays, anniversaries, and so forth) are personal celebrations, special days celebrated among family and friends. Today these may include newly emergent customs and ceremonies such as those accompanying divorce.

Humans have celebrated holidays or festivals in every country and culture and in every era of history. Many of our major holidays are sponsored by institutions such as the church or the government and have official meanings derived from these sources. For instance, in the church's liturgical calendar, Lent begins on Ash Wednesday and culminates on Easter Sunday. Within Lent we have Holy Week, from Palm Sunday to Easter, which is intensely sacred and more specifically a sequence of events that builds on what has gone before. Within Holy Week, the three days of Maundy Thursday, Good Friday, and Holy Saturday constitute an even more sacred period. The entire season is based on ancient events, following the narrative of those events and ritually recreating them.The closer we get to the holy day of Easter, the more compressed and focused and intense the sequence becomes. It is like a season within a season within a season. Each is contained in the larger cycle.

In communist countries, holidays may be adapted to state ideology, but they are still celebrated. For instance, Fidel Castro has moved Carnival to the summertime in Cuba, so as to dissociate it from the liturgical calendar. (Carnival is usually celebrated prior to Lent; it culminates in Mardi Gras, the day before Ash Wednesday, the first day of the somber Lenten season.) Moreover, along with all these official meanings, people adapt holidays and special occasions to their own experiences and their own special days. One person told me, "In my parents' circle of friends, 'Holy Week' means the third week in March, which contains something like four birthdays and three anniversaries, in addition to the occasional intrusion of either Easter or Passover." Although our holidays are nationally celebrated, they are always personally interpreted.

Festivity in its many forms has assumed an enormous importance in recent years, with many elaborate events completely separate from traditional holidays. The spectacle of the Super Bowl, for instance, is now routinely called an unofficial national holiday. So too are other sporting events such as the World Series and the Olympic Games. The quadrennial U.S. presidential election and subsequent inauguration have much festival in them (witness the Democratic and Republican conventions to nominate the candidates). We celebrate other aspects of our lives with ethnic festivals, for instance Puerto Rican Day in Boston and New York, or Hispanic Day in Washington, D.C. (both in August), or Finnish-American Day in Michigan.

Along with our sense of ethnicity and the need to celebrate our origins, many other aspects of our lives are recognized and celebrated through ritual and festival and holidays. For instance, our religious ties are expressed and reinforced through such holidays and celebrations as Passover, various saints' days, or Tet (the Vietnamese festival of the New Year). Our occupations are ritualized and celebrated with outings, parties, retirement ceremonies, and official, calendrical days of recognition such as Labor Day. Likewise, we have celebrations that reflect the places we come from, the friends we have known, and the families we have grown up with. Some of these are national, some are local, and some are personal. Many holidays are established to honor historical events, such as the birth of a president. In fact, historical components form the basis of holidays such as Thanksgiving, Memorial Day, Presidents' Day, and Veterans' Day (formerly Armistice Day).

In this book we will look at examples of celebrations that range from small events such as parties to larger festivals and national and international spectacles such as the Super Bowl or the Olympics; and also from spontaneous events such as the celebrations following the return of the American hostages in 1980 or a sports victory, to elaborately planned events such as the Macy's Thanksgiving Day parade and formalized ritual events such as a Passover seder. Through this book we will look at all of these and others—their histories, their regional variations, and their contemporary celebration. As often as not

Holidays such as Presidents' Day honor historical heroes such as Lincoln. Courtesy of the Center for Archival Collections, Bowling Green State University.

I will relate my own experiences of the holidays. We will look at local and regional celebrations, religious celebrations, and occupational celebrations, all of which contribute to the multicultural nature of the American holiday cycle.

*All Around the Year*

# 1

## Holidays in America:
## Ritual, Festival, and Celebration

Whatever their focus, holidays are usually rather complex events. The emphasis may be on one particular aspect of our identity, but the celebrations generally incorporate many facets of our lives: family, religion, ethnicity, politics, economics, and so on. Christmas, for instance, is both a national holiday and a Christian holy day. It is a period of family reunions as well as parties with our friends and colleagues. In this way, it is both sacred and secular. Politicians use it as an occasion to woo their constituents by sending greeting cards and making speeches. It is perhaps the single most important economic event of the year: many businesses survive or fail depending on their Christmas sales. Different Christian denominations celebrate it in different ways. Likewise, its customs vary in different regions of the country or among different ethnic groups. In Louisiana, for instance, many Cajun people light bonfires near swamps on Christmas Eve; in Texas, Mexican Americans reenact the search of Joseph and Mary for shelter in processions that often last for several nights, called *las posadas*. Christmas is all of these things and cannot be reduced to or explained by any one of them alone. The same is true of our other holidays.

### The Sense of Seasonal Time

Just as there are regional and ethnic variations in the ways holidays are celebrated, so too are there personal variations, innovations, and creations. Ethnicity, occupation, religious denomination, citizenship— all of these aspects of our being, and others, have their own grids, their own particular cycles, their own ebbs and flows, and their own celebrations. Each person has his or her own cognitive map of the year: special anniversaries, holidays celebrated or ignored, ethnic, religious, and occupational celebrations. A student, for instance, cer-

tainly has a distinct and pronounced year, which begins in late August or early September, includes winter, spring, and summer breaks,
is divided into semesters or quarters, and culminates in exam periods. A student lives in that year and may view Christmas primarily
as a semester break. However, the same student also has a sense of
identity that involves all those other aspects mentioned above, living simultaneously in a religious or liturgical cycle, and in political,
athletic, familial, and other cycles, all of which have important dates
to be celebrated. Writing after Thanksgiving in a university newspaper, a student sums up the scholastic holiday grid this way:

> Christmas is the day people get greedy, New Year's the day people get
> drunk, Saint Valentine's Day is the day people get romantic, Saint
> Patrick's Day is the day people get drunker, and Fourth of July is the
> day people turn into pyromaniacs. Thanksgiving is the day people
> should get stuffed. I did. . . . Now that Thanksgiving is over, let us be
> thankful that it won't be around again until next year. However, we
> still have to survive the Christmas season, and after that we have New
> Year's Day. After that, we have a nice long period of rest until Spring
> Break. Until then, our only concern will be getting to class, but if we
> classify that as a winter sport, then it should be fun. (Dawson 1987)

A somewhat less cynical view of a holiday cycle as seen through a
particular grid based on religion was put forth in 1952 by Clarence
Seidenspinner's *Great Protestant Festivals*. His point is that festivals
and holidays, including secular ones, are noted and celebrated among
Protestant denominations, despite the image of Protestantism as nonritualistic. Many of the events he describes fall on or near other, sometimes related, secular holidays. World Peace Sunday is set on the Sunday nearest Veterans' Day, and the Festival of the Christian Home in
May is Mother's Day broadened and redefined to emphasize the entire family. The author begins this volume with Rally Day, which he
describes as "a warm-hearted homecoming when friends greet one
another again" (Seidenspinner 1952:1). Rally Day falls after Labor Day
but near to it, and it functions in much the same way, initiating the
autumnal cycle after the seasonal summer break. Seidenspinner states
that although Advent is the official beginning of the liturgical year,
Rally Day is the unofficial opener.

An important but emphatically secular contemporary day of note
is April 15, the day income taxes are due to the Internal Revenue Service and we assess our past year's financial business. Invariably, people rush to the post office at the last moment to get their returns in
the mail, and in some of the larger cities, the pubs have begun to have

IRS Day specials and parties. The philosophy is not unlike that of an Irish wake or a New Orleans jazz funeral: celebrate rather than weep, and thus defeat death or, in this case, taxes.

The cycles coexist and sometimes collide. IRS Day usually comes sometime around Easter. So do collegiate athletic championship tournaments, academic semester breaks, and, every four years, presidential primary elections. In April 1984, I thought about, worried about, and finally paid my taxes for the previous year. Taxes are part of a civic (and economic) cycle, and I assumed my role in it like any conscientious citizen. That same week I watched the Georgetown University basketball team's march to win the championship of the National Collegiate Athletic Association. The basketball season is both a scholastic and an athletic cycle, from the pre-season training through the first game of the season through playoff eliminations to the finals. Since I was teaching at Georgetown that semester, I was particularly interested and felt myself to be a part of the community that was swept up in the momentum of the season. Meanwhile, I paid close attention to the Democratic national primary elections, part of the quadrennial political cycle that leads ultimately to the presidential elections. As it happened, I taught on Tuesdays, the day elections are held, so I would leave the Georgetown campus, buzzing with basketball, and return home to watch the primary election results on television. Moreover, as a Roman Catholic, I engaged in the Ash Wednesday–Lent–Easter cycle, while at the same time some friends invited me to a Passover seder. These are components of religious cycles: the forty days of Lent that culminate with Easter, and the eight days of Passover. In 1984, Passover coincided with the final week of Lent. On Palm Sunday, I attended mass with my wife in Philadelphia; on Monday and Tuesday I was invited to Passover seders; I attended Maundy Thursday services with my in-laws at a Presbyterian church outside of Washington, D.C.; I drove to Boston on Good Friday and attended mass with my mother in Boston on Easter Sunday. These holidays are religious, but we use them to affirm family ties and the responsibilities of friendship as well.

We operate simultaneously on different levels. While in church on Palm Sunday, my mind occasionally wandered to thoughts of as-yet-unprepared income taxes, which were due the very next day. It seemed to me a bit sacrilegious to be thinking of income taxes during a beautiful Palm Sunday service, but I could not help it. It was then that I realized how we exist in so many different cycles at the same time. Each of these cycles, each role we play, is almost like a separate language: we might understand more than one, but we speak

Attention is drawn to the fact that both IRS Day and New Year's, each in its own way, signals the beginning of a new cycle. Copied with permission, © 1984 American Greetings Corporation.

in one at a time. When the pub had its IRS Day celebration, there was no sense of its being connected to Easter, even though Easter was but a few days away. The celebration of IRS Day belonged to a different system, a different cycle entirely. Similarly, when the students of

Georgetown celebrated their team's victory with a beer-fueled, spontaneous crowding into the streets, even though Georgetown is a Catholic, Jesuit university and it was Lent, a time of self-sacrifice and somber reflection, not to mention sobriety, the Jesuit fathers allowed and even approved of the outburst. The religious cycle and the athletic cycle were seen as two different tracks, like concentric circles that paralleled but never crossed each other.

In the same way that members of various ethnic groups have their special holidays, new year's days, and saints' days, the academic community—an occupationally defined group—has its own symbolic interpretation of the year. A look at my own department, Popular Culture at Bowling Green State University in Ohio, will help to show the formal and informal celebrations and rites of passage that mark the year.

Sometime early in the fall semester, perhaps on Labor Day weekend, we have an annual picnic. This is usually held in the backyard of the department's chairperson, and is intended as an opportunity for students to meet each other and the faculty. Although the barbecue is always a pleasant affair, the new students are shy and retiring, while faculty members talk amongst themselves and with returning, familiar students. Later, in December, some student will initiate a pizza party at a local restaurant for all faculty and students to mark the completion of the first semester. This is a more raucous affair. After the semester break over the December holidays, spring semester begins without a party.

In about the middle of the spring term, however, comes spring break. While the students go home or make a trip to a student vacation spot, the Popular Culture Association holds its annual meetings. Throughout academia, these meetings of professional associations and societies are in fact occupational festivals that act as rites of intensification for the more senior scholars, and as rites of initiation for graduate students. In them, both work and play are elaborated. The central skills of the occupation are exaggerated, as scholars read one paper after another to rooms full (ideally) of people, nodding either with interest or with drowsiness, much as we lecture and present research in a more leisurely pace through the year. Graduate students make their first professional presentations, gain experience, and perhaps make professional contacts at these meetings.

At the end of the spring semester, our department has a chili cook-off, which often coincides with the first of May. The cook-off marks the end of the term and, for the new students, the completion of the first full year of graduate study. The mood at this party, held in a professor's home, is noticably different than that of the fall picnic. For one thing, the party centers around a competition: humorous prizes are awarded for the best all-around chili, for the hottest, for the most unusual, and so on. Anyone can enter, and for the first time all year, the students are on an equal footing with the professors. Second, the food competition provides the party with a focus and a purpose; and finally, since everyone tastes all the entries, much of the afternoon and evening is taken up with the eating of the chili. Status differentiations which were so painfully obvious at the first party are dissolved at this one. So we see that beginnings and endings are ritually marked during the year, but the nature of each of these events shifts as the roles of the participants change and as they mark different points of the academic calendar.

A sense of seasonal time also affects the way holidays and seasons are often anticipated far in advance of their arrival. Many people feel that the anticipation of a holiday too far in advance of its time is inappropriate. For instance, on July 10, 1987, a Toledo television weatherman began his report by displaying an advertisement from the newspaper and saying to the news anchor, "Just a week ago we were all celebrating the Fourth of July. And today it's ninety degrees. Look what ran in the paper. This ad ran in the paper last week—a going-back-to-school sale. Talk about rushing the season!" This man's sense of violation is similar to the feeling we get when we receive Christmas catalogs in August, or see Christmas decorations displayed in stores in October.

The day the television weatherman complained of the sale, the times for sunrise and sunset the following day were 6:11 A.M. and 9:10 P.M. On another station on the same day, after the weather report, the news anchor commented, "All I see is a day with less than fifteen hours daylight. We're begining the long stretch into December!" Thus on one day, comments were made on two different television stations concerning seasonal time. Ironically, one man rejected the image of returning to school because it was being introduced too early, for commercial purposes, while the other noted the solar phenomenon of shortening days that does signal the inevitable, though not imminent, approach of fall. Later, on August 9 of that summer, the man who had complained of the early advertisement said, "We are rapidly proceeding into mid-August and to Labor Day, [which] means summer's over."

We talk generally of four seasons, but within any one given season, there is flux and change. Moreover, the perception of seasonality varies according to the grids mentioned above. For instance, the well-known mud season in northern New England, which generally corresponds to the beginning of maple-sugaring activities and to town meeting days throughout the region, is fully a fifth season in that area. The holidays not only tell what what time of year it is, they also tell us about the coming and going of seasonal time. People are as concerned with the changing of the seasons as they are with the season they are in at any given moment. We notice it when the days begin to grow perceptibly longer or shorter. We look for early-budding bushes, for birds returning from winter migrations. Perhaps we listen for the geese flying overhead, south in October, north in March. People talk about the weather, not only, as Mark Twain suggested, because they cannot do anything about it, but also because it is ever-changing and therefore always remarkable, always interesting.

These nameless periods of transition are fascinating. For instance, a newspaper columnist offers several suggestions for "what to do during that farewell-to-winter month called March." On the same day in the same paper, another columnist states his (unexplained) opinion that spring begins on February 4 (*Washington Post*, 24 Feb. 1984). We have our own sense of the seasons that does not depend on a rigid adherence to the calendar. For instance, a September 7, 1983, *Washington Post* article suggests that harvest festivals are appropriate up to the Super Bowl in January. An August 18, 1984, *Boston Globe* editorial devotes several paragraphs to the final two weeks of August, a time, it says, that is still summer, but when the humidity is gone and the average mean daily temperatures begin to drop. Although it is still hot, in a matter of only a few months people will be complaining of the cold and remembering August wistfully. Enjoy these days while you can, the newspaper suggests. "Change is here and more is on the way, as the sun moves south and the heat chases it. Hard to realize, in these moments, that in less than four months the afternoons will start getting longer as the cycle begins once again."

Many industries and occupations demand a unique sense of the year and its seasons. At the American International Toy Fair, held in February, decisions are made about the toys that will be marketed during the following autumn, for Christmas. On Valentine's Day in 1984, the *Wall Street Journal* ran a story that began, "Happy Fourth of July, John Hildebrandt." This man, the article explains, is marketing director of an amusement park, where the work for all the summer's activities is in full swing behind the scenes by Valentine's Day. The article is about occupations that are out of sync with the seasons, for which the holidays measure a different rhythm. Former first lady Nancy Reagan's press secretary Sheila Tate is quoted in the article as saying, "We begin [planning for Christmas] in July and August. By that time the Christmas cards have been selected. . . . the first year we were here we set up a Christmas tree in the middle of the August heat in order to help a women's magazine meet its November Christmas issue deadline." A program director for UNICEF (United Nations Children's Fund) reveals that on Valentine's Day her mind is filled with thoughts of pumpkins and goblins and the drive scheduled for the following Halloween. On the plus side, a man who works for the Toro Manufacturing Company in Tomah, Wisconsin, says, "The most depressing months for most people in the northern part of the country are January, February, and March. [But] now, while I'm surrounded by snow and ice, I'm thinking about sunshine and lawns. That's definitely an upper."

Holidays are times of much spending in the United States, and so there is a commercial grid associated with them as well. The motion picture industry recognizes two seasons: Christmas, which begins on Thanksgiving weekend, and summer, a "15 week period between Memorial Day and Labor Day" (*USA Today*, 31 Aug. 1984). These are the times when most people, especially the young, have free time and use it to watch movies. For the same reasons, the comic book industry releases a great many special issues and increases the press runs of its regular titles during the summer and at Christmas. These special commercial seasons have their parallel in the television industry's ratings "sweeps" months, November, February, and May, when the viewing audience is at its greatest. A calendar of retail business activity for the year shows February and July as the two months of lowest trade, October and November, the months leading to Christmas, as high, with December by far the busiest and most profitable. Business drops off quite a bit in January, is at its lowest in February, builds again until May, slacks until July, when everyone is outside vacationing rather than in the stores buying. Then the Christmas buying cycle begins again in August.

### Native American Ceremonies, Rituals, and Festivals

The aboriginal peoples who inhabited this continent prior to and during the European conquest and colonization consisted of many different nations, and these in turn consisted of different tribal groupings. The peoples we call Indians are really a great number of different cultures, some more closely related than others, all with their own languages and traditions. Likewise, their festivals, rituals, and celebrations are legion, and I cannot describe them in anything resembling reasonable detail, but we cannot overlook them, either. The tribes lived in all the various regions of the country, on terrain that ranged from seacoast to eastern woodland and forest, to the Great Plains and the deserts of the Southwest, to the West Coast. If we look at some examples of the many ways American Indians understood and celebrated their society, the yearly round of calendrical ritual, and their lives, then we will understand better their festivals and celebrations. We might also see that there is an intimate relationship between celebrations and society.

Among the Indians of the eastern woodlands, the Iroquoian-speaking group, which included the five Iroquois tribes proper (Mohawk, Oneida, Onondaga, Cayuga, and Seneca) as well as the Huron, Erie, and the Susquehannock, among others, was related by custom as well as language. Along with important rites of passage of the life cycle, such as the spirit quest undertaken by young men, they celebrated many important rituals and festivals that were tied to the natural year. These included the maple ceremony, held when the sap began to run in the trees; the planting ceremony, when seeds were sown; the green corn ceremony, celebrated after the first ripening of corn for eating; the strawberry ceremony, at the time of that berry's ripening; the green bean ceremony; the harvest festival in the fall; and a midwinter ceremony held after the new moon when the Pleiades hung directly overhead.

These ceremonies and rituals indicate the cultural and social concerns of these peoples, that is, successful planting and growing of subsistence foods. The midwinter festival was also a new year celebration, at which time rituals of renewal were held. In the ashes-stirring ceremony, ashes of old fires were used to kindle new ones, a new year's practice that is apparently close to universal. Other Indian rites were also performed at midwinter, such as the renewal of the dreams and the renewal of the cures. These are based on beliefs that sacred cultural knowledge, such as the power of healing, is communicated to people through dreams. These rituals are performed to recognize and thank the spirits for having shared such important knowledge, as well as to renew the cures. Likewise, the seasonal festivals also give thanks that the sap rises, that the strawberry and corn and beans and squash grow (see for instance Tooker 1979:63).

Among Indian groups who live in the Northwest, one of the most important rituals is called the potlatch. This is a highly important festive event, called by a chief at certain key times (often during times of social stress). Central to the potlatch is a ritual giving of gifts, often quite elaborately done. According to anthropologist Stanley Walens, "at one Kwakiutl potlatch, the chief not only fed several hundred guests during the two-week-long ceremony but distributed to them 18,000 Hudson's Bay blankets, . . . 700 carved silver bracelets, a dozen canoes . . . sewing machines, outboard motors, pots and pans, clothing, hundreds of sacks of flour, sugar, fruit, and other food, [and] a large amount of cash" (Walens 1982:178).

Lavishness of this magnitude is rare, but the potlatch is a ritual of giving, whether on a large or modest scale, rather than getting. The potlatch is a symbolic redistribution of wealth in which the giver attains "purity through philanthropy," as Walens puts it (1982:179), and each receives according to his status and station. Central to the potlatch is the formal aspect of the ritual: that the wealth be given away in the appropriate, prescribed manner. Since the Great Spirits created the world as a gift to people, the giving of gifts is said to put one in harmony with nature and so echoes a divine act.

Important tribal myths and dances are enacted during potlatches. Families use the ceremonial occasion to recount their history and lineage. The potlatch is described by anthropologists such as Walens as nothing less than the symbolic recreation of the universe itself and the acts of its gods in human society, in such a way as to strengthen ties of mutual interdependence, to create bonds necessary to the functioning of the group, and to reaffirm the status and authority of the chiefs.

## Ritual, Festival, and Symbol

Rituals, both formal and informal, sacred and secular, play a major role in holiday celebrations. While some writers assign the term *ritual* to any repeated action (for instance, brushing one's teeth at the same time every day), throughout this book I prefer to use the term in its more specific sense, to refer to repeated and recurrent symbolic enactments, customs, and ceremonies that are often carried out with reference to the sacred, or at least to some overarching institution or principle: the state, the government, the alma mater, and so forth (see for example Turner 1967). Having said that, I interpret this broadly enough to include events that are not specifically religious in nature. For instance, the family feast at Thanksgiving, while not always marked by religious observance, is in its own way a historically and politically sacred event that celebrates the domestic values of family and also refers to the beginnings of this country.

Many of our holidays are rites of season. Christmas is a winter celebration, Easter celebrates the spring, and Independence Day is inextricably tied in with summer. These days become associated with the seasons in which they occur, and seasonal symbolism is part of their particular appeal. Snowmen and winter scenes are a part of our Christmas iconography, despite the fact that there would have been no snow in Bethlehem, and even the Victorian associations given to Christmas by the works of Charles Dickens do not explain it, since snow is relatively rare in England. Rather, Christmas operates as a midwinter festival as much as, if not more than, a religious one, and so snow and other symbols of the season are regularly associated with it, even in such sunny places as Florida and California. Our more modern occasions for festivity, such as the annual Super Bowl football game played in January, are also rooted in the seasonal progression of the year. Thus the Super Bowl can be said to be an annual festival, with an athletic contest at its ritualistic center.

The stages of the life cycle are marked by rituals such as christenings, circumcisions, first communions, confirmations, bar mitzvahs, weddings, and funerals. These rituals, and secular ones such as graduations, coming-out parties, retirement parties, and more recently, divorce parties, not only mark our transitions from one stage of life to another; they are the means of accomplishing them. A wedding, for instance, is the way we make the transition from being single to being married. Rituals change things: they make us married, give us a name (a social identity), or ceremonially take us from being a student to being an adult, or from being a member of the work force to no longer being a worker. At festivals such as Mardi Gras, New Year's, and Halloween, people gather in crowds and engage in normally forbidden behavior such as semi-nudity, open homosexuality, and open drinking and drug-taking. The festival is a time of license, when the rules of society are suspended or flouted. While rituals, as we have seen, support the social order, festivals subvert it (Abrahams 1987). Many of the other family celebrations are commemorations of these rites of passage: anniversaries recall weddings; decoration day homecomings recall deaths; birthdays, births; name days, christenings.

Although less obviously so, calendrical holidays are also rites of passage, in this case, seasonal passage. New Year's Eve is the most clear-cut example: it is a ritual celebration of the moment of transition from one year to the next (Van Gennep 1960). Christmas is also associated with the end of the year and the beginning of a new one; historically, it is related to the winter solstice (December 21), the day of most darkness, after which the days begin to lengthen. Other holidays are related, some more directly than others, to the solstices of summer and winter (longest and shortest days) and the equinoxes of autumn and spring (days of equal daylight and darkness). The cus-

toms and symbolism are often derived from these sources and need
to be understood in terms of them. However, these ancient symbols
have acquired new and various meanings. We should not confuse the
contemporary uses and meanings with ancient ones; they are not necessarily the same.

Different ethnic groups have their own calendrical holidays. Chinese New Year usually occurs in February, and many Italian Americans celebrate March 19 as Saint Joseph's Day. Oftentimes these smaller religious, ethnic, or regional celebrations grow into national
celebrations. In America, for instance, Saint Patrick's Day is not the
quiet day of churchgoing and devotion that it is in Ireland. Instead,
it is a major celebration of Irish-American ethnicity, a parade of roots.
And it has even transcended that to become a great American celebration open to us all. In some summer resorts, such as Ocean City,
Maryland, some of the bars celebrate Saint Patrick's Day on Labor
Day weekend, so that summer residents can celebrate themselves and
their temporary summer community, and perhaps the end of summer itself, before they all go home for the season. Although everyone in the tavern sports fake Irish derbies, and the bands play popular Irish tunes, the point of this celebration is not ethnic pride but
rather the dissolution of the summer community. They use Saint
Patrick's Day symbolism—the "wearin' of the green"—probably because a regular Saint Patrick's Day celebration is the kind of celebration they need. This also points to the fact that, although we have a
national holiday that is said to be the close of summer, Labor Day
has no specific rituals, customs, or symbols that make it particularly
appropriate for marking the end of summer for the beach crowd. So
instead, the people in Maryland borrowed traditions from another
time of the year, traditions that involve drinking and celebrating in
large groups. As in the case of the divorce ceremonies referred to
above, we create new rituals, celebrations and holidays as we need
them in our changing world.

These "borrowed holidays" are common to temporary summer
communities. A Boy Scout camp counseler from New Mexico told me
that he regularly celebrated the year's holidays with the boys through
the summer; Christmas on July 25, New Year's on August 1. A Friday was chosen as Hanukkah, and other calendrical days were celebrated as well. One year, he even staged a kind of nativity play based
on the Mexican tradition of *posadas* he had witnessed in New Mexico, borrowing some domesticated llamas to be used as camels. I have
found similar phenomena in other summer communities such as Cedar Point, Michigan, and Put-In-Bay, Ohio. These celebrations are

more than occasions for friends to celebrate together holidays that they could not share otherwise. The summer is made to contain the entire year, so their relationships are felt to be complete.

We all have an idea in our minds as to what properly constitutes any one particular holiday; the appropriate images seem self-evident. A shamrock can only represent Saint Patrick's Day, of course; a red heart, Valentine's Day. Firecrackers? The Fourth of July. However, in many parts of the United States, including rural Pennsylvania and Ohio, and also Hawaii, firecrackers are set off at New Year's. Moreover, as the people in these places will tell you, they are set off for different purposes. In Hawaii, the custom involves the traditional beliefs of the native Hawaiians, who say that the fireworks scare off demons. In Ohio, they are used as noisemakers, often instead of a gun, since "shooting in the New Year" is the tradition. The fact is that holidays are made up of many different components, and although we associate certain customs with certain holidays exclusively, these vary from place to place and from time to time. We may feel that trick-or-treating belongs exclusively to Halloween, but the tradition of dressing in costume and going from home to home in search of food and drink is found at Christmas in Newfoundland, among the Norwegians in Minnesota, where it is known as *Julebukking* or Christmas mumming (Moore 1986), and among Hungarian Americans in Toledo, who conduct an annual Christmas procession that begins as a door-to-door revel through the neighborhood and culminates in a dramatic presentation of the Nativity and the Adoration of the Christ Child by the Magi in church. In Shakespeare's time, children roamed from home to home, reciting little rhymes, for which they received a penny or some other reward, on Valentine's Day, while today English children do this for the Fifth of November, Guy Fawkes Day. Virtually any custom or symbolic element that today we associate with particular holidays can be found at other times of the year, either in ethnic and regional variations or at some other time and place.

A holiday can have many such components. A partial, and by no means exhaustive, list would include certain foods and beverages (as well as the act of feasting), music, noise (as distinct from music—firecrackers, for instance, or the popping of the cork on a champagne bottle), costuming, masking, parading, dancing, playing games and watching them, decorating, and performing religious rituals specific to the holidays, such as going to midnight mass at Christmas or to temple at Yom Kippur.

Different holidays focus on different components—Thanksgiving has the meal as its center, for instance—and any one holiday may not have all the components. Each of these components is symbolic; that is, each has meaning greater than itself. A turkey dinner on Thanksgiving is more than just another dinner; we do not eat it simply because we are hungry. A rendition of a heart with an arrow through it is a valentine, which has meaning only in the context of the holiday and has personal meanings to those people who exchange it.

Anthropologist Victor Turner has said that symbols, which include actions, words, and objects, are the minimal building blocks of ritual, and to understand ritual we must first understand symbols (Turner 1967). Some of the properties of symbols were brought home dramatically to me once in the early 1980s. I was giving a lecture on symbols and folklore to a general audience in Washington, D.C. As part of my presentation I held up a long, narrow piece of yellow crepe paper and asked the audience to identify it. At first, no one could. They needed a little bit of coaxing. "It's a piece of paper." "But what color is it? What shape? What does it look like?" Then somebody got it: "It's a yellow ribbon."

When the American hostages were held captive in Iran in 1979 and 1980, people in this country took to the custom of displaying yellow ribbons on their doors, on gates, around trees, in sympathy for the hostages and their families, and to display anger and impatience with the situation. The yellow ribbons were intended for the whole world to see, from the American politicians to the Ayatollah Khomeini, from one's neighbors to the relatives of the captured Americans. In Washington, the yellow ribbon phenomenon grew to the point where small businesses and large government buildings (including the Library of Congress) had them prominently attached to their doors and displayed in their windows. When the hostages returned, there was a motorcade parade through the streets, and those of us who worked nearby were allowed time off to go out and see them. As the buses rolled by, yellow ribbons were everywhere. People threw them like confetti; they hung from every lamppost and street sign along the way. In the crowd, as I waved to the returning heroes, I recognized a certain value in these pieces of paper and ribbon that had become so heavily symbolic, so I took one with me. This was the piece of paper I showed to my audience at the lecture.

The yellow ribbon had become the central symbol of America's hopes and fears and frustrations during the hostage situation. Why the yellow ribbon? In large measure it was because of the popularity of a song entitled "Tie a Yellow Ribbon 'Round the Ole Oak Tree," which told the story of a man returning home from prison. The man had arranged with his lover that she could leave a sign if she was still interested in him after "three long years." The sign, of course, is a yellow ribbon tied around a tree, and when the man returns home he finds the entire tree covered with yellow ribbons. People also associated the idea with the title of a popular film of the 1940s, *She Wore a Yellow Ribbon*, which starred John Wayne. The title aside, however, the plot of this movie did not resemble the hostage situation in any way. Nevertheless, people somehow had a feeling that the yellow ribbons were a traditional sign for waiting for someone to return from a far distance. In fact, wearing ribbons, or leaves and branches of a tree, is quite traditional in Anglo-American folklore, as illustrated in the old folksong "All Around My Hat":

> All around my hat, I will wear a green willow,
> And all around my hat, for a twelvemonth and a day,
> And if anyone should ask me the reason why I'm wearing it,
> It's all for my true love who's far, far away.

When the authors of "Tie a Yellow Ribbon" were asked about the ideas of the song, they said that they used the color yellow because it scanned better within the verse and melody. Originally, they had planned to use white. Yellow is in fact a curious choice, since it is often associated with cowardice. In any case, these many strands of folk and popular tradition all fell into place during the hostage crisis. The idea of wearing something, a flower, branches, or a ribbon (traditionally green); the movie title which probably influenced the writers of the popular song, and the custom of displaying holiday-related symbolic objects on the facades of our houses all came together to produce the yellow ribbon phenomenon that helped Americans get through a period of self-doubt and humiliation. Moreover, the people invented this symbol themselves, out of various bits and pieces of popular culture. Based on tradition but new to the situation, the yellow ribbon carried the authority of tradition with it. Although essentially a new usage, the yellow ribbon seemed as if it had been with us forever (see Parsons 1981, 1991; Santino 1992).

So there I was, in front of a hall full of people a couple of years later, a piece of darkening yellow crepe paper dangling in my hand. At the time of the parade, with the flood of intense emotions that accompanied the return of the American hostages, the yellow ribbons had taken on an almost sacred aura, like the flag or a religious icon. I had been afraid that people might view my taking one as a kind of sacrilege. Certainly, if I had removed one from a street signpost before the return of the hostages, people would have considered it some kind of violation. A couple of years later, in the lecture room, I held a piece of darkening paper, but one that once had many associations, some specific (the hostages), some less so (nationalism, defiance, pride). It had been the focus for our anguish, the expression of our patriotism and our confusion over the new realities of international politics. It had been a statement of our solidarity. It had been all these things and others, more than we can articulate. Stripped of its context, it has no monetary value, and in fact, seems highly disposable. This does not matter. It was not intended to last. To examine this piece of paper solely through its formal elements is to miss its essential value. Since that time, variations have developed, such as the wearing of red ribbons in commemoration of Black children who were being slain mysteriously in Atlanta in the early 1980s and in commemoration of AIDS victims in the 1990s. In 1990, when Saddam Hussein held hundreds of Americans in Iraq against their will, the yellow ribbons were again seen adorning homes and office buildings.

This is the nature of symbols: they have meaning only in social contexts. Also, it is what I think ultimately separates us from the other species of life on this planet. All living things are born, mature, mate, and die. However, only humans see these as discrete stages and have developed elaborate rituals to mark and guide us through them: rites of baptism, christenings, brisses, bar mitzvahs, weddings, funerals, and holidays to mark passage through the seasonal changes of the year. Like the spontaneous yellow ribbons at the time of the hostage crisis, or the calendrically regular holiday decorations, these deeply cultural forms surround moments of life crisis and temporal passage and give us a sense of control over events that are uncontrollable. The yellow ribbons and the holiday decorations come and go. But that does not mean that they are not important, indeed centrally important, to our lives. Celebration, symbol, ritual, festival, holiday, folk custom—all too often these are viewed as fun, pleasant, perhaps even beautiful upon occasion, but also as frivolous, never as primary to life. I suggest that in fact they have to do with those parts of life, both biological and social, that are of the *most* importance to us, with birth and death, with life and growth. We should not be fooled by the comic and joyous nature of so many of these, or by their ephemerality, or by the fact that, outside of their proper context, the customs and festive objects may appear silly and worthless. Where we find elaborated symbol and ritual we find issues and events that are of central importance to human beings.

## The Syntax of Holidays

If we look at the holidays side by side, in the sequence in which we celebrate them, the symbols of each can be read in light of the pre-

As the months progress, the wreaths change. This wreath has (top) a bunny, (middle) a heart, and (bottom) a baby chick, combining the symbols of two holidays of the spring quadrant, Valentine's Day and Easter. Photo by Jack Santino, Bowling Green, Ohio, 1984.

ceding and following holidays, and this helps unlock some of their meanings. For instance, between Christmas and Easter, each of the more traditional holidays says something about the approaching spring, and each holiday is more overtly about the coming spring than the one before it. Groundhog Day says that spring is really coming, sooner or later (maybe in six weeks, maybe less); Valentine's Day celebrates love and warmth in late winter; and Saint Patrick's Day celebrates the full green of spring with drinking and public festivity in a way that is reminiscent of ancient fertility rituals. Finally, the symbols of Easter and Passover are overtly related to the rebirth and renewal of spring: lambs, rabbits, eggs, even the dying and resurrected God suggests the miraculous return of the verdancy of spring. The fact is that the world is always turning, always moving from winter solstice to spring equinox to summer solstice to autumnal equinox, back to winter solstice. The holidays of the year mark this ongoing change. This is part of their ancient message, making us aware of how one season turns to another. In this way, the holidays provide us with a symbolic syntax of the year, a kind of running commentary on this process.

An illustration from *The Village Voice*, February, 1985, which beautifully depicts the relationship of the holidays of the spring. The Valentine heart bursts open like an egg, as a hatchling finds its way to the sun. Walter Gurbo, artist. © 1992.

In order to understand our holidays today, we need to find out about their origins and the ways in which they have developed over the centuries. There are a few basic principles that recur for almost every holiday. They almost always have their beginnings in ancient festivals, both religious and agrarian, that predate the coming of Christianity by centuries. Roman festivals especially have been important to our holidays of midwinter and spring. Another important point is that, although festivals and celebrations occur around the times of the solstices and equinoxes, the actual dates of the celebrations do not correspond exactly to these solar events, due to a variety of historical factors. A major influence on our various holidays today is the development and adaptation of the calendar that is in use today in the Western hemisphere and is rapidly being accepted throughout the world.

The word *solstice* comes from the Latin word *sol*, for sun. The solstice of the sun occurs twice during the year, when the sun appears at the northernmost or southernmost point of the earth's ellipse. The winter solstice occurs around December 21; the summer solstice six months later, around June 21. These days are often called midwinter or midsummer, and today we in America consider them the first day of winter (December 21) and the first day of summer (June 21). The winter solstice is the "shortest" day of the year in that it has the least amount of daylight. The summer solstice is the longest. Likewise, the equinoxes are the two days of the year when the amount of daylight

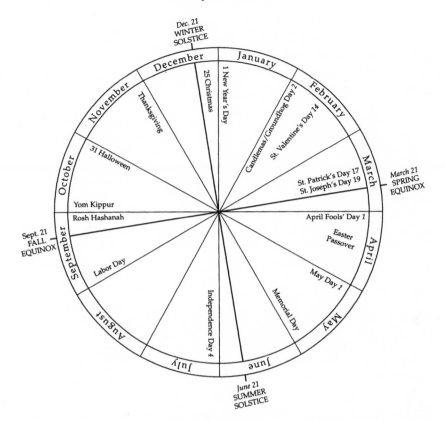

and darkness are just about equal: March 21 (vernal, or spring equinox) and September 21 (autumnal, or fall equinox). These four dates divide the year into four equal quarters.

Long before even the time of Julius Caesar, the Roman calendar was divided into only ten, not twelve, months. It is from this ancient system that we get the names September, October, November, and December. Once, these were the seventh, eighth, ninth, and tenth months of the year. Unfortunately, this calendar inaccurately calculated the length of time it took for the earth to travel around the sun, and as a result, it lost time over the years. By the time of Julius Caesar's reign, the calendar—although by then using twelve months—was wildly out of phase with the seasons. Winter fell during months that were thought of as spring months, and so forth. Caesar took it upon himself to reform the calendar and make it consistent with the natural year. This he did, and, after a modification centuries later by Pope Gregory XIII, we still use the basic Julian calendar. Gregory's calendar used the birth of Christ as the starting point to count the years, and since this system has been generally adopted, we record the date of Julius Caesar's introduction of the new calendar as 46 B.C.

The names of our months are Roman. January is named for Janus, a Roman divinity who could see into both the past and the future; he is depicted as having two faces: one views the past; the other, the future. The name February is derived from the Latin word *februare,* "to purify," in reference to the festival of purification known as the Lupercalia, which was held in early spring. March is for the war god Mars, April from a Latin word which meant "to open," reflecting a time when the new year began in the spring. May is named for the Earth mother goddess Maia; June is named for the goddess Juno. July and August are named for Julius and Augustus Caesar.

On the other hand, the English names of the days of the week are Germanic. Sunday is of course named for the sun, and Monday for the moon, but Tuesday is named for a Norse war god named Tyr. Wednesday is for Woden (Odin), chief god of the Norse pantheon; Thursday for Thor, god of thunder; Friday for Frig, wife of Woden. Saturday breaks the pattern since it is named for the Roman Saturn. In countries that speak the Romance languages, the days of the week are named for Latin gods. The north European gods in many cases correspond, day-by-day, to the Roman deities: in French, for instance, *lundi* is Monday, from the Latin root *luna* for the moon; Tuesday is *mardi,* for the Roman god of war, Mars; Wednesday is *mercredi,* for Mercury, who was associated with Woden by ancient Romans interested in Teutonic myth; Thursday is *jeudi,* for Jove, or Jupiter, the Roman thunderer. Thus were the gods of northern Europe identified with the gods of the south (see Colson 1926:110; Strutynski 1975:364; and Zerubavel 1985).

January 1 marked the end of the Saturnalia festival which began at the time of the solstice. In Caesar's scheme, the year began after this important period of festivities. Our situation today is very much the same. New Year's Day marks the end of the Christmas festivities for most of us and is at the same time a beginning, the first day of the new year. This is how and why we have our New Year's Day when we have it, and shows that New Year's is related to the winter solstice by virtue of being the end of an ancient festival that was held at the time of the solstice. Likewise, many of our other holidays through the year are based in some way on old festivals of other cultures that started the new year. Even Halloween in late October is descended from an ancient Celtic new year festival that was held on the eve of November 1. Other peoples have marked the year as beginning in the spring, around the time of the equinox, and many of our holidays are vestiges of old springtime festivals of the new year, of rebirth and renewal, as we shall see.

The Gregorian calendar was introduced by Pope Gregory XIII in 1582, and it was officially proclaimed on October 4; the next day became October 15. The Julian calendar had added months and shifted dates; now the Gregorian calendar changed the date by weeks. As a result, and also because no calendar perfectly measures the time of the earth's orbit around the sun, holidays no longer fall on exactly the solstices and equinoxes that they once presumably celebrated. When the new calendars were introduced, some people accepted the shifts in days that came with them, but other people went right on practicing the old ways according to the old, familiar dates. The Russian Orthodox Church still keeps to the Julian calendar. Christmas is celebrated on December 25, but this falls on January 7 on the Gregorian calendar. The Christmas festivities begin only after a long night of fasting and worship, followed by a long morning's Christmas service, according to Russian Orthodox tradition. After services, those of the Orthodox faith in Alaska go "starring," an old Russian custom that has become an Alaskan custom. It is a form of Christmas caroling in which people carry a twirling star that represents the star of Bethlehem from home to home and from village to village.

Some countries did not accept the Gregorian calendar until the twentieth century: Russia in 1918, when it was introduced by Lenin; Greece in 1924; Turkey in 1927. As the world's communications systems become increasingly sophisticated and we are in ever more frequent and direct contact with other cultures, we see countries with their own traditional calendars beginning to use the Gregorian, or Western calendar, oftentimes alongside their traditional calendars, much as Jews have done for centuries. This kind of calendrical shift has sometimes given rise to two or more festivals or holidays arising out of a single original source. This is true of Groundhog Day, Valentine's Day, and Mardi Gras as well. All three of these have their source in the Roman Lupercalia, and in European carnivals of spring.

Although the solstices and equinoxes are not as obviously or directly important to us today as they have been in other places in the past, many of our holidays fall near these four points in the year. Our New Year's Day is ultimately, if indirectly, related to the winter solstice through the Saturnalia. Other peoples have preferred to set the first of the year in the spring, closer to the turn of the seasons and the return of animal and vegetable life, while yet others have set it at the beginning, rather than the end, of winter. Given the range of possibilities, it is not too surprising to find not only that our holidays can be traced to ancient festivals, but also that these festivals were oftentimes celebrations of the new year.

## Solstice Parties

Today, parties that celebrate the solstices and equinoxes hearken back to a largely imagined past in which so-called pagans celebrated these solar events, rather than more culturally specific ones tied to their own history or belief system. For instance, some friends of mine held a "paganing" instead of a christening for their newborn baby. The same couple sometimes has solstice parties in place of Christmas parties. Although this tendency might be viewed by some as antireligious and blasphemous, people do not do it in a mean-spirited way. Instead, they feel that they are returning to the pre-Christian origins that underlie many of today's religious festivals. Obviously, a "paganing"— just a party, really—is held with a sense of humor. My friends feel they are cutting through centuries of historical, cultural, and religious baggage and going back to the pre-Christian roots of the rituals and celebrations.

Such parties are examples of what Hobsbawm has termed "invented traditions" (Hobsbawm and Ranger 1983). These solstice parties really tell us more about our society today than about the root nature of the symbolism. In fact they are modern reinterpretations of our festivals and holidays for a pluralistic society. Solstice parties and the like are ecumenical rather than secular, although they accomodate secularism. They allow people to celebrate together despite differing beliefs. Additionally, solstice celebrations are increasing among atheists and other people who specifically do not want to engage in Christian ritual or tradition. Thus, the Christmas tree becomes the solstice tree, and the major celebration happens prior to December 25.

Historically, however, perhaps because holidays actually celebrate so many aspects of our lives at once—the social, the economic, the spiritual—festivals have not always fallen precisely on the solar turning points of the year. Many people do not like the contemporary movement toward making every national holiday fall on Monday, but most are loose about such things as solstices. A festival that takes place during the summer satisfies the summer holiday urge; typically, summer holidays and festivals are held anywhere from June to August; winter festivals from November to February, and spring festivals from March to May. True harvest festivals (such as strawberry festivals, cherry festivals in Michigan, tomato festivals in Ohio, state and county fairs that award prizes to the biggest and best produce and livestock) occur throughout the summer, since various crops come in at various times. Many so-called solstice celebrations such as Christmas, Hanukkah, or Saint John's Eve are not celebrated on the solstice, but rather, near it. Even that statement is imperfect, since the actual date of the longest or shortest days in any given place may be a few days away from the date the sun "crossed' the equator, due to the refraction of the sunlight through the earth's atmosphere. In this way, dates such as December 25 and June 24 (Saint John's Day) correspond closely to the actual solstices, but the match is not exact. Perhaps this range in the timing of seasonal festivals is the best indicator we have of our sense of season. The map it provides is appropriately overlapping; there are no sharply defined demarcations from season to season. Rather, there is gradual change, and our holidays reflect this.

The turning of the seasons (and the chores this brings) along with the journeys of the sun, moon, and stars, while they may have been the primary inspirations of many of our feasts, festivals, and celebrations, are in themselves not enough to explain them. One can only speculate about some prehistoric time and place where festivals of the solstices were that and only that, pure and simple. In any recorded history, no matter how ancient, festivals are dressed in religion, politics, commerce, and society. That is, festivals, as they are understood by their celebrants, are culturally specific: they honor deities, commemorate significant historical events, and solidify social ties. In *All Around the Year* we will look at holidays horizontally and vertically; that is, through time (vertically) and across space (horizontally). We will examine the past of the holidays we celebrate today, their histories and pre-histories, and we will look at the many ways they are celebrated in today's world. We will also examine the many ways people invent traditions and use traditions creatively in their lives.

# 2

## Homemade Holidays:
## Making Symbols, Making Meaning

The holidays and the seasons touch us daily, in tiny ways we do not even notice. A sales receipt from a bookstore reads, "April is the foolest month—spring returns and tax returns." A parody of T. S. Eliot's famous line, "April is the cruelest month," evoking a customary holiday, the seasonal flow, and the civic cycle, all on a small sales receipt that we normally would toss out without reading. How many other mundane, everyday aspects of our lives take on a seasonal holiday glow? Everyday household objects, especially those in the kitchen, are often seasonally related. In modern homes, the kitchen is the equivalent of the hearth. Its ovens and stoves provide warmth in the winter and food the year round. Of course, the kitchen is also largely the domain of women, upon whom it generally falls to maintain holiday traditions. Holiday mugs and plates, pot holders and dish towels, dust covers and rugs embroidered with holiday symbols, or even simply of different colors appropriate to different times of the year, are used accordingly. In these cases, the seasons stretch. Perhaps there are only two long seasons for some things, summer and winter.

People take part in holidays in an almost infinite number of ways. Holidays require *actions:* giving gifts, traveling, sending cards, making foods, decorating. All of these are to a greater or lesser degree creative. We each choose just how much of ourselves to invest in the effort: how much money, how much personal creativity. Some people decorate their houses elaborately each holiday, marking the seasons and the ongoing year. Others make homemade gifts. For many, it is the preparing of special holiday foods that is the source of the most satisfaction.

The anthropologist Mary Douglas has said that a meal is a poem that is created within certain rules and that expresses much about the family as a group (1975). In this regard, the woman is the poet who cooks the meals. The woman also generally buys the clothes and sees to the spiritual care of the family. Often, men are allowed to be careless in their religious obligations, to arrive at church late and to leave early. Piety is seen as a feminine virtue, and for men, femininity is no virtue at all. Wives and mothers are charged with getting the men and children out of bed and into church on Sundays, and they are the keepers of the faith during the week. Barbara Myerhoff has called this "domestic religion" (1978:37), and the making of the holiday crafts is a part of this. A woman pays attention to the ongoing processes of life: birth, feeding, growing, nurturing, sheltering. She also pays attention to the symbolic overlays on life that enrich it and give it meaning. By making the holidays apparent on everything from pot holders to Easter egg trees, she engages in the creation of the holidays themselves, since they need to be recreated every year. Decorating for the holidays adds an extra dimension to the quality of her family's life, which they may take for granted.

The Johnson family of northwest Ohio is an excellent example of a family group who decorate elaborately, indoors and outdoors, for all the holidays through the year. Mrs. Louise Johnson, fifty-nine at the time of this interview, is the primary artist in the family. She explains her involvement as such:

> I have decorated like this for at least twenty years. Before that I worked in a factory, but I quit when my mother died. I like doing the crafts. I like holidays—Halloween, Easter, Christmas are my favorites. It keeps you young, doing it. I started doing a little at a time. Now I do too much! I do Saint Patrick's and everything. I learned by myself, not from *McCalls* [magazine] or anything, just by tinkering around. I'd see things at bazaars. If I see something I like, I go ahead and make it. Sometimes I make things in between time and wait for the holidays to put it out.
>
> Holidays keep you young. I used to make egg trees and I thought, 'I ought to make a witches' tree.' Some of the stuff is bought, but I made the ghosts and witches myself. I made that outdoor witch. That scarecrow, my brother Stanley and my husband made the scarecrow and the ghost. They like to do it every year. My husband Wayne feels like I do it and he's glad for me. It gets me in the mood for the holidays. . . .
>
> Down the street they buy four different size of pumpkins, one for each in the family, then each one puts his own features on them and he cuts it out. Then he takes poles and puts Christmas lights in there—twinkling lights—and then at night he's got the corn stalks next to it. And he does this every year, and it's pretty. It's a big letdown when everything is down and it looks so *bare*—and there's a lot of cleaning, too!

After Halloween, she says,

I'll be taking this stuff out and I'll have my pumpkins and turkeys and stuff. I'll take the ghosts off and the witches off. You can leave some stuff up like the pumpkins. I've got some pilgrims I made out of clay pots, then I'll have a basket with some fruit and little pumpkins. There won't be too much of that. For Christmas there'll be a lot. We have Christmas decorations up 'til January sixth (my mother's birthday) and Three Kings' Day. You celebrate up 'til Three Kings' Day and then it's over. That's the Polish tradition.

I start in the first part of November. I clean the woodwork and the drapes and all. I start decorating the first part of December. I used to make a Valentine tree and put hearts on it, but I don't do that anymore. I don't like to do a tree every time because it gets to be the same idea. The only time I do trees are for Easter and Halloween.

Dressing the house with seasonal items for the holidays is an old idea. In an excellent little book called *4000 Years of Christmas*, Earl W. Count writes, "We do not have to go back far in time to see the peasants of Europe setting up and decorating trees on almost every important holiday. The Maypole itself was a tree, and it even bore the same ornaments which were used on the Christmas tree; but garnished trees stood also on Shrovetide, Palm Sunday, Easter, Ascension Day, Harvest Home, Saint Martin's, Saint Nicholas's, New Year's, and even others" (1953:86). Newspaper accounts of Halloween parties from the turn of the century mention that evergreens were used as decorations, and today they still are: a twenty-one-year-old man has told me that he once hung an evergreen tree with a lot of little tiny pumpkins.

Today, Easter egg trees are common too, and Mrs. Johnson, for one, makes a Halloween witches "tree" as well. She recognizes that the ephemeral but cyclical nature of the holidays creates fresh anticipation on a regular basis. New decorations are always necessary, and this eternally recurring sacred time keeps her young, returns her to her youth, in that it reconnects her with her creative resources, her vitality. Also, as she explains, decorating the inside of the home connects neatly to the domestic work cycle.

Although women are often responsible for the in-home holiday crafts, the porch and lawn displays are another matter. Sometimes the man of the family is the active tradition bearer in this regard, sometimes the children, as seen in this statement: "Now that my son is thirteen going on fourteen years old, he's the one who is the guiding force for our holidays. A week before Halloween we'll come home from work and everything will be done, all the decorations. The picture window is decorated. He makes sure that we get the pumpkin on time. We visit my mother's house twice or three times a week and her house is still festive, so he might have absorbed some of the atmosphere from her."

Making holiday craft objects is an outlet for personal creativity, and the holidays provide an unending reason to create. There is always a holiday approaching, always a reason for more work. Also, it is in the nature of holidays to combine the old with the new. Holidays themselves are old things made new annually, so that gifts and ornaments from the past take on special, nostalgic meanings with the passage of time, and new ornaments and decorations are required each year.

Mrs. Linda DeWalt, of Bowling Green, decorates her house extensively, indoors and outdoors, for each holiday, because, she says, it helps her enjoy the holidays, but also because "it is a challenge. You have to come up with something new each time. I actually lie awake at night dreaming up new ideas. . . . And people love it. Strangers who wouldn't otherwise say hello come and ring the bell, or wave from their cars as they drive by. It's almost a performance on my part. I think it adds a lot to the neighborhood if *everybody* decorates, not just me, and it's just a lot of fun." Although Linda has no formal art training, her porch decorations are holiday sculptures, and she recognizes that the holidays provide an ongoing outlet for her creativity that she can share with others.

Usually, one member of a household, a holiday-lover, is responsible for initiating the creative effort, such as this woman from Maine: "I remember very fondly my mother's Thanksgiving invitations to my grandparents. Every year she would think of something different. It was never the same. One year she had a roll of paper, and she wrote the invitation on twenty-five yards or so of paper and they had to unroll the whole twenty-five yards to get all the details. One year she cut things out of a magazine and put it together that way. One year she cut it up into a puzzle and they had to put the puzzle together. I just remember her being so excited about the holidays. They were a real avenue of self-expression for her" (Northeast Archives, University of Maine, Orono).

## The Hungry Hog Society

People invent their own traditions. Sometimes they even invent their own holidays. The Blaho family of Ohio, for instance, has invented an elaborate comic ritual that, although born in the summer, has become a part of their New Year's celebration. They call the tradition, and those who participate in it, the Hungry Hog Society. Jean Blaho, a student in a folklore class I taught, wrote up her description and analysis of the Hog Society as part of her class assignment. She describes the beginnings of the society as follows:

> Eleven years ago, in a small, unheated summer cottage on Catawba Island, in Lake Erie, a tradition was born. I was ten years old at the time, and my brother was thirteen. My mother, father, brother, and I had been going up to the cottage in the summer for a year, so this was our second summer. . . . One bone-chilling evening, when we were all bundled up drinking hot chocolate, we did not have any munchies, and no one wanted to go out to get any. It was then that my mother baked the first of what we would come to call "hog cakes." Hog cake is just ordinary coffee cake, but it hit the spot, and the oven warmed the place up, too. We gobbled it down until there was only one piece left to fight over. My brother, the "growing boy," felt that he should have the last piece and asked if he could have it. My mother said he could have it, but only if he got down on his hands and knees and said, "I am a hog. A hungry hog." He did it, and that marked the beginning of the Hungry Hog Society.

Within a short period of time, the Hungry Hog Society had become associated with New Year's Eve and Day.

> My uncle, who is my mother's brother, and his family have always come over to our house for our annual New Year's celebration. We eat and drink all evening until midnight. At midnight there is a toast. Then we eat a special dinner, which Mom has been fixing. My uncle's family always spends the night at our house and stays for dinner on New Year's Day. The Hungry Hog Society seems to have nestled right in with this New Year's tradition. Pat and Donna and Scotty have come over to our house for New Year's Eve and New Year's Day for as long as I can remember. It seems to follow naturally that the Hog Society would become associated with New Year's.
>
> When the children were younger, we used to beat on pans (after midnight) with spoons, but now we just set off firecrackers. We eat a large quantity of food. After midnight we have a big meal: we have fun foods like fondue, Chinese, tempura, or shish-kebob. For breakfast we have hogcake, egg casserole, and fruit juice. The casserole is made of eggs, cheese, and bread, mainly. It is very filling, and it keeps people until dinner. In the afternoon, we have dinner. We have traditional foods, roast pork and black-eyed peas.

Setting off firecrackers after midnight and eating black-eyed peas on New Year's Day are traditional to New Year's. Along with these customs, however, the Blaho family celebrates special Hog Society traditions as well. During breakfast, someone, usually one of the males, is the "presiding hog," and eating is accompanied by "much grunting" and sometimes singing:

> Give me some hogs who are
> Stout-hearted hogs who will
> Fight for the cake they
> Adore!

The family even has a proverb that sums up the importance of the Hog Society: "As long as we get our stomachs in gear, it is obviously going to be a good year." Jean recounts other Hog Society traditions: "We always kept an eye out for hog memorabilia. Somehow, someone came up with a hog placemat. One year at New Year's, Donna brought iced pig-shaped cookies. Another year she brought a ceramic pig set, consisting of a whole hog family."

Interestingly, this family custom moved from the summer to become chiefly a New Year's event. The image of the hog, and of overeating, makes a natural symbolic fit with the idea of beginning a new year. Seen this way, the celebration of the Hungry Hog Society is what Roger Abrahams calls a festival of increase (1982). One eats heartily at this special time in hopes that one will eat heartily through the entire year. Moreover, the abundance of food stands for the abundance of fellowship this family enjoys with one another. More important than the eating is the fact of eating together. The Hog Society celebrates family ties as well as family security. In her paper, Jean Blaho addresses the relation of the family tradition to the larger New Year's holiday:

When the hog society did begin, it was only natural that it become centered around the time when all the members already had a big celebration. But New Year's makes sense as the chosen holiday for another reason. New Year's, as a holiday, has fewer strong traditions or symbols associated with it than others such as Halloween or Christmas. As George R. Stewart says in *American Ways of Life*, "New Year's in the U. S. lies under the shadow of Christmas and has comparatively little character of its own." For this reason, there is more reason for personalization of this holiday. The Hungry Hog Society moved in and filled a niche. We already had a New Year's celebration with all the members of the Hog Society; eating was already a big deal, with dinner after midnight and a big breakfast in the morning. And, since New Year's does not have any strong symbols of its own, the hog society naturally fit right in.

The Hungry Hog Society is classic in its elements: what it celebrates, the way it is celebrated, and when it is celebrated. Like many of the most succesful "invented" traditions, its symbolism is appropriate to the occasion because it is based on a deeper, more general, society-wide set of symbols, in this case the linking of the new year celebration to a family "pig out." Like the turkey at Thanksgiving, the hog is a symbol of plenty for the Blahos, and it fits perfectly with the needs and intents of this family group.

Another former student, Deborah Dawson, tells how her family eats all the Christmas leftovers on New Year's Eve, so as to begin the new year with an empty refrigerator. They then fill up the refrigerator with food acquired after New Year's Day, so as not to carry last year's food into the new year. It is traditional to New Year's customs to pay all debts and resolve all outstanding accounts (spiritual as well as physical) before the turn of the year; otherwise it is considered bad luck to carry the old into the new year. The Dawsons' cleaning the refrigerator of the foods of Christmas is a concrete way of realizing this idea.

At New Year's, the Dawsons, like the Blahos and thousands of others, explode firecrackers. We find similar customs the world over. In many areas of the United States, including Pennsylvania, North Carolina, and Detroit, people "shoot in" the new year with guns. The mummers who parade in Philadelphia on January 1 call themselves "shooters," probably because they once practiced this custom. In Japan and Hawaii, firecrackers are set off to scare away demons during what is said to be a dangerous time of transition when everyone and everything is vulnerable. Some people beat pots and pans. The Dawsons save some of their fireworks from the Fourth of July. They once had a scale-model Mount Vesuvius (no one remembers why), and they set off their fireworks inside it so it would look like a real volcano erupting. As wear and tear has taken its toll, they have replaced the volcano with a more conventional champagne toast.

The explosion of summer's fireworks at the end of the midwinter festival that is the beginning of the year provides another kind of continuity. Fireworks are traditional to both the Fourth of July (the American midsummer festival) and New Year's. By putting away some of the explosives on Independence Day, we look across the circle of the year to the opposite point. Exploding them on the last night of the year calls us back to the high summertime, reminding us sharply of the ever-turning quality of the year and of the lives we live. In *All Silver and No Brass*, Henry Glassie mentions an old tradition among

Irish mummers, in which they burned their straw hats in a bonfire during a Saint Patrick's Day party. They had worn these straw hats during their Christmas mummings, and so, Glassie says, "The oat straw of the hats brought a memory of the past year's harvest into winter, and the hats carried a reminder of the winter celebration into spring" (1975:100). Something similar to that is going on in the Dawsons' family holiday traditions, in which the link between Christmas and New Year's is made tangible. Likewise, summer and winter, another set of measures (we define these oppositionally; one is not-the-other) are linked in a concrete way, forcing us to think of the one when we are still in the middle of the other.

People infuse meaning in holidays in any number of ways. Mrs. Marion Strickling, for instance, who lives in an apartment complex for elderly people, makes new holiday cards from recycled old ones. She charges a nickel apiece for them and gives the money to charity. In 1985 she made almost four hundred dollars! These homemade Christmas cards have become a year-round and communal activity for the residents of the apartment complex in which Mrs. Strickling lives. Still, it is linked to the seasons and the holidays (the peak selling seasons), and it is also a perfect Christmas activity, for it is done in the Christmas spirit of helping. The profits go to help others, the cooperative stores are rewarded with the women's business, and the creation of the new cards recycles the old and prevents needless waste. The finished products are handsome and affordable. The activity is creative and engrossing, so that it involves people, gives them purpose and satisfaction. Christmas and the other holidays remain vital and fun. She says,

> We have about three sales a year and the rest of the time they just come to my room. Now I've set it up out at the common room, and they just come and take what they want between sales and bring me the money. The big sales are before holidays, of course. In the fall, I have one sale for fall and Halloween and Thanksgiving, then I have another sale for Christmas, then I have another sale for Valentine's Day and Easter. There isn't a week that I don't get cards just dropped in my door and people cannot get out here, they don't drive, and they don't want to pay a dollar and a dollar and a half for a pretty card. They seem to enjoy giving me what they would normally throw away. Plus, when they close an apartment here at somebody's death, oftentimes . . . they bring them to me because I can get more for them by making my cards. It gives me something to do all the time.

Many people make and keep scrapbook albums of the holiday greeting cards they have received through the years. These capture the past cycles of holidays and are a way of retaining the years of our lives, quite literally. And they can be very beautiful. Several cards placed artistically on a page are bright and colorful and create an effect that transcends the relative artistic merit of any individual card. These calendrically based scrapbooks are really a kind of folk art. Each album tells a story of an individual life or of a family in terms of the holidays, the rituals of the life cycle (cards reflecting births, marriages, deaths, birthdays, graduations, and anniversaries are included), and also events of personal significance such as trips, recitals attended or participated in, and so forth. They are, however, made up entirely of cards—greeting cards, perhaps a postcard or two, and maybe an invitation or a program note. No letters or photographs are found in them. They express the past tangibly through physical, material objects associated with the events—the cards that remain of the rituals, festivals, and celebrations after these have passed. Although such books are fairly common (I have examined several from the Great Lakes area), they remain a largely unrecognized phenomenon.

All this—the hogcake, the Fourth of July firecrackers at midwinter, the homemade cards—has to do with making symbols and making meaning. If the holidays that once seduced us as children are less compelling as we get older, or if religion provides less reassurance as life gets increasingly complicated, and if we no longer live in a society in which a single mythic belief system permeates all aspects of our lives, we nevertheless still need artistic and expressive outlets for our creativity and our beliefs and values; we still need what myth and religion and festivals and holidays provide. But today, in a secular society, we have to construct—or reconstruct—our meanings from the ground up. Rather than passively accept the dogmas and creeds and liturgies, people use these as the raw materials from which to build acts and symbols that are meaningful to themselves and to their friends, companions, and neighbors. Referring to holistic societies in which a single belief system prevails, and to societies that are less secularized or pluralistic than ours, Barbara Myerhoff has noted the apparent lack of a fully realized system of ritual that is relevant to contemporary American life. "Where did all that ceremony go?" she asks (1982:126). In other writings, she recommends that people actively create their own rituals to mark the important events and times of transition in their lives.

In fact, I think people have already begun to do this (as Myerhoff herself has attested in her works). For instance, as our society becomes increasingly mobile and neighborhoods become residentially less stable, new forms of ceremony have arisen that mark the special situations associated with frequent moving. Moving parties, like the barn raisings of old, involve a social group of friends, neighbors, and relatives who come together to make the vast task of moving simpler and more pleasant. The larger the number of people, the fewer objects and boxes they have to carry into, or out of, trucks and homes. The grateful host provides food and drink as small but sincere thanks at day's end. Another example is the going-away party. As we relocate more often for reasons of school or work, we have developed a format to mark the dissolution of the ties we develop along the way. Usually, a going-away party will consist of a reasonably small, intimate dinner with one's closest friends, followed by a larger, more raucous party that includes a wider range of acquaintances. And our potluck dinners and parties, which we take for granted, are a form of friendly celebration in which everybody contributes something to the overall effort. The result is a meal, a festive get-together that is greater than the sum of the parts, which everyone enjoys. Potlucks remind me, in their way, of the bonfires in traditional communities where everyone contributes an ember from the hearth to make the large public fire. They also recall Mardi Gras stews and gumbos, to which everyone contributes something , then all eat the hearty results. Potlucks carry this quality into our lives: each contributes, each helps create the event, and all enjoy it.

Just off Interstate 75 in Sydney, Ohio, north of Dayton, there is a cedar tree. Every Christmas for years, nurses from the Dettmer Hospital in nearby Troy have decorated this tree, which stands on state-owned land. At first, they decorated for Christmas, but then they decorated for Valentine's Day and, soon, for all the holidays, with shamrocks and eggs and flags and so on. An electric wire was connected to it, with some difficulty, so as to allow for illuminated candles at Christmas. The tree is visible from the highway, but only from the highway. The nurses had "adopted" the tree, and decorating it was a gift for everyone.

In 1987, an eighteen-year-old boy vandalized the tree. He cut it down and left a hand-painted sign reading "Bah! Humbug!" next to the felled cedar. The townspeople of Sydney were dismayed but undaunted. They took up a collection and raised two hundred dollars to replace the tree. In a "small but special ceremony," as it was called in the newspaper, they replaced the vandalized holiday tree with a green hill spruce. The holiday tree of this small town had become more than a symbol to the community. It was a statement of community spirit, and of holiday greetings as well, to the world at large.

The holidays provide us with a national language—in some cases international—which we can use to communicate with strangers. We can document single households which use their public space to mark the succession of holidays. Putting up holiday decorations, and subsequently taking them down again, marks the movement into and out of a socially-defined period of calendrical time. These decorations embody both historical and contemporary attitudes and beliefs about the seasons and their holidays.

## Holiday Assemblage

In recent years there has been a remarkable growth in the popularity of outdoor house decorations for holidays other than Christmas. Halloween decorations, for instance, are increasingly widespread and elaborate. I am refering to the Halloween dummies, harvest displays, hanging ghosts, paper cutouts, and Indian corn that dot the countryside, suburban lawns, and city porches every October. The making and displaying of Halloween decorations is a contemporary custom that continues ancient folk traditions. The symbols of Halloween are attractive and fun, and they provide food for thought. Also, at this time of year, there are garden materials and harvest items that need to be used so as not to be wasted. As a result, the lamppost in the front yard may be transformed with corn shocks into a scarecrow-like figure. In addition, a giant ghost might sway in front of a house, and sometimes a macabre figure is hung from a tree in the front yard.

We have all seen these elaborate displays: many times they are organically-based figures, pumpkin-headed and straw-legged, stuffed with rags, placed next to cornstalks. These dummies are often part of a larger display that includes paper cutouts of jack-o'-lanterns, ghosts and witches, and seasonal fruits and vegetables such as squash, gourds, and apples. All of these together are seen from the street, framed by the facade of the house. The front of the house becomes the canvas, as it were, of a three-dimensional work of art. Also, displays of fruits, vegetables, and sheaves of wheat might decorate a front porch by themselves. If humanoid figures are present, they often look like scarecrows (which, although agricultural, have more to do with planting and growth than with the harvest). Of course, rarely are the fruits and vegetables or the figures brought *directly* from the fields to the home. The harvest we celebrate is the result of someone else's work, and the symbols refer to a romanticized view of an idealized past.

As a term that would be more useful and more precise than *har-*

A jack-o'-lantern as a full, standing harvest figure. Photo by Lucy M. Long, Boone, North Carolina, 1981.

*vest figure,* I would suggest the term *assemblage,* which refers to a category of art, a genre of sculpture done with found objects, a kind of three-dimensional collage (Santino 1986). The groups of objects that people use to make a public holiday statement are something like a folk version of that, a folk assemblage. Other calendrical holidays too

An old orange ball and a blue plastic hand are pressed into service to make a distinctive Halloween decoration. Photo by Lucy M. Long, Nova Scotia, 1982.

are marked by the display of assemblage: certainly Christmas, as we have seen, but also Easter, with its egg trees and rabbits, and to lesser extents, most of the others. But Halloween is a major time for these homemade creations, and if we look at them closely, we find that there is more to them than meets the eye. They are another example of the ways people use holidays creatively to situate themselves in the larger scheme of things, using familiar symbols with socially accepted meanings to make personally meaningful statements to themselves and to the world.

Think of the assemblage as a whole, which is how it is created and presented to the public, not just as unrelated elements. One man, for

As a jack-o'-lantern rots, its visible decay is part of its aesthetic effect. Photo by Jack Santino, Washington, D.C., 1983.

instance, a farmer, transformed an old orange rubber ball into a Halloween figure by painting a face on the ball and impaling it on a stick which served as a pole. On top of the ball he placed a blue hand on a spring, the kind we see waving from the back windows of cars. He said he did so because he had these things lying around. It was getting toward autumn ("beginning to feel fallish," as he put it), so he painted a face on the ball, and since he had this toy blue hand, "Well," he said, "why not?"

It is this act of combining elements that are varied but limited (one is generally restricted to the symbols of the particular season), bounded but infinite (no two assemblages are the same), that is the outstanding characteristic of these works. They can be as modest as a discarded Clorox bottle used as a head for a figure, or as resonant as culturally oppositional symbols of life and death in single displays. For instance, a jack-o'-lantern, a creature of the otherworld, often associated with death, may be placed in a garden of flowers, a symbol of life. A witch, a figure of evil, may appear with pumpkins and harvest sheaves.

As the jack-o'-lantern rots and sags, its persona changes. With the passing of time, the straw men decay visibly, publicly. Earlier the jack-o'-lanterns and pumpkins and humanoid figures announced the approach of a holiday. Now they testify to its passing. As we move through the festival period, so do they. Comparisons to the Easter egg are instructive. Like the Easter egg, jack-o'-lanterns are ephemeral. Like the Easter egg they are artistic and decorative, and they exist in a transitory context of social holiday and calendrical ritual. To the extent that ritual, festival, celebration, and holiday overlap, these assemblages share a great many characteristics with ritual objects. In fact, they are a kind of ritual object deeply rooted in the temporal context, and must be seen as such. If we displayed these at any other time of the year, they would look out of place. They would be out of time.

Today, holiday decorations are often personalized, sometimes in ways that are not immediately obvious. A few years ago, I was photographing Christmas decorations in Washington, D.C., near where I lived at that time. In the window of one house I noticed what seemed at first glance to be a rather modest decorative statement, a single strand of holiday tinsel draped in a window. I found its apparent simplicity charming, but not overly beautiful. It seemed to be an effort on the part of someone who probably had meager resources to join in the spirit of the season, but the tinsel appeared to be haphazardly strung in the window. As I raised my camera and focused the window in the lens, I realized that the hanging that I thought was random and sloppy was in fact shaped like a hand with the thumb, index finger, and little finger extended. Then I remembered that I was standing within a few blocks of Gallaudet College, the nationally known school for the deaf. As it happens, I know a bit of American Sign Language , and I finally recognized the shape as a rendering of an extremely popular hand sign. It is a combination of the finger signs for the letters I, L, and Y, which when extended simultaneously stand for "I love you." The window display that I had condescendingly thought a poor attempt at holiday decoration was actually a Christmas display with a double layer of meaning. For those passers-by who celebrate Christmas, the tinsel said, in its way, Merry Christmas to you, we in this home join you in your celebration. But for those who were also deaf, this single bit of tinsel said much more. It said, we in this home are deaf, we are of a smaller number of Americans who share our own language and our own traditions as deaf people. If you can read this sign, (deaf or not) you are one of us, and you know the message: we love you.

A Christmas tree high atop the steel frame of a building under construction is a similar phenomenon. The tree says that it is Christmas, and that this great day permeates our society and reaches into every corner of it, even way up to the top of skyscrapers. But then we must stop and think about the fact that someone put the tree so high above us. We are reminded that people work up there; someone builds the buildings that we all take for granted. In this case the Christmas tree demonstrates participation in the general round of social holidays, but it is also an occupational symbol that calls attention to the ways workers in this job are set apart from the rest of us.

Building symbolic statements such as assemblages is parallel to creating rituals out of meaningful symbols. The two concepts meet when people use outdoor house decorations in conjunction with the rites of passage of the life cycle, rather than with calendrical holidays. Increasingly, people decorate their houses to announce to the passing world an event of importance to their family: the birth of a baby, the marriage of a child, the retirement of a father, the fortieth birthday of a member of the family, and so forth. Of all the rites of passage through the life cycle, only the rituals of death have not yet entered the realm of this new form of public statement. In fact, the old custom of placing a wreath on the door to signify the death of a family member (who is being waked inside) is no longer widely practiced. As we have denied death its role in the life of the family in recent years, our calendrical holidays of Memorial Day and Halloween have absorbed some of the active rituals of the recognition of death. However, perhaps in the future we will see a trend toward the return of the home wake, just as we have in recent years seen a return to the practice of home births.

Life-cycle rituals have always depended on the presence of family members and community representatives who act as witnesses to the social change that occurs. The tendency to advertise the events publicly, to make signs and decorate the house, is part of the growing tendency to decorate the house for social holidays, possibly because the days of the old, small-scale neighborhoods and communities are changing. As in the case of the Ohio holiday tree, people who walk by the houses or drive by in their automobiles become witnesses to these personal transitions, even though the people inside are strangers. Communities filled with people who are tied together through kinship and friendship are being replaced in a mobile society by apartment complexes where people often do not know their neighbors very well, if at all, and by neighborhoods with rapid rates of turnover. Perhaps these public statements of private ritual reflect the fact that many of the old ties of mutual dependence and reciprocity are changing. This represents a loss, but also a kind of gain at the same time. The holiday decorations, the assemblages, the birthday balloons, all are statements to an audience that shares the same language and participates in the same social events. Maybe this shows that despite the anonymity of today's world, we are still a closely-knit society—a large one, related through the media, but in touch. After all, these decorations are a kind of communication, and the communication is expressive, artistic, rich in meaning, and traditional in origin.

The most successful holiday creations are those that use the time-honored and meaning-drenched symbols of our culture, such as the Halloween assemblage. Although their antecedents can be traced to a variety of customs the world over, they are actually rather unique creations; neither scarecrows or harvest dummies exactly, they are an urban as well as a rural phenomenon. They are, in fact, something new, derived from tradition, with centuries of meaning behind them, but with a contemporary twist reflecting their own time and place. Again, the most successful "invented" personal traditions are those that plug into already established seasonal celebrations. All of these examples represent attempts to create ritual where there is a need for it, where none exists or where that which does exist is tired and in need of reinterpretation, of re-creation. If this all sounds terribly solemn, remember that above all else, these events are fun. Re-creation and renewal is joyous. Overly serious affairs defeat the purpose. Stepping outside the rules of society once in a while, celebrating in the streets, dying eggs with our children, lighting the menorah and quietly enjoying the lights, these are pleasant activities, the heart of the holidays after all the commercialism and pre-holiday apprehensions and housecleaning and gift buying is done.

Being creative with holidays also means being playful. I know a man who leaves his Christmas porch lights strung all year, and he occasionally lights them for various occasions during the year. His neighbors have actually complained to him about it; they feel it is not right, that it is somehow blasphemous. In certain ways it is. Since Christmas is a religious holiday, to subvert any aspect of it, no matter how playfully, can be taken as an insult to its religious nature. Also, he is parodying his neighbors' own tendencies to decorate elaborately for Christmas, making fun of them by decorating at the wrong

Handmade Festival of Life poster that inverts Memorial Day symbolism. The crossed flags which commemorate past wars are joined by the doves of peace; the honoring of the dead becomes the basis for a festival of life. Photo by David Hampshire, Instructional Media Services, Bowling Green State University.

time of the year. He freely admits this: "I see people competing with each other over who has the most elaborate decorations," he says. "I think that's all wrong. I believe holidays should be fun. Do I bother these people? Good."

One way of making holidays meaningful in contemporary society is to reinterpret the meanings of the symbols associated with the day. For instance, an anti-war Festival of Life was held in Orono, Maine, on Memorial Day 1986. Since Memorial Day is set aside to honor the war dead, this event was conceived as a way of celebrating the efforts of certain organizations to avoid war and celebrate life. The principle themes of Memorial Day were changed, but in a positive and ultimately patriotic way that did not clash with the fundamental symbols of the holiday.

Other organizations use traditional holiday imagery and customs toward very specific goals. A good example of this is the American Dental Association's declaration of Ash Wednesday as No Sugar Day. Since many Catholic children traditionally give up eating candy for Lent, this effort draws attention to the health benefits of not eating sugar. Similarly, the American Heart Association holds its Save a Sweet Heart program during Valentine's week. This is an anti-smoking educational campaign that uses the Valentine symbolism of the heart, and of the "sweetheart," to educate high school students about the health risks involved in smoking. Smokers are asked to pledge to stop smoking for one day—Valentine's Day—and non-smokers are asked to pledge not to start. Those who pledge are given badges that say "I'm Kissable; I Don't Smoke."

The Heart Association also holds a fund-raising ball on the holiday. In 1986, the guest of honor at the ball was a student, Donna Ashlock, of Patterson, California, a heart transplant patient. The Heart Association recognizes the opportunity to use Valentine's Day and its primary symbol of the heart as a means of raising the public's awareness of the organization and the importance of its work. In this way, the Association works within the traditional language of the holiday to extend the basic Valentine's Day imagery beyond sugary confections.

People develop rituals and celebrations unique to themselves and their families (see for example Baker et al. 1982). William and Amy Baldwin, of San Jose, California, for instance, are both big fans of the German composer Richard Wagner (1813–83), whose operas tell stories from the old Germanic myths. Since the early 1970s, the Baldwins have been celebrating their admiration for his music by holding Ring Day.

> On the Saturday closest to Wagner's May 22 birthday, we gather together with friends and play a recording of the entire *Der Ring des Nibelungen* [The Ring of the Nibelungs] cycle (four whole operas!) without stops, from dawn to sunset. This lasts about fourteen and a half hours, which coincidentally corresponds with the number of daylight hours on the day we meet.

To decorate the house, we display Wagner posters, statues, books, props, and the complete vocal scores of the four operas. We dress a mannequin as a castle witch. We videotape comments from the participants throughout the day, and stage selected scenes from each opera. We've done the ride of the Valkyries, Siegmund meeting Sieglinde, Siegfried slaying Fafnir the dragon, Siegfried waking Brunnhilde, and many others. Our costumes and props are whatever we have on hand or can devise in a hurry.

Our favorite scene is one we reenact each year. We build a model Valhalla [the hall of deceased warriors], then incinerate it on the barbecue grill to the closing strains of "Gotterdammerung." It's quite a sight.

Other ritual features of Ring Day include hanging the w flag from the roof. This flag is modeled after the one flying at the Bayreuth Opera House, which Wagner designed especially for staging *The Ring*. We make and hang an opera banner that features Wagner's name, current age (if he had lived) and the names of, and symbols from, each of the four *Ring* operas.

Since this is a birthday party, we serve birthday cakes—four bundt cakes (round like the ring), make flags for each one, naming them after the operas, and load the cakes with the appropriate number of birthday candles. In 1988 he will be 175. During the "Magic Fire" music at the end of *Die Walkure* [The Valkyrie], we light the candles, sing "Happy Birthday" to Wagner, and frantically take pictures. This is our favorite ritual, and we take bets on which cake will catch on fire first.

The day is also educational. Wagner wrote thematically. We name the musical themes as we hear them, so the entire day is punctuated by shouts of "Horn call!" "Redemption-through-Love theme!" "Valhalla theme!" And so on.

After several moments of blessed silence after the close of the last opera, we play back the videotape we made during the day. If we have the stamina for it after that, we might play Anna Russell's piano parody of Wagner and *The Ring*. That concludes the day. Everyone staggers home.

Bill has also designed a Wagner calendar consisting of thirteen months of twenty-eight days each. The year begins May 23 with the month of *Feen*, Wagner's first opera. The months are named after Wagner's thirteen operas in the order he wrote them. This totals 364 days, so an extra day is added every year on May 22. It is the "Day Without a Month," and is, of course, Ring Day. Every four years, another day is added after February 13, the day Wagner died. This is another "Day Without a Month," and is called "Siegfried Idyll."

Needless to say, despite the generally serious tone of the music, we take our celebration very lightheartedly. We hope this description of our own very special homemade holiday gives everyone a chuckle!

Not all ceremonies celebrate community or togetherness. For better or worse, divorce has become a frequent event in modern life.

Since the dissolution of a marriage is certainly as much a rite of passage as a wedding, we might wonder if new ceremonies are springing up to mark this aspect of contemporary life. Not surprisingly, people are developing personal rituals to help get through this often difficult transition. For instance, a friend once told me a story of a couple who invited some of their close friends to their home for a dinner party. Because they were a sociable couple, there was nothing unusual in this. Indeed, the night was quite a success; everyone enjoyed the dinner and the after-dinner drinks and conversation. Toward the end of the evening, the gentleman of the house made an announcement: he and his wife of twenty years had decided to call it quits. He then got up from the table, put on his coat, and left the house.

When the transition is one of parting, rituals provide closure. I first realized this when my father died. I found the funeral and wake surprisingly effective. I was twenty-three, and I had thought that such rituals were nothing but empty ceremony. After my father's death, I found myself saying that if I had not experienced the death rituals, I always would have felt incomplete somehow, as if he hadn't really died, but had merely gone away. Many people feel the same need for ritual or symbolic closure at the end of a marriage, a marriage that was, after all, entered into as a sacred, or at least life-long, commitment. So not only are people marking divorce with ritual; they are frequently using the sacred symbols provided them by their religions to do so.

In *Festivals* magazine, a periodical devoted to "the creativity needed to adapt old traditions and build new ones," a woman writes of the ritual she developed to help her get through the painful ending of a twenty-five-year union. She used the Roman Catholic Liturgy of the Hours and held her ceremony in a chapel. Religious advisers, close friends, and family members came from as far as four hundred miles away to share in the event. She used songs, prayers, psalms, readings, a homily, and chants. She explained the need for the ritual to the participants, and asked each for a sign or gesture of support and affirmation. After each person spoke, she shared a cup of wine as a sign of thanks and fellowship. The service is obviously derived from standard religious ritual, but is at the same time idiosyncratic, derived out of personal need and social fact.

In order to promote the concept of the "faithfully divorced," a minister in Kansas City has declared Good Friday "Ex-Spouses Day." Being faithfully divorced means that ex-spouses forgive each other and try to be helpful to each other. The Reverend Roger Coleman says that

Good Friday is a perfect day for such an event, because forgiveness is at the root of the Christian holy day, and forgiveness underlies his idea of what this observance should be. "If you want to talk about suffering and forgiveness," he says, "you're talking about divorce."

The minister has had badges made with a proud *I'm OK—You're History* emblazoned on them, along with an Ex-Spouses Day logo, and in small letters on the bottom of the badge, *Good Friday* is written. "I'm not saying history in the sense that you're out of my life," he says, "but you influenced it." The ex-spouse is still a major part of the former partner's life, so the idea is to recognize this and go on with life.

Finally, I want to close this chapter with an example of an occupational tradition unique to the stock exchange: Triple Witching Day. On Friday, September 19, 1986, newspapers and television programs carried stories of the Wall Street phenomenon called the triple witching hour, when the stock market undergoes an hour of unusually unpredictable shifts. The term refers not to broomsticks but to a time when "stock index futures and options on individual stocks expire simultaneously." The results of this are mercurial, unpredictable swings in the underlying value of most stocks. These "Triple Witching Days" occur four times a year, on the third Fridays of September, December, March, and June.

I do not know much about the stock market, but I found the name for this financial day extremely interesting, and of course the newspapers did too, prominently headlining the term *witch*. Within the stories, however, they indicated that there was really nothing supernatural about the day at all; rather, it was simply a colorful name for a volatile day. I think there is a lot of belief in calendrical magic to it, however. First, it is always a Friday. Business hours might dictate this, but Friday is traditionally a day of ominous power. Friday the thirteenth, for instance, is a day of bad luck, probably because of the intersection of Friday, an unlucky day, with thirteen, an unlucky number. Some say Friday is cursed, because Christ was crucified on a Friday, but Friday was treated in special ways long before the advent of Christianity. It is the Sabbath in Islam, for instance, and it is possible that, as a sign of a rival religion, Friday was considered evil by Judaism and Christianity. Whatever the case, Fridays have always been considered days of great and dangerous power.

Second, the Triple Witching Day takes place on the *third* Friday of every *third* month of the year. This may be why it is called a triple witch, along with the fact that three major kinds of stocks expire on this day: stock index futures, stock index options, and individual stock options. The number three, like the number thirteen, and like the day Friday, is a number that has tremendous symbolic significance in our society: we think of the Holy Trinity, for instance. So the triple witching day combines the power of the number three (or three times three, since it is on the third Friday of the third months) with the power of Friday as a day. Finally, in addition to all of this, I cannot help but notice that the months in which it occurs are the months that contain the equinoxes and solstices. The third Fridays of these months is, in effect, the Friday closest to the equinox or the solstice, since these solar events take place on or about the twenty-first of September (autumnal equinox), December (winter solstice), March (vernal equinox), and June (summer solstice).

The Triple Witching Day, then, combines several strands of folk belief, including those concerning points of calendrical transition. Like other times of transition, they are considered uncertain and dangerous, especially in occupations and industries that are themselves fraught with uncertainties and uncontrollable variables. For the stock exchange, these days when so much investment can succeed or fail are both extremely important and wildly unpredictable. On March 20, 1986, the Dow-Jones average took its fourth largest drop ever, during the Triple Witching Day, whereas on June 20 it jumped 23.68 points. The Triple Witching Day is a time of marginality, when the stock market can either surge or plummet. It is unpredictable and uncontrollable, and so is surrounded with magical belief by people who are involved in the stock market. It is tied, unconsciously, to the seasonal equinoxes and solstices, and represents yet another deeply rooted set of beliefs that are a part of the calendrical flow that we practice unselfconsciously, so it is quite consistent with traditional belief and custom, yet it is specific to a certain group of people. The rest of us have probably never heard of it.

These have been a few examples of the ways some people have adapted holiday symbols to their own particular situations, or have created new ones. Even the most traditional of customs, however, reflect the personal, familial, and social lives of the people who enact them. In the following chapters we will examine the seasonal cycle of these celebratory events as they occur through the year.

# 3

## Winter into Spring: Celebrating Rebirth and Renewal

> The mistletoe hung
> From the dead oak tree
> A Merry Christmas
> Come to thee
> An acorn fell
> A Young Oak grew
> A Happy New Year
> Spring up for you!
> —from a turn-of-the-century
> greeting card

Spring begins in the dead of winter. December 21, the winter solstice, is the shortest day of the year, and from then the days grow longer. The eight days of Hanukkah and the Christmas–New Year week are festivals of candles and light. Is it any wonder that they come at the darkest time of the year, when daylight is at its ebb? People all over the world celebrate festivals at this time of year, and it appears they always have. In ancient Babylonia, the new year was celebrated at the time of the solstice with a festival called Zagmuk, which lasted twelve days. Likewise, the ancient Persians celebrated the Sacaea, during which time masters and slaves exchanged places. The slave became the head of the household, while all the family did his bidding. Later, the Roman Saturnalia festival, also twelve days long, continued this tradition of inversion at the time of the new year. The slaves chose one of their class to be Lord of the Revels and leader of the household.

During Saturnalia, the Romans decorated with candlelit trees, and exchanged gifts. Obviously, we practice similar traditions to this day during our Christmas–New Year festivities, and more than likely we inherited them from the Romans, through the early Christians, who adopted much of Roman liturgical practice for their own rituals. The Roman Lupercalia, held in February, contributed traditions to the many other winter and spring celebrations found throughout Europe during the Middle Ages and later. The late-winter carnivals of the Mediterranean area and central Europe are enjoyed today as Carnival, Fastnacht, and Mardi Gras, and these in turn were brought to the New World by the European colonizers. The social inversion found in the Saturnalia, when slaves took control of the household, is mirrored in the medieval Feast of Fools, December 28, when peasants dressed as clergy and led a donkey into church in parody of the sacred rites. Social inversion is found too in the central and south European winter carnivals, when revelers, masked and rowdy, ridiculed the clergy and demanded gifts of food and drink from wealthy members of their villages, often after demanding entrance to their homes. Of course, this mockery of everyday rules was limited and ultimately controlled by those in power. After all, the Roman masters *allowed* their slaves to take control. Nevertheless, these festivals, in Rome and later in Europe, provided the opportunity to express hostilities and aggression, and sometimes they resulted in riots (Ladurie 1979). Inversion of this sort is a key aspect of most celebrations and is central to the modern carnivals as well, as when transvestites dress outrageously and parade openly in New Orleans at Mardi Gras masquerades.

Many other aspects of our spring holidays, such as the love and sex motifs of Valentine's Day, the drinking and frivolity of Saint Patrick's Day, and the hint of fertilty symbolism in "the wearing of the green" on that day owe at least part of their existence to these ancient festivals. Out of one tradition, that of the masked carnival of late winter, which anticipated early spring, came many of our contemporary holidays.

Whether they are set at the time of the winter solstice or spring equinox, or according to phases of the moon, the stirring of hibernating animals, the return of migrating birds, or the early signs of reborn plant life, new year celebrations have rebirth as their central motif. Any of these signs will do; different peoples have counted the new year as starting at each of these events. January 1 sometimes seems a wrong point to begin. Sometime in the spring might be more appropriate, or feel more right. It is largely due to the connection of New Year's to the solstice, a turning point in the solar year, that has led to its occupying the premier position of all our holidays.

Although January 1 opens the new year, it also closes the Christmas holiday period. In fact, New Year's is so closely associated with the end of the year and the Christmas season that sometimes it is difficult to think of it as a first day rather than a last day. In Northern Ireland, December 31 is Old Year's Night; January 1, New Year's Day.

Medieval woodcut depicting the Baby Jesus bringing New Year greetings, a forerunner of the contemporary greetings card. Photo by David Hampshire, Instructional Media Services, Bowling Green State University.

In Boston, they call their citywide and city-sponsored New Year's Eve celebration First Night, even though it is held on December 31, the last night of the old year and the first morning of the new year. Such public, citywide New Year's celebrations are increasingly common and popular throughout the country.

After our New Year's celebrations, we may be exhausted and glad the holidays are over. Two weeks of feasting and drinking, not to mention visiting relatives, is quite enough. Holidays are meant to be temporary releases from our daily routines, and if they go on for too long, revelry becomes drudgery. Still, although people complain that they need a vacation to recuperate from the holidays, moods are better, office workings are smoother in the first days of January. People are psychologically refreshed because of the holiday break. Recreation does not mean doing nothing; it means doing something different. In the early days of January, we may feel "festivaled out," but as the days go by, we will need more holidays to continue to refresh us.

## Three King's Day

Many Americans celebrate January 6. For some, including Orthodox Christians, Christmas is celebrated on this day. For others, it is known as "little Christmas," when a final gift of the Christmas season is exchanged. For some it marks the end of the Twelve Days of Christmas and is the Feast of the Epiphany. It is often called Three Kings Day, as Western tradition has it that on this day the three kings, or wise men, reached the crib of the Christ child in Bethlehem. In the Eastern church, the Epiphany celebrates the baptism of Christ in the river Jordan. The Greek Orthodox Church celebrates the blessing of the waters on this day, and in Tarpon Springs, Florida, sponge divers of Greek background join with church officials to perform this ritual for spectators. The gospel is read in both English and Greek, after which a dove is let loose. This dove represents the Holy Ghost, who appeared at Christ's baptism. Then the archbishop tosses a cross into the water, and the divers compete to retrieve it. The successful diver receives a special blessing. After these ceremonies, the evening is spent feasting and dancing. This custom, originally found only in Greece, has spread to other parts of the United States, such as Long Beach, California, where the January weather is mild enough to permit outdoor diving and swimming.

### The Super Bowl: An Unofficial American Holiday?

A few weeks after New Year's Day, many Americans attend a Super Bowl party, usually a day-long event at a friend's house, replete with chips, beer, and a potluck supper. For fans whose team wins, extra measures may be in order. When the Washington Redskins won the Super Bowl in 1982, people in the District of Columbia began to pour out of their homes and into the streets. Within a few minutes of the victory, police had closed off Pennsylvania Avenue to traffic: there were too many people to fit on the sidewalks. The police recognized the need to be tolerant. The crowd was giddy, openly waving bottles of beer and bourbon at the police cars, many people wearing hognose masks in honor of the Redskins' linemen, affectionately known as the hogs. The celebration was spontaneous, but it displayed many of the features we have seen in other festivals, most notably inversion, public intoxication, and masking, in this case focused on a professional sporting event.

The Super Bowl has become largely a media event. The first Super Bowl game was played in 1966; its mass popularity is due almost entirely to television. There seems to be a concerted effort on the part of those involved with it to turn it into a kind of national day of celebration, or at least to create the impression that it has become a kind of folk holiday. In fact, they have not been totally unsuccessful, perhaps because the Super Bowl is a ritualistic contest at the beginning of the year. Like ancient ritual contests associated with the beginning of a new year, the Super Bowl is the result of a long series of elimination games that culminate in a single showdown. The winner is truly a national champion, America's best. However, the reign is for a short time. The competitive cycle begins again in a matter of months, and the team must again fight its way to the top for the privilege of defending its title. So the professional football grid, with its cyclical nature that culminates in the first month of the new year, acts as a metaphor for the year itself. Anthropologists such as Clifford Geertz have said that our rituals, spectacles, and sporting contests such as the Super Bowl are symbolic events that help us make meaning out of life (Geertz 1971). What kinds of meaning do we find in the Super Bowl?

Football has been described as a corporate sport due to the fine specialization of the players' positions. The play-offs and championship game also mirror the competition involved in climbing the corporate ladder, which is for many of us the definition of success. The players are masculinity personified. Their uniforms exaggerate their muscular appearance. As in any corporation, most of the workers are anonymous. We do not know who they are; they simply do their jobs in order to contribute to the overall effort. There are, however, stars and leaders, for instance, quarterback Jim McMahon of the 1986 Super Bowl Champion team the Chicago Bears. McMahon became famous for the headbands he wears when he plays football; sometimes these have political messages written on them, such as POW-MIA (Prisoners of War—Missing in Action, a reference to American soldiers still unaccounted for in Southeast Asia.) McMahon is an aggressive individual, politically conservative, but rebellious when it comes to authority: in short, the ideal of the All-American boy. After scoring a touchdown, he butts heads with his teammates in a show of great masculine prowess. During the regular season he was told to cease this custom because of potential health risk, which he did, but he began butting heads again in the Super Bowl.

Some say football is too violent a sport. Others counter by saying it is actually a game of great skill and strategy. Although football involves all of these things, it is not *about* any one of them. Rather, in football all of these are used in an effort to overpower the opponent, to invade and take his territory (as opposed to baseball, for instance, where the object is to get "home") Appropriately, the Super Bowl trophy is named for one of football's enduring heroes, Green Bay Packers' coach Vince Lombardi. His game plan, as one former player remembers it, was "Attack! Attack! Attack!"

In 1986, a tribute to Lombardi was aired prior to the game itself. In the tribute, Lombardi was shown as a tough man who settled for nothing less than excellence. Sometimes he would motivate his men by threatening them during a game: "You won't have a job here next year if you don't perform better than that!" He was depicted as competitiveness and aggression personified, and these values were presented as crucial to winning and success, particularly in highly prestigious public endeavors. This connection was underscored in an interview with President Ronald Reagan, who spoke fondly of his college days when he too played football, and mentioned that Presidents Kennedy, Nixon, and Ford had also played football. The implication was clear: the values learned in football can carry a man to the highest office in the United States. The fact that the Super Bowl trophy is named for Lombardi honors not only the man but also the values he espoused and exemplified.

The referees in football have absolute authority, but their decisions are always challenged by the players and coaches. The law on the football field is paramount, but those who enforce it are distrusted. There is an attitude toward the authorities manifested in professional football that is similar to that expressed in hugely successful films such as *Rambo:* those who play the game appear to resent the officials, who, the players feel, do not really understand what is going on out there. McMahon, with his headband and his attitude, make the similarity to Sylvester Stallone's movie character that much more striking.

The 1986 Super Bowl game was called "An American Celebration" throughout the telecast, and was referred to on at least two occasions as an "undeclared national holiday." As a media event, nationally viewed but locally celebrated (everyone witnesses the same television show, but people experience it with their own friends, so no two gatherings are the same), the Super Bowl has a twofold relationship to television. First, it depends on television, a national, electronic medium that provides us with nationally shared experiences, for its claim as a national holiday. And second, the Super Bowl, like all professional football, makes money for television. They interact and influence each other as elements in capitalist enterprise. So television is important to the popularity of football as a medium and as an industry (Real 1977).

Sports, whether professional, amateur, or scholastic, have their own seasons, marked by peak events such as play-offs, tournaments, and championship games. The progressive elimination of rival teams and players through the playing season lends sports a ritualistic quality that audiences can hang their identity on. The Olympics are a good example of the ritualistic aspect of sporting contests, and the Super Bowl is such an event on a national level. Universities, high schools, and elementary schools all have an athletic grid. In many small towns, the athletic cycle of the local high school team provides community focus and identity and serves as a seasonal marker.

Massilon, Ohio, is one such town. Known to its residents as Tigertown, Massilon sees football as fundamental to its identity, and the final game of the season is the basis of a townwide celebration that rivals New Year's Eve in New York or Mardi Gras in New Orleans in its intensity. People paint their faces and dress in tiger colors, and parade through the streets, their cars and pickup trucks transformed into impromptu floats.

The major professional sports in America constantly lengthen their playing seasons and are in some danger of losing their identification with specific calendar seasons. In 1988, the National Basketball Association playoffs and championship series ran well into June. The final game between the Los Angeles Lakers and the Detroit Pistons was played on June 21, the first day of summer. One newspaper account sarcastically said this meant that basketball was now officially a summer sport. Baseball's World Series, while still an "October Classic," has been moved to later in the month, thus increasing the chances of chilly night games for the boys of summer.

Nevertheless, sports still mark seasonal change. The beginning of the professional football season in September indicates the arrival of autumn, while the pre-season exhibition games foreshadow its coming. In 1990, when a players' strike was settled on March 21 (the first day of spring), newspapers heralded the coincidence: "Spring Is Here!" shouted the headlines. Baseball's opening day is a major festival in many cities; in Cincinnati, among others, children are given the day off from school. Sports calendars are demarcated by intermittent events such as the National Collegiate Athletic Association Final Four, the Indianapolis 500, the Stanley Cup playoffs, the Triple Crown, and the All-Star game. Many of these have become popular events through media exposure, of course, but nevertheless they now mark seasonal change. These peak events also penetrate worlds generally unaffected by such sports. Many people who do not follow horse racing, and know little about it, watch the Kentucky Derby, especially if they have been invited to a Derby Day party.

The Super Bowl's relationship to American capitalism is basic to its success and to our understanding of it as an event that tells us something about ourselves. With a playing season of only sixteen games, the outcome of each professional football game is crucial (baseball, in contrast, has a playing season of 162 games, so it is rare for the season's outcome to depend on any single game). Because so much hangs on every game, professional football has developed yet another vast commercial enterprise: gambling, both legal and illegal. The media declares "Super Sunday" a national holiday because it is profitable to further the sport, but may be more correct than it realiz-

es when it defines the Super Bowl as essentially American. Money—
television money, players' salaries, fortunes bet—is a factor in all professional sports, but in none so much as professional football, and
never more pronounced than during the Super Bowl. Commercial
television time is more costly then than at any other time of the year.
Money is of course won in victory, but success on the field also translates into increased salaries the following season. The Super Bowl
crystallizes American capitalism.

In the 1986 broadcast, the Super Bowl was identified with other
national causes, and with the concept of America itself, in a number
of ways. A special football video collage was run with rock singer
John Cougar Mellencamp's "Pink Houses," with its refrain "Ain't that
America," as a soundtrack. Mellencamp has himself been associated
with traditional American values through his efforts as an early sup-
porter of the charitable relief effort known as Farm-Aid and in his
numerous references to small-town America in the songs he writes
and records. This video was followed by an interview with President
Ronald Reagan, who said that both teams playing in the Super Bowl,
the New England Patriots and the Chicago Bears, represented traditional American values: the Patriots because they were a come-from-
behind, underdog team; the Bears because they had achieved success
through hard work.

The Super Bowl's rituals, more elaborated and more numerous than
those of a regular season game, heighten the sense of the contest as
something special, and also provide it with a link to games of the past.
For instance, Most Valuable Players from each of the previous Super
Bowl winning teams are called on the field to witness the coin toss.
This link to the past is compelling; I could not help but think that
these men represent the elder heroes of the sport, and as time goes
on, there will come a day when no one is left alive from Super Bowl
I, or II, and so forth. I was also struck by how male-oriented this so-
called American celebration was, from the men witnessing the coin
toss to the song and video collage that was used to end the telecast,
"Forty Hour Week" by the country music band Alabama. This song
pays respect to working Americans, but with the exception of one
very brief shot of a female cashier, all the people depicted in the video were male.

The Super Bowl is a masculine power fantasy set at the top of the
year, a time when we need to "recharge." Male values dominate
throughout. Presumably, the viewers at home and the fans in the
stands relate to the players in some vicarious way. What we see is a
display in which one organization, hierarchically arranged, disposes

of another such organization by overpowering it, using aggressive traits that, if otherwise left unchecked in regular society, would be dangerous. The viewers see "real men" down there on the field, men who know the rules of the game and who test the limits of them, who play within them but are dictated to and frustrated by officials who are ignorant of the realities of the game. The viewer sees traits that lead to success, to Lombardi trophies, to the presidency—in short, to power. Football has been criticized for being too violent, but violence is not the focus. The ultimate value of the game is power. The Super Bowl is about power, who gets it and how to use it, in a way that is relevant to contemporary America. For many, this relevance is found in watching men butt heads. It seems inaccurate to call the Super Bowl an "American celebration," given the virtual exclusion of women as anything other than cheerleaders, and given its huge commercial emphasis. However, it does provide a great many of us with a sense of renewal, and sets forth ideals of masculine leadership at the beginning of the new year.

The Super Bowl is like an annual slaying of the old king and installing of a new king whose reign will bring us, the commoners, some measure of security, some protection against chaos, during the coming year. The timing of the Super Bowl may have something to do with its success: it is close enough to the beginning of the year to give us a feeling of sequence, that the turning of the old year to the new, the replacing of the past with the present, is being acted out, dramatized by the players on the playing field each year battling it out to become the "new king."

We should not stretch this Frazerian analysis too far. After all, people enjoy a good game, and they enjoy a reason to socialize. Perhaps. But we do find that the ancient, traditional holidays continue to change and have meaning in the context of the flow of the year. The Super Bowl is an example of a new, contemporary event that has meaning and importance for us which we might not think about too often but which is there nonetheless.

## Martin Luther King's Birthday

If the Super Bowl is an unofficial holiday that celebrates capitalism, January also has a new official holiday. After several years of resistance on the part of both President Reagan and the Congress, a national holiday on the third Monday of January celebrating the birth of the great civil rights activist Martin Luther King, Jr., was passed into law in 1985. Although some states had already recognized this day as a state holiday, the first national commemoration occured in January 1986.

Unfortunately, the holiday is a controversial one because of the racism that lingers in our society. President Reagan, who was initially against the establishment of this holiday, said his opposition stemmed from the fact that never before has the United States so honored an individual who has not held high public office. Today, all fifty states observe Martin Luther King's birthday. But some states, such as Arizona and New Hampshire, steadfastly refused to recognize the holiday for years. Others tried to compromise it somehow. Virginia, for example, declared the day "Robert E. Lee–Martin Luther King Day," in an attempt to please everybody that of course pleased nobody.

When a holiday commemorates persons known to us in historical time, such as Washington and Lincoln and now King, we turn the events of their lives into something of an "official" narrative that places the individuals among the extraordinary; we retell episodes from their lives that encapsulate the man's special qualities. We are doing this now with Dr. King. In January, we are treated to brief excerpts from his most famous speeches—oratory was King's special gift—and so we hear the great "I have a dream" refrain repeatedly on television and radio. We are reminded that King gave his life to the cause of equal justice and human rights, that he was a martyr, a prophet, a holy man killed before his time. This is all true, of course; Martin Luther King was a great man who suffered greatly for what he did. Now that he is honored by a national commemoration, we find the events of his life and his accomplishments being interpreted and reconstructed so as to conform in a kind of cultural shorthand to our mythic narratives and hero stories. Martin Luther King's holiday in January allows us to watch the way this is done, to see a holiday develop its symbols.

## The February Holidays

Symbolism of spring and rebirth and fertility underlies all of the older holidays in the spring quadrant. One of the first harbingers of spring is Groundhog Day, February 2; and not by accident, February 2 is also Candlemas Day. It is also related to Valentine's Day and to the medieval carnivals that we still celebrate today as Mardi Gras.

We all know the story: on February 2, groundhogs are supposed to emerge from their underground homes after their long winter's sleep. If they see their shadows, the legend has it, they will be frightened back into their homes for six more weeks, and this means there will be six more weeks of winter. But if it is overcast and no sun shines, the groundhog will stay out, and spring is here to stay. This has always seemed to me a curious piece of reverse magic: if the weather is bad, it will soon get good, and if it is good, it will only get worse again.

Few of us admit to taking Groundhog Day seriously, but the day sparks more interest than we realize, especially if we judge by the media. Not a February 2 goes by without a mention of Punxsutawney Phil of Pennsylvania, Buckeye Chuck of Ohio, or some other "official" groundhog. They may be stuffed animals, or real groundhogs forced from their hutches against their will and made to enact some empty ritual for the amusement of a distant, unknown audience. The town fathers even decide in advance what the groundhog's "prognosis" will be, as reported in this news item, headlined "Groundhog's Forecast Due":

> PUNXSUTAWNEY, Pa.-Punxsutawney's groundhog emerges for his 97th wintertime prediction today, this year braving pot shots from college know-it-alls and woodchuck rivals. "Phil," Punxsutawney's latest woodchuck, was to be pulled from his electrically heated burrow on Gobbler's Knob shortly after sunrise to the traditional cheers of tuxedoed members of the Punxsutawney Groundhog Club and hundreds of chilled spectators. "Phil's all ready," said 60-year-old James Means, a local contractor and club president who is said to be the only translator for the groundhog. Folklore dictates that if the groundhog sees his shadow—even through the rain and snow of a miserable dawn—six weeks of cold weather follow. If he doesn't, spring arrives soon. Last year, the groundhog failed to see his shadow through the rain, predicting early spring for only the fifth time. The groundhog's prediction is secretly made several days in advance by the club's 12-member "Inner Circle" of area businessmen. (*The Daily Pennsylvanian* 2 Feb. 1983: 1)

In spite of all of this obvious phoniness, we still pay attention to the groundhog's prediction, as trumped up as it may be. This probably has to do with the fact that Groundhog Day is the first time that we direct our attention in any formal way toward the coming, much-anticipated spring. It works for us because after a long January, winter is getting old. February is a difficult month to get through, even though it is short. Any indication of an early spring is eagerly welcomed, and Groundhog Day is the first tentative look ahead.

Television weather reporters condescendingly tell us that groundhogs do not predict the weather, that this is an old wives' tale, a mere superstition. The whole idea behind Groundhog Day is not as silly as it seems, however. The customs we associate with it were brought to this country by European settlers, principally the Germans who settled in Pennsylvania. The lore that they introduced to this country was not simply that a groundhog may or may not see his shadow on February 2. In the Old World, farmers in Germany and France once looked to the stirring of the bear, the king of the hibernating animals, as a sign of coming spring. Later, when bears were fewer, people watched for other hibernating animals, such as hedgehogs in Ireland, or badgers in Germany. As a German proverb tells it, "the badger peeps out of his hole on Candlemas Day, and, if he finds snow, walks abroad; but if he sees the sun shining he draws back into his hole" (Brewer 1970). In America the humble groundhog has fallen heir to this tradition. Upon him has descended the mantle of the mighty bear, and, by extension, all the creatures who sleep in the earth in the winter. When these creatures become active, it is a sign of the earth itself rumbling back to life. Groundhog Day is not some sort of magical divination; it is rather a custom derived from the return of hibernating animals as one of many natural indications of seasonal change.

Such natural indications are true signs because they are the results, not the causes, of the seasonal changes. The appearance of the animals after their winter sleep does not *cause* the return of spring, but it is a reliable sign of its coming. Groundhog Day is steeped in the rhythms of the earth and its creatures, and, the phoniness of Punxsutawney Phil notwithstanding, its hold on us has not entirely diminished. But if the outward *form* of an old custom is seized upon and inflexibly adhered to, without appreciation for the nature or purpose of that custom, the old ways seem quaint at best. As modern society has become increasingly industrial, the agrarian-based customs become stranger to us, of no apparent relevance. Groundhog Day is an example. The animal's return cannot be rigidly set at any one particular day. It varies from year to year due to several factors. Over time, however, February 2 has become the day we remember this old folk custom. In fact, February 2 is a bit early for groundhogs to appear, and for this reason, the day seems a bit silly to us today. Still, Groundhog Day is an early reminder that spring is indeed on the way. The idea behind the tradition, being attuned to the natural signs of life as winter turns, is sound.

Before the adoption of the Gregorian calendar, Groundhog Day fell later in the month, on the fourteenth, and not surprisingly the additional eleven days led to a split. Some people held out for the old date, and right up to recent times, farmers in Missouri and Arkansas stubbornly kept February 14 as Groundhog Day because it made more sense to them on that day. It was meaningful and useful on the fourteenth, when farmers considered whether to till their soil in preparation for the spring planting. There the tradition was still relevant to real life, as it had been once wherever it was found.

In the Christian calendar, February 2 is Candlemas Day, forty days after Christmas, and February 3 is Saint Blaise's Day, when people go to church to have their throats blessed with two crossed candles. February 1 was one of the four major Celtic festivals, known in past times as Imbolc; today in Ireland it is Saint Bridget's Day, and the Saint Bridget's Day hedgehog looks for its shadow on that day. China and Vietnam celebrate a lunar new year (first full moon after the winter solstice) which often falls at this time. Saint Valentine's Day occurs on February 14, the time of the original celebration of Groundhog Day. Often, when two holidays occur on the same date or around the same time, they may have had a common origin, perhaps the same ancient, pre-Christian festival. The beginning of February may be the first day of the new year for some peoples, a day of religious significance for others, and a day of agricultural import to still others. Or it may be all of these things at once, as were the old carnivals and masquerades in which people often dressed as the Candlemas bear, whose appearance implied the coming of spring. Today we have three different traditions sprung from these medieval celebrations—four, counting Valentine's Day, which is celebrated on the original date of Groundhog Day, and for which masquerading was once important— but the Candlemas bear suggests they were all part of a single multi-faceted celebration. A Scottish rhyme relates the weather tradition directly to Candlemas:

> If Candlemas Day be dry and fair,
> The half o' winter's come and mair;
> If Candlemas Day be wet and foul,
> The half o' winter was gone at youl.

Underlying these many holidays are ultimately the same natural events: the early signs of spring. The original impetus for Groundhog Day was more likely earthly than heavenly: the return of the denizens of the earth and the coming of spring, rather than a lunar or solar phenomenon. As the calendar of Pope Gregory was slowly, grudgingly accepted throughout Europe, the day shifted from the middle of February to the beginning. Candlemas and Saint Blaise were heir to these traditions: by the sixteenth century the Candlemas bear was a regular character in the masquerades of February in France and throughout Europe.

There is another principle at work here. We saw that Christmas was set at the time of the Roman Saturnalia, and other midwinter festivals, because people were already celebrating at that time of the year. In the same way, many other church holy days were set at the time of preexisting festival days of non-Christian peoples. The blessing of the candles on Candlemas Day may well be a Christian adaptation of a torch ceremony held during the February Lupercalia, a major Roman festival, and one in which we find customs we associate today with Candlemas, carnival, Valentine's Day, and Groundhog Day.

The Lupercalia festival was a torchlight parade of purification, and this may be where the church's custom of blessing the candles used in its liturgical services arose. Roman Christians borrowed the practice of using candles in religious services from the Romans, and in A.D. 494 Pope Gelasius I set the day of the Feast of the Purification of the Virgin Mary at the time of the popular Lupercalia.

The Lupercalia was held in honor of the wolf who mothered Romulus and Remus, the mythical twin founders of Rome. The name of the festival is derived from the Latin word for "wolf," *lupus*, while the city of Rome takes its name from one of the brothers, Romulus. In some of the Lupercalia rites, two boys came to the cave where Romulus and Remus had been nursed. These two boys were anointed with the blood of sacrificed goats, and then they would gleefully spend the day running through the streets whipping people lightly with strips of goatskin. These strips of goatskin were called *februa*, from a Latin word meaning "to purify." The month of February, which celebrates the Christian Feast of the Purification, or Candlemas, on the second, actually got its name from this Lupercalia custom. The festival was in large part a fertility rite, held to protect the fields and herds from wolves, and to protect the agricultural and pastoral pursuits of the people. It was also a festival of increase, much like the Greek festivals to Pan, the goat-god. Festival-goers drank openly, and in large quantities, in the streets.

During the centuries it was celebrated, many animals and nature gods were associated with the Lupercalia, such as the wolf who mothered Romulus and Remus, and also Faunus, a bestial divinity, sort of a Romanized version of the Greek god Pan. Eventually, these deities were consolidated into a hairy, lupine god called Lupercus, whom the people asked to protect their herds from wolves. We can begin to see how historically interrelated all these contemporary holidays of February are. For instance, the connection with wolves continues to this day in Europe, where Saint Blaise is said to protect herds from wolves. Also, he is thought to bring an early spring, like the Candlmas bear, or the later American groundhog. At the same time, Blaise is connected to Candlemas. He is a martyr who once saved a boy from choking to death on a fishbone. The candles that are purified on Candlemas Day (February 2) are used to bless peoples' throats on Saint Blaise's Day (February 3), to keep fishbones from getting stuck and to ward off colds. Thus, the ritual use of candles in the pre-Christian Lupercalia was adapted by the church in its own holy day ritual of purification, which is in turn connected to Saint Blaise, who is also heir to the beliefs associated with the Candlemas bear and the hairy beast of the Lupercalia before that. Even the custom of exchanging Valentine love notes can be traced to the Lupercalia. During that festival, boys drew names of girls from a box and would escort the girl whose name they drew to the festival, a custom that has obvious parallels with the schoolroom Valentine boxes of today. In yet another interconnection, when Christmas was celebrated on the sixth of January, Candlemas was held on February 14, the day we celebrate Valentine's Day.

As a child, I used to line up in church on Candlemas Day to have my throat blessed by a priest holding the two candles, joined in a cross, against my neck. This act was supposed to protect me from coughs and colds for the rest of the winter. Looking back on it, it seems a very magical ritual, and yet a very practical one (February is cold season, after all), much as waiting for a groundhog to "predict" the season is both magical and practical.

In 1988, I held a party on February 1, Groundhog Day Eve. In honor of the occasion and in recognition of its history, I asked guests to bring a candle of any kind. My wife and I provided a traditional Louisiana dish of red beans and rice, to suggest New Orleans carnival, which was approaching. One guest brought a stuffed groundhog from a museum. Another guest brought a candle shaped like a bear, the only Candlemas bear at the party, she proudly pointed out. (The invitation to the party read like an essay on the history of the holiday, in which I explained the connection between all these festive events.) All the guests, who were from a variety of occupations and ethnic backgrounds, responded enthusiastically to the idea. Although I mixed symbols a bit freely from a few different holidays, the holidays in question were all related historically, and ultimately the symbols did not clash, the way Halloween symbols would at a Christmas party, for instance. I had one, but only one, Valentine candle: a white candle in a clear glass holder that had red hearts painted on it. The red hearts of the Valentine candle fit well with the carnival-like atmosphere of the other symbols. Too many images related to Valentine's Day would have dominated the party, since the symbolism of Valentine's Day is the strongest of all the special holiday symbols between the first of January and Easter. All the other symbols centered around the groundhog and his quest for the warmth of spring, and the celebration of life and love that accompanies the searching and the eventual finding. Since we all have some of the groundhog, and the bear, in us, Groundhog Day works, and the party has become an annual event.

### Asian New Year

Other special days around this time of year are timed according to the cycles of the moon, often celebrated on the first full moon on or after the winter solstice. Southeast Asian peoples base their calendars on lunar cycles. Both Chinese and Vietnamese people celebrate New Year at the same time, for instance. The Chinese lunar calendar, said to be 2,000 years old, was used until the adoption of the Gregorian calendar in 1912, after the fall of the last emperor of the Qing dynasty (1644–1912). According to legend, the Chinese zodiac of twelve animals who represent each year in succession came about in the sixth century B.C. when Buddha issued an invitation to all the animals in creation to come to him. Only twelve animals responded: the tiger, rabbit, dragon, snake, horse, goat, monkey, rooster, dog, pig, rat, and ox. As a result, Buddha rewarded these particular animals by giving each of them a year that would carry its name and its traits as well.

Chinese New Year celebrations have become popular public celebrations in the United States, and the Vietnamese Tet, now an "ethnic" festival in the United States as many Vietnamese immigrate here, is also being celebrated by non-Vietnamese. Many of us enjoy watching the dragon dance and the lion dance of the Chinese and Vietnamese new year celebrations. These events are full of symbols that are meaningful to the Chinese and the Vietnamese participants in the festivals. Each of these celebrations prominently feature flowers and the wearing of new or special clothes that symbolize new hope and the rebirth of oneself as a new person, symbolism that we might find more familiar from our Easter holiday. Although the customs and symbols of these festivals are culturally specific, similar kinds of symbols are found in new year celebrations and spring celebrations elsewhere.

Other Southeast Asian peoples celebrate the new year a bit later in the spring. The people of Thailand conduct an annual plowing ceremony in May, for instance. In traditional costume, people lead oxen into a field as part of a plowing rite that is used to predict how the year's weather will affect farming, a custom reminiscent of our

Groundhog Day. In Laos and Cambodia (Kampuchea), the New Year is usually celebrated in April. It is said that ancient astrologers set the New Year at the arrival of the Spring Moon, when nature begins to reawaken and spring showers bring greenness to the earth. The New Year marks the time when light, a symbol of happiness, becomes more abundant as the days increase in length. The light of April represents prosperity and brightness for the coming year.

Although Laos and Kampuchea are different in important ways, they share many of the same New Year customs. The last day of the year is filled with preparation for the New Year. People clean their houses so as to drive away any evil spirit or disaster from the past year, a custom that calls to mind spring cleaning, or the proverbial phrase "making a clean sweep." The next day is an interim day, a day of rest during which all work is forbidden. The day after that is the New Year. This period is a religious time as well as a festive one.

Recognizing the growing national participation in Chinese New Year celebrations, some of the large Chinese food manufacturers have capitalized on it in their ad campaigns. "Share a tradition. Create a Chinese New Year feast" they exclaim in newpaper advertisements, "with CHUN KING"; or "Win the DOLE Chinese New Year Sweepstakes," this accompanied by a rather nice painting of a Dragon Dance in San Francisco's Chinatown. Both of these ads ran in various newspapers on February 2, 1986.

Always a pluralistic society, the United States today is enjoying an influx of new citizens from Southeast Asia. American culture can no longer be said to be exclusively western European in heritage or dominated exclusively by white males. Like so many other groups before them, Southeast Asians bring to this country their distinct cultural heritages. Like the Vietnamese, however, Laotians and Cambodians find that what was for them a national holiday suddenly becomes "ethnic" in the United States, with new meanings in their new country. Very often, the celebrations are carried on in large public halls and the public is invited to participate. In this way, Southeast Asians use their holiday traditions to introduce their culture to other Americans. The celebrations include paying respect to the Buddha by sprinkling statues with water and asking for happiness for the coming year. In the United States, some immigrants are converting to Christianity, and many people of the Buddhist faith feel awkward about publicly displaying their Buddhist traditions in a largely non-Buddhist nation. Nevertheless, this custom of pouring water over the head of the Buddha is a deeply ingrained part of the New Year festival, and it has continued in America. People spend the day visiting and feasting. In the streets, people sprinkle each other with water as a sign of purifying each other.

The New Year festivals are both secular and sacred. The Lao celebration begins with the *Song Phra,* the pouring of water on the statue of the Buddha as a sign of respect, and the *Kharava Song,* which pays respect to the holy monks. After these, people tie cotton strings around the wrists of their friends and loved ones for good luck. These are worn until they fall off naturally. After blessings for the children, and the *Kharava Phou Thau* ceremony, which is a show of respect for the elders, people visit at each others' homes, eat special foods, and dance. The Cambodian celebration begins with the *Bach Phaka* or *Robam Choun Por.* This is the "wishing dance," in which the dancers wish prosperity on everyone present. This is followed by the *Chhayam,* or Long Drum Comic Dance, during which dancers sing humorous verses for the coming year. A fashion show of traditional costumes is a major component of the festival, as is the traditional dancing known as the *Ram Vong.*

All of these ceremonies and customs have been brought to the United states, where they are practiced both publicly and privately. Not every aspect of the New Year celebration translates so easily in America, however. In Laos, the end of the ceremonies are marked by the building of small sand shapes on the banks of the Mekong River. When topped with streamers and zodiacal signs, these are still another way of asking for happiness from the gods, but there is nowhere to build these sandcastles in an American city. Cambodians end their New Year period with traditional games and sporting events, including martial arts demonstrations, and dancing all night long.

The Vietnamese New Year is called Tet. After the Chinese conquered Vietnam in 111 B.C., Tet was institutionalized and incorporated other spring festivals. Like so many festivals of both the spring and the new year, Tet is concerned with the renewal of humanity and the regeneration of nature. As at Easter in the United States, the people of Vietnam wear new clothes for the three days of Tet. In a way that parallels the American New Year's resolutions, all bad entanglements of the previous year, including debts and quarrels, are discarded. And the custom of taking a last bath on the last day of the old year recalls water purification rituals the world over.

The preparations for this major holiday of the year begin months in advance of the actual celebration. Fairs are held during the last month of the lunar year, *Thang Chap.* On the twenty-third day of Chap, Tet officially starts with the sending off of the kitchen god, *Ong Tao* or *Tao-quan,* to give a year-end report on the household to the Celestial Court. At midnight, the god of the departing year gives dominion of the world to the god of the new year. An altar is set up by the head of the household to perform a ritual to expedite this transference of heavenly power. Upon completion, firecrackers are exploded to usher in the new year noisily but joyfully (see Abrahams 1987).

The adults are up again early the next morning, the first full day of Tet. They must erect an altar and direct their first thoughts on this special day to their departed ancestors. At the same time, the eldest members of the house take their places in the best chairs of the best rooms of the house and are met there by the children, who present them with their best wishes for the new year. The entire family is present, and the ceremony is very formal. After the youngest bestow their good wishes upon the eldest, the elders in turn give the children small red envelopes containing money for good luck and prosperity in the new year. Red is the color of Tet; it is symbolic of happiness. This ceremonial custom is called *mung tuoi,* or *li xi* in South Vietnam, and it signifies that everyone is a year older. Tet is in part a communal birthday party.

No one cooks during Tet, because the kitchen god is away reporting to the highest god on the year's activities in the household. So all food has been prepared in advance. As in any major festival, food is an important component of the celebration. Special foods for Tet include dried watermelon seeds, fruit preserves called *mut,* and steamed rice cakes called *banh chung.* Beliefs that we find associated with New Year's holidays everywhere concerning the first visitor to the house are also an important part of Tet. A happy visitor means a good year, so when someone comes to call, they are treated with great hospitality and served the special treats of Tet. The second day is often spent visiting friends and relatives; the third, visiting one's teachers.

## Celebrating Tet in Virginia

Vietnamese people in a Virginia suburb of Washington, D.C., celebrate Tet in a high school gymnasium that they transform into a beautiful ceremonial site by decorating it with red scrolls and flowers such as chrysanthemums, which stand for longevity, and narcissus, which represent purity. Although very much a community effort, the celebrations are open to the public, and I attended one in February of 1980. A New Year oration was delivered in Vietnamese. It is an example of the use of a traditional form, the oration, to address contemporary concerns. That these should be included as part of the most important festival and holy day of the year is no surprise, because among other things, our festivals, holy days, rituals, and holidays are precisely about our contemporary lives. Here, in part, is that oration, translated from the Vietnamese by Nguyen Ngoc Bich. It was delivered on New Year's Day, 4859 by the Vietnamese calendar, the Year of the Monkey, corresponding to February 16, 1980.

> We, the children of Lac Viet and refugees in this land, having built the Vietnamese Senior Citizens Association, gather the blood brothers and sisters of the three regions of Vietnam who are now residents of Washington, D.C., and the surrounding areas.
>
> We hereby establish an altar, add our voices in unison, directed at our Homeland, pay our respects to Heaven and Earth, remember the holy name of our Founder King, and call on all our heroes to witness:
>
> We bow down our heads in front of the Altar to our Ancestors
> And respectfully set up these few offerings of tea and fruit
> We set up an incense stick and put in it our piety
> Our hearts in pain as we remember the Old Country
> Our souls . . . dreaming like butterflies
> Our eyes filled with tears as we remember all that is far away
> We pledge to keep our roots and morality in wait of that day
> We pledge to maintain our courage and follow our ancestors
> So as to maintain our millennium-old culture at all cost
> So as to keep our essence as Vietnamese
> We therefore make these immaculate if modest offerings
> And bow to you a thousand times, a hundred times
> Asking that you bless our land and grant it Peace
> Please accept our prayers.

Like most of our American holidays, these holidays were brought here by immigrants over the last two hundred years. America's holidays reflect the country's history of immigration. The Irish gave us many of our Halloween customs; the Germans contributed to Christmas and gave us Groundhog Day. Mardi Gras is a combination of European, Caribbean, and African traditions. New immigrants often use their holidays as a means to help maintain a sense of their unique heritage. After settling in the United States, recent arrivals from other parts of the world may find themselves categorized as minorities. Their cultural traditions are distinct from those of the dominant American society and their celebrations become ethnic holidays, perceived by assimilated Americans as quaint and curious, which means of course that they have been misunderstood. Vietnamese, Lao, and Cambodians, by presenting their traditions to their new neighbors, transform their traditional, private holiday celebrations into rites of public presentation of themselves and their cultural identities.

Pop-out valentines were very popular in the teens and twenties. Courtesy of the Popular Culture Library, Bowling Green State University.

## Valentine's Day

Less than two weeks after Groundhog Day and Candlemas comes a much bigger holiday. It is the first one after the Christmas–New Year festival that has its own set of instantly recognizable symbols: hearts, flowers, and cupids. This full complement of traditional symbols says only one thing: Saint Valentine's Day.

It is interesting how colors, as properties of some of the symbols, become traditionally associated with certain holidays. Red and green are the colors of Christmas, of course, and so is the white of winter snow, as in "I'm dreaming of a white Christmas." Halloween is orange and black. Black probably stands for death, and orange represents the fruits and flowers of the season, such as pumpkins and marigolds. Thanksgiving is yellow and brown, reflecting the late-November landscape. Valentine's Day is red and white, red hearts and red roses on a field of white. Is white for the lingering snows of February? Red and white—roses of spring in the snows of winter.

Some holidays may have a single, ancient point of origin, but over centuries they drift from date to date. As the examples of calendar reform have shown, various social and political events over history cause holidays to be redefined, to take on new meanings. For instance, most Americans did not celebrate the eve of Saint John's Day, June 24, which had been celebrated in Europe as Midsummer, but they transfered some of the traditional midsummer customs, such as burning bonfires, to the eve of the Fourth of July. Similarly, the English Guy Fawkes Day (November 5) absorbed some Halloween customs, and New Year's Day (January 1) is related to the winter solstice by being set at the end of the Roman Saturnalia. The variety of festivals that arise due to this kind of "drift," along with other factors such as the immigration of peoples from different cultures, has caused a clustering effect of festivals and celebrations that tend to occur around the same time. This is especially true in February, with Candlemas, the Feast of Saint Blaise, Groundhog Day, and Valentine's Day. Holidays and festivals that are not related historically also tend to cluster due to seasonal and celestial factors. On February 8, 1986, for instance, three stories ran side by side on a single page in the newspaper. They were "Mardi Gras Nears Climax," "Year of the Tiger Begins Sunday," and "Winter Carnival Opens in Saint Paul." Each of these very different celebrations in its own way marks the transitional February period.

There are many folk beliefs about the middle of February being a time of fertility. In the Middle Ages, it was said that birds chose their mates on February 14, as in Geoffrey Chaucer's *Parliament of Fowls*, wherein he wrote, "For this was Saint Valentine's Day when every fowl cometh there to choose his mate" (ll. 309–10). We still find lovebirds and turtledoves on Valentine cards today, as we playfully choose our mates. The fertility of the birds is yet another sign from nature, at around the same time as the return of hibernating animals, of approaching spring.

Western European and American culture translates sexuality into romantic love, and Cupid, the Roman version of the Greek god Eros, has become the god of love associated with Saint Valentine's Day. Cupid the archer was originally seen as a young man, but we picture him as a baby today. This reduction of Cupid to a baby might be related to a new year's symbolism deeply underlying Valentine's Day. As Eros, he was associated with love, but like Pan and the other gods of sexual vitality, passion, and fertility, he was dangerous, involved in great bedevilment and much sensuality. As the Lupercalia became less overtly sexual in its symbolism, Cupid, with his bow and arrows to smite us mortals with the fire of love, replaced the hairy satyr Lupercus (and the hairy bear of Europe) as the primary deity of the festival. As a baby, Cupid parallels the babies of Christmas and New Year's and is another symbol of rebirth, but he is desexualized and nonthreatening.

In A.D. 469, Pope Gelasius set aside February 14 to honor the martyr Valentine, in the hope of supplanting the Lupercalia. Valentine

A piece of music transcribed as a valentine, ca. 1400.

himself is shrouded in mystery. Some historians think there were different men named Valentine who lived at different times but who have been confused with each other. For that reason, we are not even sure just how many Saints Valentine there actually were. One story has it that Valentine was a popular Christian priest during the reign of the cruel emperor Claudius II. When Claudius tried to recruit young men to fight his wars, many were reluctant to leave their wives and families, so Claudius banned all weddings and nullified all en-

This 1985 card features all of the symbolism of Valentine's Day and its long history. The bears of winter, the valentine box, the masks, the many hearts, the homemade valentines on the table. The tablecloth quilt pattern is known as the wedding pattern. Notice the suggestion of an arrow piercing the heart shape of the male bear's chair. Family Line, Inc. Kathy Orr, artist.

gagements. The good priest Valentine went "underground" and continued to perform weddings. For this he was imprisoned and later beheaded, reportedly in A.D. 269. Another story says that Valentine cured a jailer's daughter of blindness while he was in jail. Claudius was infuriated when he heard this and had Valentine beaten to death with clubs. A common story is that Valentine had fallen in love with the jailer's daughter and secretly wrote love notes to her signed "From your Valentine." These stories, however legendary, connect the saint with love, however chaste.

There is usually a reason why we do the things we do on holidays, like exchanging Valentine love notes, even if we have forgotten it. The love notes can be traced to the Lupercalia, when boys drew names of girls from a box and would be the escorts of the girls whose names they drew. Although the Lupercalia celebrated the founding of Rome, it was, in a larger sense, a fertility festival insofar as it was held to ensure the protection of the flocks and the crops in the fields, and to ensure their increase. Such festivals, held in anticipation of spring, often invoke sexuality as part of the whole of the rebirth of nature.

As part of the overall effort to deny the overtly sexual aspects of this festival in the Christian era, the church tried to initiate a custom of drawing saints' names from a box. Participants were expected to emulate the saint whose name they drew for the rest of the year. Not surprisingly, this custom failed to take root. Like Cupid, Saint Valentine was associated with lovers, and his feast day became a time for exchanging love messages.

One of the first real valentines in the modern sense was created by Charles, Duke of Orléans. He was taken prisoner in the battle of Agincourt in 1415 and was imprisoned in the Tower of London for several years. From his jail cell, he sent Valentine poems to his wife in France. Following is one such poem, one of the earliest valentines on record:

> To Dorinda, on Valentine's Day
>
> Look how, my dear, the feathered kind,
> by mutual caresses joyn'd
> Bill, and seem to teach us two
> What we to love and custom owe.
>
> Shall only you and I forbear
> To meet, and make a happy pair?
> Shall we alone delay to live?
> This day an age of bliss may give.
>
> But ah! when I the proffer make,
> Still coyly you refuse to take
> My heart I dedicate in vain,
> The too mean present you disdain.
>
> Yet, since the solemn time allows
> To choose the object of our vows, ·
> Boldly I dare profess my flame,
> Proud to be yours by any name.
> (Staff 1969:15)

It appears to have taken some time for this custom to be picked up by common people. In England in 1667, Samuel Pepys refers in his *Diary* to giving his wife a valentine with her name in gold letters on blue paper. The custom of drawing names from a box continued, and to this day we see echoes of it in grade school parties where children deposit valentines into a large, decorated box and draw cards from it in return. Mrs. Marion Strickling, eighty years of age, of Sylvania, Ohio, remembers such Valentine boxes in school. Her reminiscence shows that in a small way even classroom Valentine's Day celebrations served as rites of passage, or at least growth.

In the little town where I lived, that was the big celebration—Valentine's Day. As I remember, we had a Christmas program and had a gift of Christmas candy or cookies, probably given by our teacher, but there was no special exchange of gifts like Valentine's Day. That was a big day when I was a little girl. We would draw names so everybody got at least one valentine. The teacher would make an elaborate box and then we would buy the valentine books, you cut them out and make them. Very seldom did you buy a valentine. Some of the bad kids would get an ugly valentine and not put their name on it and send it to the teacher, and we usually knew who the bad kids were who did it.

We would stop our studies the last half hour and the teacher would open the box, and we'd have different ones be helpers. They'd bring the valentines to your desk, and, of course, if you were real popular, you had a big stack of valentines. That was rather rough. Some of us got together and would send more than one valentine to the children we knew wouldn't get any. I mean we got real philanthropic about it. That's one way you begin to face life, that maybe you'd better sharpen up and be a nicer person. And, of course, if you got one from a boy with his name on it, that was just outstanding! Or if you drew a boy's name, there was a lot of giggling and laughing going on. I think they still have valentine boxes at school.

At one time in England, children went from home to home singing little ditties in exchange for small gifts, a custom similar to modern Halloween trick-or-treating. In Shakespeare's *Hamlet*, Ophelia sings:

> Good morrow! 'tis Saint Valentine's Day
> All in the morning betime.
> And I a maid at your window
> To be your Valentine.
> (4.5.48–55)

In Oxfordshire, boys and girls collected pennies by singing in the streets:

> Good morning to you, Valentine.
> Curl your locks as I do mine,
> Two before and three behind.
> Good morrow to you, Valentine.
> (Staff 1969:12)

In another example of floating customs, Valentine's Eve, like Halloween and April Fools' Day today, was at one time a night given over to pranks. Robert Chambers, in his *Book of Days* of 1863–64, describes some of these: "The sham bang-bangs, that bring nothing but noise and fun—the mock parcels that vanish from the door step by invisible

strings when the door opens—monster parcels that thread papers de-
nuded of their multiplied envelopes, with fitting mottoes, all tending
to the final consummation of good counsel, 'Happy is he who expects
nothing, and he will not be disappointed'" (1906[1860]:255–56).

Valentine's Day is very much the opposite of Halloween. Even
though the two are not 180 degrees apart in the circle of the year, they
both occupy similar but inverse positions relative to the seasons. Halloween is approximately seven weeks before the winter solstice and
marks the progression into the darkest period of the year; Valentine's
Day is about seven weeks after it and marks the progression out of
winter and into spring. Halloween is repesented by harvested crops
and images of death at a time when the days grow shorter, while Valentine's Day is symbolized by living flowers and symbols of life (the
heart) at a time when the days grow longer. Folklorist Henry Glassie
has said that sex is life's rage against death (1975:115), and Valentine's
Day is fundamentally sexual in its imagery, while Halloween is certainly concerned with death. Halloween activities, such as trick-or-
treating and pranking, take place outside. The pranking is largely the
domain of males; one does not find many accounts of females throwing eggs or soaping windows. On the other hand, Valentine's Day is
indoors, and the lacy, frilly, romantic imagery is considered female.
Trick-or-treating is inversive and pranking is aggressive and chaotic,
while Valentine's Day customs reinforce familial rituals of courtship
and marriage. In these ways, Halloween and Valentine's Day can be
said to represent a male/female dichotomy. Trick-or-treating involves
aggression across status lines, expressed through mischief and pranks.
Usually it is very important for the perpetrators of this mischief to
keep their identities secret. The trickery, although expected, can be
quite bothersome (finding eggs on one's house, for instance), and
implies a genuine hostility toward everyday authority. Valentine's
Day, on the other hand, often involves love notes sent by a secret ad-
mirer, but generally these are attempts to facilitate new relationships
or to reinforce existing ones.

If Halloween and Valentine's Day are similar but inverse holidays
relative to each other, it is not surprising that many of the same customs and beliefs we associate with Halloween were once also a part of
Saint Valentine's Day. For instance, a young lady writing in the 1750s
tells of a custom she followed that would predict her future lover:

Last Friday was Valentine's Day, and the night before, I got five bay-
leaves, and pinned four of them to the four corners of my pillow, and
the fifth to the middle; and then, if I dreamt of my sweetheart, Betty

said we should be married before the year was out. But to make it more sure, I boiled an hard egg, and took out the yolk, and filled it with salt; and when I went to bed, ate it, shell and all, without speaking or drinking after it. We also wrote our lovers names upon bits of paper, and rolled them up in clay, and put them into water; and then the first that rose up was to be our valentine. Would you think it?—Mr. Blossom was my man. I lay a-bed and shut my eyes all the morning, till he come to our house; for I would not have seen another man before him for all the world. (Hazlitt 1965 [1870]:610)

This description, and the poem that follows, demonstrate the belief that one would marry the first person one saw on Valentine's Day:

> Last Valentine, the day when birds of kind
> Their early paramours with mutual chirping find,
> I early rose, just at the break of day,
> Before the sun had chased the stars away:
> A-field I went, amid the morning dew,
> To milk my kine [cattle] (for so should house-wives do),
> Thee first I spied, and the first swain we see,
> In spite of Fortune, shall our true love be.

The earliest valentines were hand-made, described as "a sketch of hearts and cupids, a touch of colour, a handful of couplets written all round the page, North, East, South, and West" (Chase 1971 [1926]:58). One surviving valentine has been dated to 1750, and by 1800 valentines were being made commercially. Many of these were sold with materials such as lace and decorative hearts, which the purchaser could affix to the card so as to at least partially create the card personally.

The nineteenth century saw the rise of the comic valentine, called, as were the cheap novels of that time, "penny dreadfuls" due to their cost. The earliest one we know of was sent in England in 1817. Like "real" valentines, they were originally made by hand but by 1840 were being mass-produced. The penny dreadfuls were, as one might guess, insulting and sometimes quite cruel cards that were sent anonymously. "Ugly, Fat, and Forty" proclaims one. Another, addressed to an "Old Maid" carries the verse,

> If you'd lassoo a real live man
> and dope him, as you only, can,
> Then cut his throat and shoot him through,
> He might be coaxed to marry you.

While regular valentines speak seriously and solemnly of love undying, the comic valentines show us the other side of the Victorian

A heart-shaped wreath for Valentine's Day. Photo by Jack Santino, Bowling Green, Ohio, 1984.

obsession with an unrealistic, one-dimensional notion of love. These cards, usually cheaply printed on only one side of a rectangular piece of paper like a postcard, are hostile. Masked in this case behind simple anonymity, the sender attacks the unwitting object of his or her affection. Love—and possible rejection—forms a double-edged sword. Besides tenderness, vulnerability, and pathos, it can bring out uglier emotions as well.

Valentines today reflect the realities of contemporary social life, including single-parent families, couples who live together but are not married, and gay and lesbian relationships. For this reason, Valentine cards have changed tremendously, at least visually, since their lacy heyday at the beginning of the century. Graphic styles have become quite modern, and the images often very topical, but the cards continue to use the symbols of hearts, flowers, and cupids in very creative but traditionally consistent ways. In fact, with the increasing tolerance in our society toward alternative relationships and a growing openness regarding sexuality, we see a return to some of the older and deeper themes of Saint Valentine's Day. Fertility, passion, even lust have rejoined the platonic, flowery, Victorian concepts of love, and along with the cupids we find a return of the hairy beasts of the Lupercalia and Candlemas: bears, gorillas, even bears *disguised* as gorillas. These themes appear in the most unlikely places, such as the small town of Bowling Green, Ohio, where I work. In 1989, the Bowl-

A new wave cupid. The phallic nature of the arrow piercing the heart is made graphically obvious, as is Cupid's erotic, lusty, and sensuous nature. Henry Buerckholtz, artist. © 1985.

ing Green Flower Service offered a special deal for Valentine's Day: for a small fee, you could order flowers sent to someone and the carrier would wear one of three costumes: clown, ape, or Playboy bunny. They each epitomize the fundamental themes hidden deep in Saint Valentine's Day: the masquerade (the clown), the hairy beast (the ape), and sexuality and fertility (the bunny). Somehow, these symbols continue to emerge in connection with this ancient day that honors love but recognizes the fragility of affairs of the heart.

We can learn a lot about holidays by examining our contemporary greeting cards. These are consciously designed to frame certain holiday-related symbols in certain ways. The greeting card industry, which had its commercial beginnings in the middle of the nineteenth century, is a showcase of the continuity and change in the symbols themselves, the ways we perceive them, and the meanings we invest in them. For instance, a perusal of contemporary commercial valentines reveals layer after layer of symbolic meanings related to Valentine's Day. The idea of disguise is especially important. A great many Valentines show clowns, harlequins, masks, masquerades, or costume balls. This takes us from the present, back through the European tradition of ballroom dancing as part of the Valentine's Day activities, to the days of the winter carnivals and masquerades that in turn have become the pre-Lenten carnivals and Fastnachts, Mardi Gras and Shrove Tuesday celebrations of today. Once, this costuming and masquerading tradition belonged to Valentine's Day, and to an extent, it still does. The images on the cards reflect this.

The cards also very often rely on verbal puns, a kind of verbal or semantic misdirection, for their humorous effect. A pun is a word with two meanings at once, just as a person in a costume is a person with two identities at once. A costume or a mask is also a kind of misdirection. This misdirection and masquerading shows up throughout our valentines, as in the case of the bear dressed as a gorilla: he is a monster on the outside, but a teddy bear on the inside. This motif is typical of many of our national heroes. How many of our film heroes can be described that way? How many of us feel that, in order to make it in this world, we have to put on a tough front, but underneath it all we are tender and vulnerable, if only people could see through the mask?

Perhaps this theme is related to some other aspects of Valentine's Day, like the giving of cards, and the primary symbol of the day, as Charles Lamb described it in 1823: "This is the day on which those charming little missives, ycleped Valentines, cross and intercross each other at every street and turning. The weary postman sinks beneath a load of delicate embarrassments, not his own. . . . In these little visual interpretations, no emblem is so common as the *heart*—that little three-cornered exponent of all our hopes and fears,—the bestuck and bleeding heart" (1903 [1823]:56).

The exposed heart of Valentine's Day signals vulnerability. When we give someone a valentine, we are wearing our heart on our sleeve, so to speak. We are taking a risk, a chance that we will be rejected. How many of us have sat during a grade school Valentine party, pretending not to notice how many cards the other children received, while we got only the occasional card from the unpopular kids in the class, written perfunctorily because they wrote one to *every* kid in the class? "Here's hoping you'll be my Valentine," a contemporary card proclaims on the front. And on the inside: "If not, here's hoping you won't blab it to everybody that I asked you!" The inside of the card reveals the hedge: I want you to be my valentine, but if you do not reciprocate, I do not want everyone to know about it. I do but I don't. I love you . . . maybe. Just as a mask lets us take this risk by means of a visual dodge, so does the verbal dodge in this card. Many Valentine's Day cards depend on a pun for this verbal dodge. Valentine's Day has a dark underside that has to do with the fear of rejection. When we put our hearts out there, we hope they will not be bruised.

Along these lines, it is worth noting that the valentine image of love, the heart pierced with an arrow, can also be seen as a sign of

death, and another representation of the vulnerability of the unpro-
tected heart, of open, exposed emotions. Cupid's arrow through the
heart connects love with death, a time-honored theme. It can also be
seen as a symbolic representation of the male and female principles,
the round and open heart shape indicating the female, the arrow
through it a phallic male symbol. The heart and arrow would then
represent the union of these two forces in sexual coition. Consider-
ing Valentine's Day's roots in ancient fertility-related festivals, this
reading of the symbols makes sense. For instance, during the Roman
Lupercalia, when members from two colleges of priests gathered at
a cave in one of the seven hills of Rome, the Palatine, supposedly
where Romulus and Remus had been raised by a she-wolf, the priests
sacrificed goats and a dog. Two young priests were then smeared on
the forehead with the blood of the sacrificed animals. Their foreheads
were wiped with wool dipped in milk. The two youths were stripped
down to a loincloth made of goatskin, and they ran around the Palatine striking people, especially women, with thongs made of goatskin. From this ritual came the more generalized custom referred to
earlier, wherein young men ran through the crowds of Rome with
their strips of animal hide. This was meant to promote fertility in
women. The colors of blood and milk are red and white, the colors
of Valentine's Day. Goats are to this day considered a particularly
potent symbol of sexual drive, and February is in fact the time of their
mating.

If the heart and arrow represent the merging of the male and female principles, so might this dual symbolism be seen throughout the
history of the customs and symbols of the day. Red is the color of
passion, white of purity. Blood is the force of life, milk is the maternal and feminine sustenance of life. Red is the color of the devil, of
Hell; white, of angels and spiritual purity.

Valentine's Day brings these opposites together, combines them the
way they need to be combined in life. Red and white make pink, the
color used most frequently in valentine cards after red and white.
Valentines often depict flowers, another sign of spring and renewal,
and birds, turtledoves mostly, who mate at this time. But Valentine's
Day is for most of us a winter holiday, perhaps the final winter holiday of the season. To me, the overriding message of Saint Valentine's
Day is that life is soon to come, that spring may bloom from the melt-
ed snows of winter, and that February is dreary but short. Both it and
Groundhog Day ring full with promises of the future, of resurrection
soon to come. Both recall in their own way the awakening of sleeping animals, the stirring of the deepest earth, and the powerful sexual life force deep within us. As the days grow longer, these holidays

Older St. Patrick's Day cards show the shamrock, the harp, and Irish castles as symbols of Ireland. Courtesy of the Center for Archival Collections, Bowling Green State University.

lead us into the next season. They only tease us about the future, however. Then Saint Patrick's Day explodes in March, and everywhere is seen the shamrock. Suddenly, everything is colored green.

### Saint Patrick's Day

According to Irish folklore, every other day between Saint Bridget's Day (February 2) and Saint Patrick's Day is supposed to have fair weather, and after Saint Patrick's Day every day is fair. This belief connects the February 2 saint's day with March 17 in much the same way that carnival links January 6 to Lent and Easter. In pre-Christian Ireland, February 1 was one of the four major festival days of the year and was considered the first day of spring. Saint Bridget's Day, February 1, has taken on many of the customs of the ancient Celtic festival on February 1 that preceded it. March 17, on the other hand, is very close to the spring equinox, which is the first day of spring by the Gregorian calendar. This belief in alternately good days from Saint Bridget's until Saint Patrick's Day, and all good days thereafter, connects both days to the coming spring, Saint Patrick's Day directly and Saint Bridget's Day more remotely. As in the American Groundhog

Day, there is a Saint Bridget's hedgehog whose behavior on February 2 is said to predict the upcoming weather. Each of these days relates to different calendars in which they are associated with the beginning of spring, the old first of spring in the beginning of February and the modern first of spring in mid-March. The two calendars, one traditional and one contemporary, are brought together and the two different opening days of spring are reconciled by relating Saint Bridget's Day with Saint Patrick's Day.

Much of the Irish year consists of observances of days that relate to either of these two calendars. The various customs and festivals celebrated on and near the first of November, February, May, and August reflect the ancient pre-Christian Celtic calendar, while those of the Gregorian calendar (January 1 as New Year's, for instance) represent a more recent overlay. Saint Patrick, who brought Christianity to the Celtic Irish, is according to legend the agent of this change. In one of the stories, Patrick lights a paschal bonfire to celebrate Easter, on a hilltop across a valley from the site of the druidical bonfires. The druids insist he extinguish the fire, but Patrick replies that the fire he brings—the Christian faith— can never be extinguished. Here we have an example of a missionary redefining traditional symbols and customs in Christian terms. Patrick's actions were in fact probably viewed as blasphemous or sacrilegious by the druids since he was using a sacred custom of theirs outside of what they considered its appropriate context. It is easy to forget that what we call paganism is simply non-Christian religion.

Patrick and the druids both burned bonfires, but they gave different meaning to what they did (see for example Gailey 1977). In this action we can see two interesting facts about traditional ritual and symbol. They often are formally similar; that is, they outwardly resemble each other. This is true of customs throughout the world. But that does not mean they are the same, or that they have the same meanings. For example, the wine and communion wafer of the Roman Catholic Church outwardly resemble the wine and matzo of the Jewish seder, and they are in fact historically related, since the Last Supper of Christ and the apostles is generally believed to have been a Passover seder. However, the current meanings of the two, and the contexts in which they are used, are drastically different (see for example Feeley-Harnik 1981, and Fredman 1981). In much the same way, Patrick (and the other missionaries) redefined the symbols and customs of the traditional Irish religion.

The shamrock was probably associated with the earth and assumed by the druids to be symbolic of the regenerative powers of nature.

Interestingly, the shamrock is also held in special esteem in Iran, where it is said to cure the bites of scorpions and snakes. There may be nothing to the coincidence of these beliefs, although one may speculate that cultural contact could have occured in the past between the Irish and the ancient Persians (today's Iranians) through the intermediary of Rome. Patrick himself was probably educated in Rome, and many Roman legionnaires were Persian. So it is possible, even though highly speculative, to think that Irish and Iranian folk beliefs might be historically related.

Nevertheless, the shamrock, whatever its history as a folk symbol, today has its meaning in a Christian context. Pictures of Saint Patrick depict him driving the snakes out of Ireland with a cross in one hand and a sprig of shamrocks in the other. As the serpent was driven out of Eden, so were the snakes driven from Eire, returning it, perhaps in some people's minds, to an Edenic state in which it remains to this day. The shamrock has a cross-like shape, especially if the cross is rendered in the Celtic style, and this physical property of the herb also helps to explain its special position in Irish and Irish-American culture. Today it retains an intrinsic connection to the coming of spring and the rebirth of the earth for those who wear it, almost as a totem, during the public celebration that takes place very near the spring equinox.

Saint Patrick's Day evokes the earth's fertility through another custom, that of planting something new in the garden every day during the week that follows the saint's feast day, known as Patrick's Week in Ireland. Because the entire week is marked as Patrick's Week, the equinox is included in the festival period. Even leprechauns remind us of the fertile land: dressed in green, they are said to live in the hills and hollows of the earth. Said by many scholars to be the contemporary versions of ancient gods and goddesses, shrunk to miniature size over the centuries due to the effort of Christianity to abolish belief in them altogether, leprechauns, like elves and dwarves, are busy, magic spirits associated with nature.

Many of the major components of Saint Patrick's Day symbolism, such as the shamrock and its connection to snakes, can be traced to a time before Patrick's arrival in Ireland as a missionary (approximately A.D. 432; he had been there earlier as a boy). Saint Patrick is said to have adapted the shamrock, already rich in native symbolism, to a Christian context, using it to explain the theological doctrine of the Trinity, the three persons in one God, to the unconverted Irish. He plucked the little plant from the ground and pointed out that the shamrock has three distinct leaves but is a single plant with a single stem, just as God comprises the three distinct persons of the Father, the Son, and the Holy Ghost. The Irish were converted, and to this day they honor the shamrock as the symbol of Saint Patrick's Day. This legend about Patrick probably arose after the fact, to justify the special esteem for the shamrock in a Christian context.

One other thing about Saint Patrick: he is said to have brought the art of distilling spirits to the Irish, a blessing certainly as important as having banished the snakes, and cited almost as frequently when recounting the saint's legendary feats. Many anthropologists, most notably Claude Lévi-Strauss (1969), see food as a primary symbol in most societies. Uncooked or raw food represents nature; cooked food is nature culturally transformed and therefore represents culture, that is, society. In the same way, distilled spirits are a cultural rather than a natural form.

All stereotypes aside, drinking is quite important to Saint Patrick's Day in the United States. Along with parades, the day is celebrated by heavy public drinking, in a show of the inversion of regular rules and licentiousness that typically accompanies large-scale public celebrations of increase and fertility. In Ireland, there is the custom known as "drowning the shamrock." Families with servants, on Saint Patrick's Day morn, put some of the plants in a bowl and cover them with good Irish whiskey. The remainder of the bottle is given to the servants. The term generally has come to mean making the rounds, pub-crawling, much like the American public drinking.

Nevertheless, despite the drowning of the shamrock, Saint Patrick's Day remains a more solemn day in Ireland, a day for attending church and visiting with friends. In the United States, it has taken on the aspects of large urban festivity, celebrated with parades that rival those of Thanksgiving and New Year's Day.

### Saint Patrick and Prohibition

During Prohibition, from 1920 to 1933, the drinking was exorcised from the festival, much to the indignation of many. The president of the Friendly Sons of Saint Patrick in 1920, Common Pleas Court Judge Joseph B. Rogers, presumably an upholder of the law generally, gave the following toast on March 17:

> In commemorating the birth of the patron saint of the Emerald Isle it is well for us to note that he gained immortal fame by introducing to our ancestors the eternal principles of Christianity. For 149 years it has been the custom of this society to pay a reverent tribute to his memory. On this occasion, sad to relate, we are forbidden by a strange legis-

lative enactment from toasting his memory in a beverage instituted by the Creator of heaven and earth and sanctioned by His Divine Son. Craving the good saint's forgiveness, I ask you to rise and drink, in uncharitable ice water, to the immortal memory of Saint Patrick.

This from a judge! Saint Patrick and the divinely instituted beverages won out in the end, of course, with the repeal of the Nineteenth Amendment.

Saint Patrick's Day is not a legal holiday in America, but it is nationally observed. Saint Patrick's Day was celebrated in America as early as 1684 in New York. The first celebration outside of a church was held by the Charitable Irish Society of Boston in 1737. In that heavily Irish city, Patrick is the patron saint of the Archdiocese and March 17 is a legal holiday that commemorates the departure of the British from Boston Harbor during the Revolutionary War. General George Washington is said to have used the word "Boston" as password, and "Saint Patrick" as the countersign, after the British evacuation of Boston Harbor on March 17, 1776. Now, on this holiday known as Evacuation Day, people use their free time to attend the Saint Patrick's Day Parade in the Irish-American enclave of South Boston. The Friendly Sons of Saint Patrick was established in Philadelphia in 1780, and a branch was founded in New York in 1784. These early Irish-American groups were made up of both Catholics and Protestants. In fact, the first president of the New York chapter was a Presbyterian.

Despite this apparent ecumenism, early Saint Patrick's Day celebrations were marked by anti-Irish, anti-Catholic, and anti-immigrant disorder. Protestants, who considered themselves "native Americans," held counter-demonstrations to protest the immigrant Irish Saint Patrick's Day parades, calling for the severe limiting of Irish-American rights. According to folklorist and social historian Susan G. Davis, on the eve of Saint Patrick's Day, the burning of effigies of Saint Patrick called "stuffed Paddies" was a "venerable nativist tradition." Conflict is very often a part of our large public holiday celebrations (see for instance Davis 1986). Like all holidays, St. Patrick's Day is affected by social issues and conflicts. Today a debate rages in Boston over the inclusion of a group of gay, lesbian, and bisexual Irish-Americans in the parade.

Although Saint Patrick's Day is sometimes beset with political problems, such as the choice of an alleged sympathizer of the Irish Republican Army to lead the New York parade in the 1980s, or the outbursts of violence that seemed inevitably to accompany the parades in the middle 1800s, the day goes on its merry way. It is a celebration of Irish-American roots and a day of social leveling when we can all be "Irish," a day of social license when we can drink to excess if we choose to, a day of good feelings toward each other, a day of green at the beginning of spring.

## Saint Urho's Day

The success of Saint Patrick's Day as an ethnic celebration that has achieved national prominence has rendered it a model for the festivals of other European ethnic groups as well as a target of parody. Saint Urho's Day, for instance, is a Finnish-American celebration that commemorates a "saint" who drove the grasshoppers out of Finland. Folklorist Yvonne Hiipakka Lockwood calls the story a "pseudo-legend written in the 1950s by a Finnish American psychology professor in Minnesota," but in her extensive work with the festival, she shows that it has grown to be a significant celebration of Finnish-American identity (Lockwood 1987). Urho supposedly saved the vineyards of Finland from a plague of grasshoppers (or, alternately, frogs). However, he is unknown in Finland. Instead, his day is vigorously celebrated throughout the upper Midwest, from Minnesota through Michigan's Upper Peninsula.

Saint Urho's Day is celebrated on March 16, the day before Saint Patrick's Day. The colors of the day are green (for the grasshoppers or frogs) and purple (for the grapes). Parades, toboggan and ski races, dancing to Finnish-American music, eating Finnish-American foods, and telling Finnish-American jokes mark the day. In fact, Lockwood says, if the same jokes were told by outsiders, they would be considered ethnic slurs. People drink green beer and purple grape juice. They dress in silly costumes, and eat and drink to excess. They act silly and they make fun of themselves, and of people who make fun of them, by speaking in exaggerated, stereotypical dialect and telling the stereotypical jokes. According to Lockwood, Finnish Americans are lobbying to have this celebration declared a national holiday.

There is obviously a good deal of tongue-in-cheek fun going on here. The celebration overtly parodies the Irish Saint Patrick's Day, right down to its date. Irish join in the fun: in one town, an Irishman has planned and hosted the celebration for ten years, while in others, Irish people participate bedecked in shamrocks. The event has become a genuinely ethnic, communally celebrated holiday despite its recent invention and parodistic origins. It is the nature of festivals to invert and subvert, and Urho Day does this while at the same time reaffirming local and cultural identities.

## Saint Joseph's Day

March 19, two days after Saint Patrick's Day, is the Feast of Saint Joseph. I entered a greeting card shop one year and noticed a group of Saint Joseph's Day cards displayed between the Saint Patrick's Day cards and the Easter cards. Most of the Saint Joseph's Day cards depicted scenes of specially baked breads, fruits, and grains along with statues or other images of the saint. Curious, I asked the woman at the cash register if they sold many of these cards. She replied that they did. "Who buys them?" I asked. "Catholics," the lady told me. I am a Catholic, and moreover, an Italian-American Catholic, but I was never involved with any folk customs associated with Saint Joseph's Day.

Catholic it is, and Italian too, but more specifically it was initially a Sicilian practice to observe Saint Joseph's Day by setting up altars in the home in honor of the saint. The greeting cards show these home altars which, as a major component of the feast day, have become symbolic of it. Like Saint Patrick's Day, Saint Joseph's Day is an ethnic festival; it "belongs" to Italians and Sicilians. Also like Saint Patrick's Day, it has strong elements of fertility symbolism: the grains, the specially prepared fish, the fruits and breads, the simple fact of abundance itself. Unlike Saint Patrick's Day, however, this celebration remains a small one. It has not become a national day of public festivities. Rather, it is celebrated throughout the country in pockets, wherever there are Sicilian Catholics. Among these people, Saint Joseph's Day is a major event, taking the place of Saint Patrick's Day as an important religious and seasonal holiday. In New Orleans, Saint Joseph's Day is part of the Carnival cycle, and Saint Joseph's altars are set up in homes throughout the city. In Milwaukee, where there is a large Sicilian population, the day is quite important.

The Sicilians of Southern California vigorously celebrate the day. A 1940 description of the foods displayed on the altars, and served for the occasion, includes fruits, fresh and cooked vegetables, cookies, cakes (often stuffed with figs), many kinds of fish, and many kinds of breads baked in decorative styles. A large baked fish, decorated with flowers and foodstuffs, claims center stage but shares it with a square Saint Joseph's cake. The cake is usually donated by a friend of the family celebrating. All of this surrounds an icon of the saint, and the rest of the altar is filled with plants and flowers. The preponderance of fish is due to the fact that the holy day occurs during Lent, but it also may owe something to the traditional symbolism of fish both in Christianity and as a fertilty sign. Because of the day's proximity to Easter, the altars sometimes include representations of lambs and other Easter symbols.

Southern Californians also have a Saint Joseph's Day custom that is remarkably similar to the Hispanic Christmas *posadas*, that of going from house to house, reenacting the search of Mary and Joseph for shelter when Mary was about to give birth. In the Sicilian version, children dressed as the Holy Couple go to three homes and ask for lodging, only to be refused at the first two. At the third house, a large Saint Joseph's altar is set up and ready for the arrival of the "saints." The hosts serve them and the numerous visitors who follow them a ritual meal, beginning with blessed wine. The meal eventually becomes a large-scale, happy event at which many visitors are fed, and any remaining food is distributed to friends and neighbors and given to the poor.

Saint Joseph's Day is not the national celebration that Saint Patrick's Day, two days earlier, is, but it is a festival of ethnic identity that comes at almost exactly the same point in the calendar. For a specific group of people, it is their holy day, it is an important part of their year, and it is part of a grid that is based on their ethnic identity. Thus it is a meaningful component in their annual cycle, but not one that is shared nationally.

## Carnival

The February masquerades and spring carnivals of ancient and medieval times are still with us as Carnival and Mardi Gras, which are linked to Lent and Easter. Easter usually falls in April, but it is a movable feast and may occur sometime between March 22 and April 25. The dates of such movable feasts are calculated according to solar and lunar events. For instance, Easter is always the first Sunday after the first full moon following the spring equinox. (Of course, the dates of Mardi Gras and Lent move with Easter.) The Easter season begins with Ash Wednesday, the first day of Lent, and in Louisiana, the day before Ash Wedneday is celebrated as Mardi Gras, otherwise known as Shrove Tuesday or Fat Tuesday. The entire period from January 6 (Epiphany, or Three Kings' Day, or Twelfth Night) to Ash Wednesday is called Carnival. The Carnival period culminates in Mardi Gras, which is always forty-six days before Easter. Carnival is celebrated in many parts of the world, including Europe, the Caribbean, Central America, and South America.

Peoples from the Caribbean make up a growing segment of the population of North America, especially in cities such as Boston, Hartford, New York, Toronto, Montreal, and Los Angeles. Not surprisingly, Caribbean Carnival celebrations flourish in these cities, and in others, including Philadelphia, Washington, D.C., and Miami. For many of the participants, Carnival is known as *Mas* (probably from *masquerade*). An individual participant in Carnival is also called a Mas or a Mas player; "doing" Carnival is called "playing Mas." Costumes are elaborate, and prizes are awarded to the most original, most colorful, best designed, and most exciting. Mas players dance to music— self-generated or recorded or both—as they parade through the streets. Carnival has become pan-Hispanic. Peoples from Panama, Costa Rica, Tobago, Trinidad, and throughout the Caribbean region celebrate together, and Mas has become a celebration of Latin American, Caribbean, and African ethnic identity. The carnivals are held at different times during the year in different cities: in New York, Mas is a part of *el Diá de la Raza,* held on Columbus Day, October 12 (Parris 1980; Williams 1980).

## Laskiainen

Although many of our carnival traditions in the United States, including those of Louisiana, are an amalgamation of African, Hispanic, and Southern European cultures, carnivals preceding the Lenten season were also celebrated in northern Europe. In Finland, a pre-Lenten festival that probably predated Christianity and celebrated the lengthening of the days was brought to the United States in the early 1800s. Today this festival is known as *Laskiainen* and is celebrated among the Finnish Americans in northern Minnesota. This name has been translated as meaning "sliding downhill," since Laskiainen was a festival that quite literally featured sliding downhill in the winter snows of Finland and Minnesota: sports familiar to the Finns such as skating, sledding, and tobogganing were a large part of the celebration. On the other hand, Thomas Vennum, Jr., says that the name comes from the festival's associations with Shrove Tuesday, which date back as far as the early 1500s. The verb *laskia* means "to settle down," and Laskiainen is, according to Vennum, a "settling down" into Lent (1980:14).

For generations, Laskiainen was celebrated by small groups of family and neighborhood friends. Besides enjoying the winter sports, people cooked traditional Finnish foods and played and danced to Finnish folk music. Around 1930, the celebration became centralized in Palo, Minnesota, overlooking Loon Lake. Two days in length, the

Palo Laskiainen is the focus of what has become a major regional and ethnic event. Perhaps the single most distinguishing feature of Laskiainen is the whip-sled, the *vipu-kelkka*. This is a sled attached to a pole, sometimes as large as a twenty-six-foot spruce, that rotates on a post frozen into the lake.

The festival's very name bears testimony to its Finnish origins and many Finnish components. Laskiainen has become more than just an ethnic festival, however. Along with the Laskiainen *voi-leipa-poyta* (buffet; literally, bread and butter table) and *kropsua* (baked pancake), the Finnish music and food and stories, and the making of *lastu* (Christmas tree ornaments) and birchbark winter slippers, the festival reflects regional culture. People come from all over the upper Midwest to attend. Winter sports are essential to the area and are a major component of the festival. Indeed, since the 1950s, the queen of Laskiainen ascends her throne after she walks through an archway made of crossed hockey sticks, held aloft by uniformed hockey team members. Laskiainen is not a frozen relic of the past; it is a dynamic celebration of Finnish identity and regional pride.

## Mardi Gras

On Twelfth Night, January 6 (the twelfth day of Christmas), the Carnival season begins with a Parisian tradition, the *Bal du Roi*, or King's Ball, and the eating of King Cakes. These round or oval cakes, signifying Three Kings Day or the Feast of the Epiphany, are among the primary foods traditionally associated with Carnival. They are frosted with alternating bands of sugar colored purple, green, and gold, the three colors that have become associated with Mardi Gras. Hidden in the cake are small figures. Originally, whoever got the king doll (today a baby) got to be king for a day. This person also has to buy the next cake or hold the next ball. Sometimes the cake contains a bean rather than a figure. The balls continue throughout the Carnival season, on a weekly or biweekly basis until a final ball is held on Mardi Gras.

A native of New Orleans describes it as "a whole season, from January 6 to March 19. It's a big continuity factor there." The Christmas–New Year period gives way to the Carnival–Mardi Gras festivities, which give way to Lent, which leads to Easter. The entire Carnival period is a time for self-indulgence before the forty-day period of religious sacrifice begins. Because Lent is a time of fasting and abstinence from meat, some think that the word *Carnival* is a corruption of the Latin *carne vale*, which translates as a farewell to meat. It is most likely that this really refers to a farewell to flesh and to fleshly delights. Street parties and parades take place throughout the Carnival season. Each parade features elaborate and original floats, and the paraders wear spectacular costumes.

*Mardi Gras* is French for "Fat Tuesday," and no one is quite certain how this name developed either. One theory is that it refers to the old practice of leading a fattened ox through the village before Lent; when slaughtered, the ox provided the final meat meal. Another theory is that the name comes from a custom of frying foods before Ash Wednesday in order to use up all the animal fat in a household, because, being a meat product, fat could not be used during Lent and would spoil. In support of this theory, most Carnival and Mardi Gras celebrations the world over include the preparation and consumption of some sort of fried dough morsel. In New Orleans it is the *beignet* (a square, fritter-like doughnut without a hole), while in the Black Forest area of Germany, and in Alsace, where Carnival is known as *Fastnacht* (in other areas Carnival was called *Fasching, Karneval, Fassenacht,* and *Fasnet* [Russ 1982:79]), the raised doughnut is called the *Fastnacht Keuche* or *Fastnachtkuchen.* The custom of preparing it was brought to this country by German and Alsatian settlers (Taueber 1933). As a result, we find the *Fastnacht Keuche* in the German areas of Pennsylvania and we find traces of it in other German-settled areas of the country. For instance, at least two Faschings were held in Bowling Green, Ohio, in 1986, one at a school and one at a church, both with fried cakes. We find related examples in the Pancake Day held in Convoy, Ohio, on February 2, and when I held my all-purpose Groundhog Day party, one couple brought homemade doughnuts as a kind of food that was appropriate to the occasion.

New Orleans' Mardi Gras was first imported from the Continent: when the French explorer Iberville arrived at the Mississippi River on Mardi Gras eve, 1699, he named his encampment "Bayou and Pointe de Mardi Gras." Later French explorers established the settlement of La Nouvelle Orleans on the Mississippi River in 1718, and they brought the Parisian Carnival tradition with them. Over the years, this Mississippi port city was heavily influenced by Africans, Afro-Caribbeans, Germans, and French Canadians who migrated from the area of Nova Scotia called Acadia. They became known as Cajuns, as the name *Acadians* was anglicized. Each of these ethnic groups brought its unique music, dance, and foodways to the region, and all of these influences melded together: the results are the famous New Orleans cuisine, the spectacular music that has come out of that city, and its many street festivals, of which Mardi Gras is the most famous.

Mardi Gras in New Orleans today is a lavish affair of private masked balls and a dizzying public spectacle of costumes, floats, parades, crowds in the streets, crowds on the balconies, crowds everywhere. The masked balls are cotillions linked to the debutante season, coming-out parties for young ingénues. Traditionally, they are upper-crust affairs, run by the socially prominent families of New Orleans, who also sponsor the oldest and most respectable krewes, that is, social organizations, each with its own king. The parades that run throughout the Carnival season are staged (and paid for) by these different krewes. In recent years, additional balls fêting young ladies from a variety of suburban and newer neighborhoods have appeared on the Carnival calendar too.

Carnival as a way of celebrating the new year is quite an old idea. In A.D. 742 Saint Boniface, also known as the Apostle to the Germans, complained to Pope Zacharias that he was close to converting the Germanic Franks and Alemanni, but that they continued to engage in "lurid carnivals." When confronted with their supposed moral laxity, they responded that they had witnessed similar goings-on "under the very shadow of Saint Peter's in Rome." In response, the pope issued a statement that forbade Romans from conducting carnivals in Rome, but the edict was unsuccessful. Carnival continued, in Rome and throughout Europe, and the French brought it to the New World.

While Mardi Gras is undoubtedly identified with New Orleans and Rio today, it actually came to New Orleans from Mobile, Alabama, where the day is still celebrated, albeit on a slightly less grand scale. In Mobile, floats had been a part of New Year's parades since 1830. Some men from Mobile brought the idea to New Orleans, but not before founding in 1831 the somewhat whimsical Cowbellion de Rakin Society, which played a large part in Mobile's Mardi Gras festivities. The Society was instigated by Michael Krafft, who was originally from Pennsylvania.

There is an interesting connection here with another large, citywide costume parade, the Philadelphia Mummers Parade. The Philadelphia parade also features groups of men who march through the city in bizarre, elaborate costumes. It has been held every New Year's Day since the turn of the century, and dates back as far as the War of 1812. It is for that city a tradition quite similar to New Orleans' Mardi Gras parades.

Krafft and some friends had been celebrating New Year's Eve. Drunk, they broke into a hardware store and stole cowbells and rakes, and proceeded to parade through the streets making noise, mimicking people, and generally raising hell. From this inspired moment, the men called themselves after the things they stole, and the Cow-bellion de Rakin Society was born. A year later they organized a noisy, costumed New Year's parade, which featured tableaux and dancing. In 1857, six men from Mobile who had been members of this society met and decided to introduce a somewhat similar society in New Orleans, where they were now living. They organized what was to become known as the Mystick Krewe of Comus. Other krewes fol-lowed: Momus and Rex in 1872, and Zulu (which was all Black) in 1909. Along with Comus, they still put on parades, joined in 1988 by approximately sixty other krewes.

Comus, the first of the krewes, took as its inspiration the works of the English poets Ben Johnson and John Milton. In Milton's masque *Comus*, the title denotes a god of mirth and "spirits." The theme of Comus's first parade was "Demon Actors of 'Paradise Lost,'" inspired by Milton's religious epic. The spellings of "mystick" and "krewe" were supposedly Anglo-Saxon, and were intended to add an "Arthu-rian fillip" to the group. At the time when Comus was organized, an English-French rivalry pervaded Mardi Gras. Thus the krewe, true to its origins in satire and rebelliousness, chose its name and its theme in such a way as to antagonize the French settlers in the region.

For its first procession, the krewe wanted to stage a "bal-masqué" similar to its literary namesake, Milton's play. Through the streets they marched, led by Comus himself on one float and Satan on the other. The floats were attended by devil-maskers who carried torches or played music. They proceeded to the French Opera House to perform scenes from *Paradise Lost* in a series of tableaux. This was followed by dancing. Although not based on folk sources as other holiday-re-lated plays are, the tableaux and krewes became traditional. Eventu-ally, the people of French descent (known as Creoles) accepted the Anglo-Saxon krewes and adapted them into the overall Carnival tra-ditions. Mardi Gras has throughout its history been quite adaptable, which has probably contributed a great deal to its ongoing vitality. Festivities were canceled during the Civil War but returned stronger than ever afterward. New krewes continued to join, and after the Sec-ond World War, the practice spread to the New Orleans suburbs. Af-ter 1951, mules were no longer used to pull the floats, having been replaced by tractors. Today, krewes parade in the metropolitan area for almost three full weeks before Mardi Gras; among them are Co-mus, Rex, and Zulu on Mardi Gras Day itself, and Momus on the Thursday before.

The krewes are private clubs; the older organizations, such as Mo-mus, Comus, Proteus, and Rex, have become quite exclusive and maintain old-line, white male-dominated social ties. The parties, parades, and balls are, for them, ways of reinforcing their status, which is linked to the social circuit of the old-line Protestant or Catholic social networks. These krewes have been challenged by upstart krewes that offer membership to anyone who can foot the bill, and crown as king an out-of-town celebrity. The maverick krewes offer participation to disaffected groups who are not part of the city's social whirl, and these krewes were at first viewed as heretics and heathens. Along with the maverick krewes' parades are the truck parades in which each float is managed by its riders rather than by formal krewes of any kind, and all the other smaller events throughout the city, especially parades of marching bands and decorated vans. Eventually, in good partygoing spirit, when it was seen what good parades the new krewes and non-aligned bands put on, they were all accepted.

So there are, interestingly, two levels of social action taking place during Mardi Gras: members of the upper levels of society link it to the debutante season and to social prominence, ritually displaying their wealth and ultimately reinforcing their social position; while at the same time, African Americans (in Zulu), other ethnics, middle-class and working-class people, suburbanites—in short, just about everybody else—take advantage of Carnival and Mardi Gras as a chance to be rowdy, spontaneous, and free, mocking and thus challenging social pretensions. One of the most fascinating parts of Mardi Gras is the parade in the French Quarter of gay men, especially transvestites, in full regalia. In fact, there are full gay balls and tableaux. If any festival in America illustrates the principle of social inversion, Mardi Gras is it.

In the medieval carnivals of France, people formed *reynages* or pretend kingdoms for the celebrations, and today's Mardi Gras krewes of New Orleans, each with its own king, may very well be a contemporary version of that custom. Scholars speculate that the parade floats are derived from religious tableaux once performed in church and later expelled into the streets as they grew increasingly rowdy. The parades too are traced to religious processions in the Old World.

The first newspaper accounts of Mardi Gras parades in New Orleans date to 1837, but this does not mean that less organized masked parades did not begin earlier. In 1806, for instance, the government prohibited public masking after sundown. In fact, masked parades are more than likely continuous with the European traditions. Throughout the nineteenth century such parades were held, featuring decorated carriages, masked riders on horseback, and maskers on foot. The paraders tossed gifts and favors to the spectators, but here too excess reigned, and after incidents in the 1850s of throwing lye, dirt, and flour onto the crowds, the city fathers banned these "throws," as they are called, and considered banning the parades.

Today these throws are back and provide some of the greatest excitement of the festivities, as people crowd and shout, cajole, plead, and try to bribe the riders to toss a trinket in their direction. In the official guide book to Mardi Gras 1984, the throws are described as "the biggest excitement . . . tossed by the tons, to the crowd." The book advises the readers to put their foot on any throw that happens to land on the street near them, because to simply reach to pick it up would endanger one's hand! What are these throws that are so important, so eagerly sought after? They are strings of plastic beads (once glass) and cheap aluminum coins called doubloons. The doubloons were introduced only in 1960 but have become an integral part of the festival since then. Some krewes, such as the conservative Comus, will toss only beads and doubloons, while others toss garters, bikinis, and underwear. Some toss ashtrays, cups, Frisbees, or umbrellas. The Zulus tossed out decorated coconuts. Although these are highly prized items, sometimes the Zulus tend to throw them *at* rather than *to* the folks in the street. As a result, throwing coconuts through the air was banned from the 1986 Mardi Gras, just as other throws, as well as masks and the parades themselves, have been periodically banned over the years.

Mardi Gras is a curious combination of the very old and the very new. In its officially accepted history as published in the program guide, it is correctly described as a modern descendant of the Lupercalia. New Orleanians themselves know this and recount it as an important aspect of the festival. They are not afraid to modernize, however. As we have seen, tractors have replaced mules, doubloons were introduced in 1960, other trinkets since then. The floats are made by only a few local businesses, whose workers view themselves as artists first, businessmen second. Suppliers manufacture the throws (often these are imported from Hong Kong or Korea), and Las Vegas–style running lights are gradually replacing the *flambeaux,* or metal torches. These in turn had replaced the torches made of pine-tar rags on wooden staves that the original Krewe of Comus carried in its first parade of 1857. Comus is today the most traditional of all the krewes (which is ironic in light of its rather rebellious beginnings), one of the few that actively seeks to maintain the type of float that was seen a hundred years earlier, a small, delicate float with a great deal of ornamental sculpture (dragons, for example) and with much gold and silver foil.

The krewe of Rex, on the other hand, combines the old with the new. Rex has reintroduced the fattened ox to Mardi Gras as a giant float. In the 1880s, this European custom was very much a part of New Orleans Mardi Gras. In an eyewitness account of an 1880 celebration, published in 1882, George Augustus Sala describes the float: "Then came the four-legged King of the Carnival—the *Boeuf Gras,* a magnificent animal, milk-white, and weighing four thousand pounds avoir-dupois, attended by a posse of Assyrian butchers, and so bedizened with decorative trappings as to recall Mr. Tennyson's 'curled and oiled' Assyrian bull. I was glad to see that the poor beast was not compelled to walk. As it was, he must have suffered enough discomfort on the sledge in which he was slowly dragged along. Has he been converted into beef, I wonder, by this time, that corpulent *Boeuf Gras!*" (Sala 1984[1892]:72).

The Rex parade incorporates the traditional tiny floats of yesterday with large superfloats of today, just as Carnival itself bridges the gap between Christmas and Easter, winter and spring. The king of the Rex krewe is called Rex, the King of Tomfools, Lord of Misrule, and King of all Mardi Gras. Rex and Comus hold their balls on Mardi Gras night. While Rex is officially the king of Mardi Gras, Comus is older and much more socially prestigious, so Rex accomodates him. At midnight, the members of the Krewe of Rex march over to meet the members of Comus for a toast that officially ends Mardi Gras and begins the Lenten fast. On Ash Wednesday morning, groups of people, many of whom have been up all night, attend a Lenten mass celebrated by the bishop at Saint Louis Cathedral in Jackson Square. The bishop wears the colors of Mardi Gras in his robes: purple, green, and gold, colors used by the Rex krewe in its first parade in 1872. Although the colors are probably ecclesiastical in origin, in a parade of 1892 called "Symbolism of Colors," they were defined as representing justice (purple), faith (green), and power (gold). They have been associated with Mardi Gras ever since (see Kinser 1990).

The event is very much a popular cultural event. Giant floats process through the tiny, crowded streets, while television cameras broadcast the sight of hundreds of thousands of people clamoring and scrambling for the coins and beads thrown from the floats. The newer krewes try to lure famous people to their parade, if they can afford them. In 1986, John Ritter was king of Bacchus, as were television personalities Henry Winkler and Ed McMahon before him.

While the celebration in the city of New Orleans is quite spectacular, wild, and licentious (women are seen in all manner of dress and undress; on Bourbon Street, women line the balconies, responding to cries of "Give us some T!" by lifting their blouses), out in the countryside it is a different story. There the Mardi Gras is in its own way wilder, less slick, less "polite" than the superparty in New Orleans. The men ride horseback, for instance. In Mamou, Louisiana, over a hundred miles northwest of New Orleans, groups of men ride horseback and in pickup trucks from farm to farm and from home to home. The leaders of these bands do not and cannot by law wear masks, supposedly because celebrations in the past have become violent. At one time in the early 1950s, they were even outlawed. Today, the leader, or captain, is in charge, and must remain unmasked so that he can be identified and assume the responsibility for the group if trouble arises. The riders are also called the Mardi Gras. From house to house they ride, through the countryside begging, "Give us a little chicken so we can make a gumbo!" A chicken, or a piece of spicy sausage, or rice, bell peppers, onions—any ingredient will do. This tradition is a form of mumming: dressing in masks and costumes, and going from house to house, demanding or begging food and drink. In this version of it, we see the communal aspect of the custom, since the women will make the gumbo for the village from the food the men collect. Each household contributes, many receive.

From the *Washington Post*, March 7, 1984, comes this account: "The farmer holds high a fat white chicken. The band plays louder. The shouts rise like ugly thunder. The old man tosses the bird above the outstretched arms of the men. It struggles to fly, but lands less than 10 yards from the frantic *courir* (the troop of masked riders), who pounce upon the poor, doomed fowl and send a cloud of feathers floating off into the heavens. . . . Carl LeBlanc, himself dressed like a chicken, rips the bird's head off and stuffs it in his Kewpie doll shorts. *'Poule grasse,'* he shouted, *'poule grasse.'* Fat chicken, fat chicken." This is known as capturing the chicken. As gruesome as it sounds, it is an ancient custom. We know that roosters were decapitated in medieval French carnivals, and it seems this custom lives on in Cajun Louisiana. It is worth remembering that the chicken is eaten and not killed solely for sport.

Although Mardi Gras is pretty well centered in New Orleans and surrounding areas, Louisiana politicians throw a big Mardi Gras Ball in Washington, D.C. More and more people are picking up the idea and having Mardi Gras celebrations in different cities and regions in the United States. In some areas of Maine, people of French Canadian background continue a traditional Mardi Gras celebration. In other parts of the United States, various kinds of new Mardi Gras traditions are springing up. Baltimore had a Mardi Gras celebration in 1984, for instance, as did a Catholic church in Ohio in 1986. German Americans hold Faschings in Ohio. Because of its public nature, and because of the late winter–early spring timing, Mardi Gras might just become a nationally celebrated event before too long. Except in the Mediterranean-influenced Gulf Coast–Louisiana area, we have lost the coherent Carnival period throughout our country, and this is a real loss indeed. I suggest, however, that the holidays of February and March act for us in much the same way the celebratory days of the late Middle Ages and early-modern periods did for our European ancestors. They may yet reform as a new Carnival tradition.

## The Feast of Fools and All Fools Day

Although not a Mardi Gras celebration, the Feast of Fools was a carnival celebrated in France and England that satirized the Church and her powerful authorities. Like Mardi Gras and other celebrations, this feast was marked by the reversal of social roles and the flouting of social rules; those on the bottom of the social ladder temporarily became the ones on top; those who had no social influence became, for a time, the ones in control. In France, the subordinate clergy, such as subdeacons, who were generally poor peasants, took on the roles of the Lord of Misrule and the Mock King. In England the feast was known as the Feast of the Boy Bishop. It was held on December 28, the day that commemorated King Herod's biblical command to slaughter all babies in hopes of killing the baby Jesus. The medieval streets were clogged with masked and costumed revelers during this festival, and as so often happens on occasions such as this, sometimes events got a bit too unrestrained.

The Feast of Fools made the clergy very nervous with its overt and implied criticisms of the Church. Parodies of the mass, celebrated by donkeys brought into the church were not unheard of, for instance. These were held in the churches and cathedrals of France, where men dressed as women and as animals paraded into the church with great pomposity. Inside, they sang and played musical instruments, gambled, burned old leather sandals in place of incense, and ate and drank from the altar itself in a kind of beggar's banquet in which the altar was returned to its original function, that of a supper table. All of this was, of course, done with great rowdiness and not a little hostility.

Ironically, the Feast of Fools had been sponsored by the church in an effort to provide an outlet for pent-up anticlerical sentiment among the people. The Church Fathers had based their approval of such a feast on two biblical texts: "He hath put down the mighty from their seat, and hath exalted the humble" (Luke 14:11), and "up with the low and down with the high" (Ezekiel 21:31). But by allowing people to mock the authority of the Church, the Feast of Fools contained the seeds of subversion, as do all such festivals of public license and inversion. Fearing that the festival undermined its authority, in 1431 the Church at the Council of Basel banned it. This festival did not die out until the sixteenth century, however, and in a way it is still with us in all our days and nights of revelry (such as New Year's Eve) and pranking (such as Halloween). Its name echoes in our April Fools' Day. The Feast of Fools was especially popular in medieval France, and in France today, April Fools' Day is widely enjoyed.

Some historians believe that our modern practice of sending friends on a fool's errand or of pulling pranks and practical jokes on April 1 has to do with the change to the reformed calendar. When Charles IX of France adopted the Gregorian calendar in 1564, switching New Year's from March 25 to January 1, there were those who insisted on maintaining the old New Year's Day. In certain areas of France, the old new year's festival stretched from March 25 to April 1 and culminated with gift giving. Those who did not modernize were sent mock gifts on April 1 in derision, and these people were known as April fools, or April fish. *Poisson d'Avril* (April fish) is still the current term in France, and there the fish is to April Fools' Day what the shamrock is to Saint Patrick's Day—the primary symbol of the holiday. Everywhere in France at this time of year one finds chocolate candy in the shape of fish. The fish may even be another sign of rebirth and fertility, since fish begin to run in the spring.

It is also possible that since under the old-style calendar the new year was celebrated somewhere near the spring equinox, very often the major Christian celebration of Easter occurred during the same week as New Year's, or very close to it. But the proximity of the sacred holy day (Easter) to the secular holiday (New Year's) was, according to this theory, too much for the churchmen to bear. Mildred Arthur, in her *Holidays of Legend*, asserts "April Fools' Day started because New Year's Day fell during Easter week. That may sound like nonsense, but those are the facts" (1971:45). It was because of this "conflict of celebrations" that New Year's Day was moved to April 1. Then the calendar reform occurred, from Julian to Gregorian, and the rest, as we saw above, is history.

What's Wrong with This Picture? Norman Rockwell painted several surreal scenes such as this 1948 April Fools' Day magazine cover as April Fools' pranks. Printed by permission of the Norman Rockwell Family Trust. © 1948 the Norman Rockwell Family Trust.

Explanations for the origins of April Fool's Day are many, and often as foolish as the day itself. A poem in the *Poor Robin's Almanac* of 1870 alludes to the fact that the exact origin of the day is lost to history:

> The first day of April, some do say,
> is set apart for All Fools' Day.
> But why the people call it so,

April Fools' Day is related to the other holidays of the spring quadrant. The rebirth and renewal imagery of Easter and spring is seen in the chicken and egg motif, while the emerging seductive woman represents the sexuality and fertility found in Valentine's Day and Carnival. Photo by David Hampshire, Instructional Media Services, Bowling Green State University.

Nor I, nor they themselves do know.
But on this day are people sent,
on purposes of pure merriment.

Some scholars contend that it was customary to play tricks during
the Roman Saturnalia festival held during the winter solstice, and that
this might be the antecedent of our April tradition. Since the usual April
Fools' prank is to send someone on a "fool's errand," others claim it
to be a farcical reading of the passion of Christ, during which Christ
was sent from official to official. Some theories point to the uncertain-
ty of the weather at this time of year: it is supposed to be spring, but
winter weather is still common. Some maintain that it has to do with a
practice of freeing insane people from asylums to temporarily enter-
tain a cruel and taunting public. Some of these theories, and others too
numerous to go into, are plausible, at least in part, but none are per-
suasive. Surprisingly, the Hindu people of India celebrate a festival
around April 1 called Holi, or Huli. It begins with the burning of bonfires, and features as one of its principal customs the playing of practical jokes on people, especially sending them on fool's errands. Some
scholars have tried to find a historical connection between the Western April Fool's Day and this almost identical Eastern custom, but no
one has really succeeded. All we can do is speculate.

Although the specifics are obscured, the custom of April fooling
spread quickly throughout France and Europe. In England, although
the calendar reform was not officially instituted until 1752, the custom had taken root in the early eighteenth century. The popular term
for the fool there is the April gob, gawby, or noddie. In Scotland, it is
the April gowk, a word that means "cuckoo," a common term in Britain for a simpleton. In Scotland the fool's errand is known as "hunt-
ing the gowk." The basic prank here is to send someone on a mis-
sion to deliver a letter. Upon reading the contents of the letter, its
recipient would tell the carrier that he had been mistaken, the letter
was meant for someone who lived farther down the road. In actuali-
ty, the letter read, "It's the first of April! Hunt the gowk another mile."
So on and on he would go, until he had been led on a complete circle. When he arrived back from where he had started, all who had
been involved in the joke gathered to shout "April gowk!" at the poor,
well-meaning but gullible individual.

Such pranks are legion. They were brought to the Americas by British and French colonists and immigrants. Today in Mexico, if one
borrows something on April Fools' Day, he is by custom not required
to give it back. The burden is on the lender, who must remember

when asked for a loan of any kind what day it is. If he is foolish enough to lend one of his possessions to the trickster-borrower, he may never see it again but will get instead a box of candy with a note that announces the April fool joke. In Ireland, one never lends on May 1, for the same reason: borrowing on that day is neither binding nor contractual. Here we have another example of a custom being associated with different holidays in different parts of the world.

One thing that is certain, though, is that April Fools' Day in America contains very little of any ancient festival other than the practical jokes. Predictably, posters advertising April Fools' Day–related events feature jesters—that is, fools—in their graphics, and in Philadelphia in 1985 a radio station sponsored a successful Parade of Fools. So the older aspects may be returning. Generally, however, April Fools' Day is a day when we can lie to our friends and cause them great anxiety, as long as we justify our actions by exclaiming "April fool!" We can, and in fact are *supposed* to, dream up elaborate practical jokes to snare the unsuspecting. But April Fools' Day revolves around only this single custom of practical joking and is no longer a fully realized festive celebration with music, dance, costumes, masks, or food and drink.

## Spring Break

We mentioned earlier spring break, which generally is in March or April, as a major period of festivity in the academic year, which is experienced differently according to whether one is a student or a professor. Come spring break, for instance, many students will sojourn in Florida, while their professors stay in town, enjoying the brief week of peace and quiet. In the academic calendar, the spring break is especially reminiscent of pre-Christian fertility celebrations traditionally held at the time of the equinox, with little cultural overlay to disguise it. Florida has become the symbolic mecca for thousands of nubile youth (*nubile* actually means "of marriageable age"; it is derived from the same root word as *nuptial*). The sun is not "worshiped" as a deity, but is held in esteem as a thing with power to transform one into a sexually attractive (tanned) creature; young people drink, dance, mate, and occasionally even die in an explosion of sex and a celebration of sexuality, fertility, potency, and regeneration. Sometimes, college spring celebrations are accompanied by excess that breaks into riot. Folklorist Tristram Potter Coffin has even referred to the "spring riot" as a genre of folk celebration and ritual (Coffin and Cohen 1975:345).

The Easter Bunny goes to war. Courtesy of the Center for Archival Collection, Bowling Green State University.

### Passover and Easter

The Lent-to-Easter season is an excellent example of the ways people symbolically interpret the year. It is, of course, a religious season, and it reminds us that the church calendar has assigned the commemoration of a saint or an event to every day of the year, so that, while we are always creating a new present, we are also reliving an eternal, cosmological past (see Eliade 1954 and Warner 1959). In our pluralistic society, many of these are no longer celebrated or even noted, but Ash Wednesday and Lent still command public attention. Easter is a major holiday despite the fact that it is specifically Christian.

We have seen that much Christian ritual was adopted from the Romans. However, Jesus and his followers were of course Jews, and so Christianity inherited—and reinterpreted—a great deal of Hebraic liturgy as well. Nowhere is the relationship between Judaism and Christianity better demonstrated than in a comparison of Easter with Passover. Ash Wednesday is the first day of the Christian Lenten season, which is forty days long, not counting Sundays. The name Lent derives from a word meaning "lengthening days." The custom for churchgoers on Ash Wednesday is to receive upon their foreheads an imprint of ashes. These are to remind us of our mortality and our dependence on God. As we receive the ashes, the priest intones,

"From dust thou art and to dust thou shalt return." During Lent, churches are decorated in purple cloth as a sign of penance. The faithful are asked to make personal sacrifices in remembrance of the sacrifice Christ made on the cross. Palm Sunday commemorates the triumphant return of Christ to Jerusalem, where he was greeted by jubilant crowds waving palm fronds. In remembrance of this, leaves of palm are given out at church to be taken home. These palms have been blessed, and so they must be burned rather than thrown away if they are to be disposed of.

Palm Sunday begins the final week of Lent, and the progressive nature of the cycle becomes clearer as the week goes on. Each day recalls a day in the Passion of Christ two thousand years ago. Thursday of the week, the night of the Last Supper, is known to Catholics as Holy Thursday, to Protestants as Maundy Thursday, because on Thursday of that week, Christ proclaimed a new commandment, that we should all love one another. Maundy is a corruption of *mandate,* from the Latin *Dies Mandati,* Day of the Mandate, in recognition of this new commandment. Good Friday relives the crucifixion of Christ. From Maundy Thursday evening through Good Friday to Easter Sunday morning is an especially somber and holy time. It is its own three-day cycle within the Holy Week period. In many parts of the United States, people keep silent between the hours of 12 noon and 3 P.M. on Good Friday, because this is supposedly the time during which Christ hung on the cross. Vigils are maintained in churches until the Resurrection is celebrated on Easter morning. In Connecticut, Good Friday is observed as a legal holiday, as it is in Canada.

As a symbol of the end of the Lenten period of mourning and the joy of the Easter Resurrection, on Easter morning the pope wears vestments of white, rather than the purple vestments of penance he has worn throughout Lent. At the midnight mass that marks the arrival of Easter Sunday morning, he lights a large white candle of "new fire" which symbolizes the new hope and new light of the world in the resurrected Christ. As in so many other rituals that we have seen, the imagery of candles and fire is put into service for this Christian feast day.

When holidays are felt to be emblematic of a people's identity, simply celebrating them is felt to be a political act. In Warsaw, before the massive political changes that resulted in the end of the Communist government in Poland, the Catholic Church existed in an uneasy tension with the Communist government. Nevertheless, Easter celebrations were quite large and passionately observed. Nor did the people shy away from overt political statements. In 1985, the Philapelphia

Passover Night, by Raisa Robbins. Courtesy of the Library of the Jewish Theological Seminary of America.

*Inquirer* reported that thousands of people in Warsaw carried their Easter baskets of egg and other foods to churches to be blessed there by priests. At Saint Stanislaw Kostka church, the grave of the reverend Jerzy Popieluszko, a priest who had been killed by the secret police a few months earlier, was decorated with flowers. Banners supporting the then-outlawed Solidarity movement were draped on the church fence, and many of the Easter baskets carried by the worshippers were decorated with Solidarity pins (*Inquirer* 7 Apr. 1985). In this case, the symbols of one grid—a political grid—combine easily with the religious symbolism of Easter to make a larger, powerful statement about national identity and freedom. The celebration of Easter, an expression of religious faith, became also a celebration of defiance.

Passover also occurs at this time of year; in fact, the Last Supper is believed by many to have been a Passover seder. The Roman Catholic Church accepts that it was, and as a result, the bread used for the communion wafer is unleavened, as it is in Jewish tradition. Eastern Rite Catholics, however, do not accept the Last Supper as a Passover seder, and use leavened bread.

Other Christian folk customs faintly echo Passover. For instance, bitter herbs are always eaten during the seder as a reminder of the

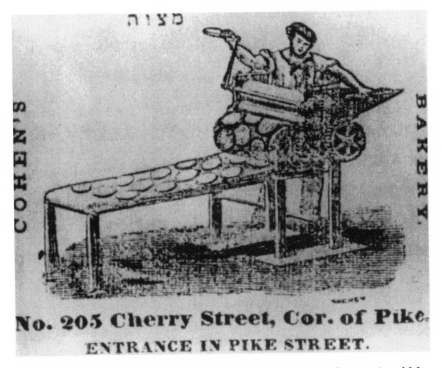

Making matzsos for Passover. Photo by David Hampshire, Instructional Media Services, Bowling Green State University.

slavery of the Jewish people in Egypt. In parts of Europe, this custom has apparently been transferred to the Christian Easter meal. Holy Thursday is called Green Thursday in Germany, because of the belief that if one eats herbs on this day, one will be protected from harm and misfortune during the coming year. In the area of Germany called Upper Silesia, lamb is eaten on Easter Sunday with horseradish, as a reminder of the bitter tortures and betrayals Jesus had to suffer before his triumphant resurrection on Easter Day; likewise, Americans of Polish or Russian extraction traditionally feature horseradish as a staple of the Easter feast (Russ 1982:46, 54).

Passover does not always coincide exactly with Easter because the Jewish system for determining the date of Passover differs from that of the Christian reckoning of Easter. Easter's date is based on a solar calendar and is specifically related to a celebration of the spring equinox. Passover is a seven-day (for Reform and Israeli Jews) or eight-day feast (for Orthodox and Conservative Jews outside Israel) that begins on the eve of the fifteenth day of the month of Nisan according to the Jewish lunar calendar, based on the number of times the moon revolves around the earth rather than on the length of time it takes the earth to revolve around the sun.

Like the eight days from Palm Sunday to Easter, the eight days of Passover relive a series of events by means of ritual. The biblical book of Exodus tells the story. The Lord intends to punish the Egyptians, who have held the Jews as slaves. An angel will be sent to strike dead the first-born son of every Egyptian household. The Jews are told to smear their doors or gates with the blood of a slaughtered lamb so the Angel of Death will know to pass over these families. Eventually the Jews are given their freedom, and Moses leads them to the promised land. From the evidence in the Bible, it appears that the Hebrews had already celebrated an ancient and now-forgotten spring festival at this time, a festival that involved the sacrifice of lambs.

Today, Passover is a festival of freedom. It is a happy holiday that, although sacred, involves a good deal of wine drinking during the seder, so that by the end of the meal everyone is in excellent spirits. The texts that are read, known collectively as the Haggadah, are about freedom and slavery, and contemporary works such as excerpts from the speeches of Martin Luther King are sometimes included. At a seder that I attended, we sang John Lennon's "Give Peace a Chance." In such ways Passover remains relevant and contemporary, while at the same time a ritual several thousand years old. The sanction of thousands of years of tradition is retained because the ritual form is retained. The content—at least some of it—is flexible and determined by the participants at specific celebrations. Thus, the holy day is still meaningful to younger generations, because it allows for creative input and participation. It breathes. Parts of it are intentionally left open-ended so that people can insert texts and refer to issues of particular importance to them.

A very holy and very joyous festival, Passover often does double duty. For a family in Philadelphia, it functions as a family reunion. In 1885, Abram Pressman and his family, Jewish immigrants from Poland, celebrated their first seder in the United States. In 1985, their descendents held their centennial Passover seder. Members of the family come from all over the country, including Florida, Michigan, and California. Now numbering about 150 members, the family has some trouble keeping up with each other. So they have evolved a family custom for the Passover reunion. Each family writes out a history of the previous year's events and reads it aloud. Thus the extended family keeps track of itself and maintains its continuity with the past.

However, the future of the family is not overlooked. Engagements of marriage are traditionally announced at the seder. If a member of the family escorts a date to the ritual meal, it is a means of announcing to the family that the couple intends to wed. So the family group has developed Passover as a ritual family homecoming in which both past and future generations of the family are recognized and the continuity of the family is assured (Philadelphia *Inquirer* 7 Apr. 1985).

When I was a child, Easter excited me very much, but as I got older, like many people, I lost much of my youthful enthusiasm for it and other more child-oriented holidays. No longer did I anxiously await the Easter bunny on Easter Sunday. As a teenager I began to question the validity of organized religion, so the day did not work as a holy day either. As I grew up, I found less and less meaning in the traditional holidays, and Easter became just another day on the calendar. I felt this as a real loss, however. I had always enjoyed the four seasons and the holidays and customs that go with them, and did not want to lose them. Many people attend church at Easter and at Christmas, not necessarily because they are believers, but because attending church is emotionally associated with the holiday for them. They enjoy the beauty of the ritual and its celebratory aspects. I think it is important to make an effort to be involved in the holidays and rituals of one's culture. Only by participating *in* them can one get anything *out* of them. They have existed for thousands of years, and when we examine them closely we find that their symbolism usually transcends any particular religion and speaks to all humanity.

Some people make the holidays particularly meaningful by an act like donating a pint of blood to the Red Cross every year at Easter, and sometimes at Christmas too. Giving blood is a somewhat unpleasant act, so it involves a bit of sacrifice, but it genuinely helps people. Blood, of course, is a very powerful symbol at this time of year, as is the idea of sacrifice, since it was the blood of slaughtered lambs that was smeared on the doors at the time of the first Passover, and Christians believe that Christ is the Lamb of God, who gave his blood for all humanity. Adding a personal dimension of meaning by conducting rituals such as donating blood can make the spring holidays hold a great deal more significance than marshmallow eggs alone allow for.

## *Family Easter Traditions*

Lawn and house decorations for holidays other than Christmas have been growing more elaborate for years. As long ago as 1961, the MacKenzie family of Lakeside, Ohio, was well known for its Easter

An egg tree. Photo by Jack Santino, Bowling Green, Ohio, 1990.

scene, which sported approximately two thousand multicolored shells on an egg tree and in the bushes and shrubs surrounding the house. Live rabbits helped the Easter Bunny give out gifts to children, and the MacKenzies also had a Maypole as part of the spring holiday symbolism. Another family keeps an egg-a-year collection that was started in 1938, the year their daughter was born. Each egg has the child's name and the year written on it. The collection and the family tradition that it represents is now entering into its third generation.

Increasingly, Jews and Christians are celebrating the continuity of their traditions. Jews invite Christian friends to seders; Catholics invite their Jewish friends to Easter breakfast. Some Catholic families have begun to have seders and invite Jewish and Christian friends to attend. Some may feel that their religious beliefs and cultural identity are compromised by such "nondenominational" events, but those who attend such events either continue to celebrate their religious customs privately or feel a need for something that addresses their situation today. Distinct cultural heritages are important and should be maintained. When we make a special meal for Passover, we are engaging in a tidal wave of tradition that may go back to an ancient Hebrew spring festival that became the celebration of the historical and religious events that are recounted in the book of Exodus; when

*The Virgin with the Dead Christ and Saints Mary Magdalen and John*, 1485, by Carlo Crivelli; from a 1985 card. James Fund and Anonymous Gift. Courtesy of the Museum of Fine Arts, Boston. Christ being removed from the cross, below a bough of fruits and vegetables. The connection of the resurrection of Christ and spring's rebirth is graphically illustrated.

we paint an Easter egg, we are involving ourselves with a Christian holiday that in its way is to Passover what Passover was to that ancient festival of the nomadic Hebrews. Just knowing of this kind of continuity adds richness and depth to our celebrations.

A lot of adults make Easter eggs with their friends as gifts for one another, not just for the children. Many Americans of European background continue to create beautiful, intricate traditional Easter egg patterns, and people of all backgrounds simply paint their own personal visions, such as a Jewish man who painted an Easter egg with Passover sayings. As natural symbols of birth, new life, resurrection, and renewal, eggs have been used all over the world. In China, for instance, people traditionally give eggs to celebrate the birth of a baby boy. Today in the United States, along with Easter egg hunts and egg-rolling contests is the belief that eggs can be stood on their ends on the vernal equinox. The oldest surviving decorated egg, found in a Roman sarcophagus in the city of Worms in present-day Germany, dates back to the fourth century A.D., but we know that eggs were being decorated even before that. In eastern Europe and Slavic countries such as Russia, long before the coming of Christianity, eggs were symbols of the sun, and it is in these countries—Poland, Hungary, Czechoslovakia, Lithuania, and Ukraine—that traditions involving eggs have remained powerfully linked to spring rituals. Coloring Easter eggs is a highly detailed and elaborate art in these places, and Americans of Eastern European background continue the tradition (see Newall 1971).

While saving eggs is a family tradition that emphasizes continuity with past family generations, people recognize the need to adapt to a changing environment. For instance, in the 1970s several Christian denominations began to hold Easter sunrise services in shopping malls. Easter is a religious holy day, but it has more to it than religious dogma. Everything about it says rebirth, renewal, regeneration. Like Passover, it comes during the period of growth of the earth's vegetation and during the time when the days begin to grow longer than the nights, until the summer solstice in June, the longest day of the year. The primary religious symbol of Easter is the resurrected Christ, who has died and is reborn. The pre-Christian symbols of rabbits and eggs are intrinsic to it; rabbits are ancient symbols of fertility and sexual potency, while eggs are universal symbols of life. Each of these symbols—the reborn God, the fertile rabbit, the new life promised by the egg—reinforces the other. The day is celebrated when the earth is reborn, when flowers bloom anew. People wear brand-new clothes for the occasion, indicating a personal rebirth. New suits and Easter bonnets adorned with the flowers of spring represent the new person we can each become. People buy new sets of clothes, launching their spring wardrobes. Easter bonnets and baskets of flowers are hung on front doors of homes.

Is all of this deliberately cyclical, as I suggest, or is it simply a random sequence of events that occurs every year? Consider this. The Church will burn the palms left over from Palm Sunday to create the ashes for the following year's Ash Wednesday. We may not all have Carnival and Mardi Gras, or the church calendar, to take us from midwinter to spring, but we have our holidays of Groundhog Day, Valentine's Day, and Saint Patrick's Day to help us along. Spring begins in the dead of winter. This year's palms of living glory become next year's ashes of death, as the cycle repeats and the year goes around, always connected to the past, always moving toward the future. The movement from dead of winter to the rebirth of spring is complete, but our march toward high summer has just begun.

# 4

## Toward Midsummer: Celebrating the Season of the Sun

The spring and fall quadrants of the year are an ascent into light and a descent into darkness respectively. The holidays that mark the route, however, grow scarce after the high spring celebrations of Easter and Passover. For the seven months of the year from October through April, we have many special days filled with old, compelling symbolism that we experience on a monthly basis. But from May through September, our national holidays lack traditional imagery such as rabbits, jack-o'-lanterns, or turkeys. The festive display of flowers that begins with Easter is the closest we come to a decorative organic item that represents the summer season. The flowers do not stand for any particular holiday of the summer, however, but rather for the season itself.

Although flowers are associated with the first of May, May Day, a major holiday in many parts of the world, is not nationally celebrated in the United States. It was in fact actively persecuted at one time in our history. In England, the government of Oliver Cromwell did not recognize most traditional holidays and discouraged the practice of calendar customs because they seemed to be forms of ancient idolatry.

The religious sect known as the Puritans continued to discourage the celebration of holidays in the New World, even after the Restoration in Great Britain abolished the antifestival laws. In the early American colonial days, a man named Thomas Morton had the temerity to set up a maypole on Mount Wollaston, known then as Merrymount, in Quincy, Massachusetts. It was promptly torn down, and Morton was expelled. Since then, May Day has been celebrated only as a children's diversion, or as part of a religious celebration of the month of May as Mary's month. Although there are some May customs in the United States today, the day has never fully recovered from the time of the Puritans' official disdain.

Flowers fill the May baskets of the first of the month, and flowers decorate the graves of fallen heroes and family members at the end of the month. May Day is descended from the Roman Floralia, which was celebrated in honor of the goddess Flora. As one of many Floralia customs, young girls would wind the columns of the temples with chains of flowers, a practice which reminds one of the maypole of more recent eras. Although originally a tree (usually birch), in the sixteenth and seventeenth centuries maypoles were built as permanent structures that often became town landmarks throughout England. The pole was hung with colorful streamers that people held while dancing around it. The patterns they formed changed endlessly. Although the Maypole is pretty much restricted to kindergarten these days, this aspect of it has not changed.

The Floralia, which was established late in the history of the Roman empire (approximately 173 B.C.) combined with Beltane, a Celtic celebration also held on the first of May. Beltane was a quarter day marked by bonfires, a day on which fairies were believed to be very active. Throughout the Middle Ages, the Renaissance, and into the nineteenth century, May Day was a nationally celebrated day in Europe and eventually to some extent even in America. Women washed themselves in the dew of May Day morning, in the belief that this would contribute to an almost eternal youthfulness. Men, women, and children of all classes went Maying, gathering flowers from the woods and fields for the May baskets and decorations. The day and its traditions were banned in England in 1644, during the time of Oliver Cromwell, but enjoyed a rebirth with the restoration of King Charles II of the Stuart family in 1660. In America, however, the Puritan influence lasted for a longer time, and the unflagging persecution of May Day, along with Christmas and other holidays the Puritans felt to be superstitious and idolatrous, succeeded in diminishing its importance. For instance, in his 1583 *Anatomie of Abuses*, Philip Stubbes railed against this May Day custom, calling the pole a "stinking idol." He wrote,

> Against Maie Day, Whitsunday, or some other time of the year, every parish, towne, or village, assemble themselves, both men, women, and children; and either all together, or dividing themselves into companies, they goe some to the woods and groves, some to the hills and mountaines, some to one place, some to another, where they spend all the night in pleasant pastimes, and in the morning they return, bringing with them birche boughes and branches of trees to deck their assembles withal. But their cheiftest jewel they bring from thence is the Maie-pole, which they bring home with great veneration, as thus—they

have twentie or fourtie yoake of oxen, every oxe having a sweet nose-
gaie of flowers tied to the tip of his horns, and these oxen draw home
the May-poale, their stinking idol rather, which they cover all over with
flowers and herbes, bound round with strings from the top to the bot-
tome, and sometimes it was painted with variable colours, having two
or three hundred men, women, and children following it with great
devotion. And thus equipped it was reared with handkerchiefs and
flagges streaming on the top. They strawe the ground round about it,
they bind green boughs about it, they set up summer halles, bowers
and arbours hard by it and then fall they to banquetting and feasting,
to leaping and dancing about it, as the heathen people did at the dedi-
cation of their idols. (1882 [1583])

Both secular and sacred May customs do continue in this country,
however. Many people recall making May baskets and secretly putting them on people's doors. Not only older people, either. Some of
my students, in their early twenties, did it in their younger years in
Ohio, and one woman tells that her teenage daughters have kept up
the tradition that she herself had grown up with and taught to them.
Children make May baskets, filled with flowers, at home. Then they
quietly attach them to the door of a neighbor or a friend, ring the
doorbell, and run off. In some parts of the Midwest, children will ring
doorbells and expect to receive pennies for their May basket creations,
a practice similar to trick-or-treating. In Iowa, children might leave
their May baskets at the door of a young friend they secretly have a
crush on, a custom that reminds us once again of the themes of love
and fertility that underlie so many of our festivals, especially those
of the spring. In this case, the custom is more reminiscent of Valentine's Day. Throughout this book, we see that the various customs and
activities we associate with certain holidays are actually quite universal, and are somewhere in the world attached to other holidays. Because of its phallic quality, the Maypole itself can be said to be related to fertility.

May Day customs are found locally and regionally in the United
States today. Rex Lowe discovered the reality of regional variation in
holiday customs first-hand when he moved from Iowa to Ohio and
found that May Day did not travel with him. He describes his experiences as follows:

When I grew up in central Iowa, on May Day, we'd all make May baskets, maybe two dozen of them. In fact, the dime store sold them, little
baskets, and we'd fill them with violets, popcorn, and gum drops, and
you'd go around to all your friends' houses, our parents would deliver us, and you'd put one up on the porch and ring the doorbell and

run like crazy. And if they caught you, they *kissed* you. And so depending on whose porch you put it on, if it was one of the guys, you know, you'd *run* like crazy. If it was a girl that you kinda liked, you'd trip or something like that.

Well, we moved to Bowling Green. Terry was four, and we were all pumped up—"All right! May Day is coming!" Terry needed to make some friends, so we fixed him up with a couple dozen May baskets, and he had a lot of little friends on his block that he had met. He went out and put them on the porch, rang the bell, and they looked down, and looked at him, and thought he was just crazier than hell! Apparently, they'd never done that here.

Sharon and I still give each other May baskets. We make them with very cheap things, you know, we put little flowers and candy and so forth in them. Everything costs less than a dollar that you fill it with, but it's just the thought of carrying on May Day. And we feel—we felt kind of, we'd been here a year and we felt really kind of displaced when May came around and there was no observance whatsoever, because May Day was kind of *important* when we were growing up. It was a fun holiday. You got lots of candy, and it was sort of equivalent to trick-or-treat night.

The month of May takes us from spring to summer. The first of May is, to the extent that it is still celebrated, a flower festival, while at the end of May, Memorial Day (now celebrated on the last Monday of the month) is considered to unofficially open the summer. In 1986, May 1 was the eighth day of Passover, and also Holy Thursday in the Eastern Orthodox Church. Insofar as each celebrates spring, they are cultural variations on a theme.

An interesting local adaptation of May Day is the Hawaiian Lei Day. Leis are traditional chains of flowers worn around the neck. Since May Day is a flower festival, in Hawaii the European holiday and the local custom combine to form Lei Day, a time for festivity when leis are exchanged as tokens of good luck and friendship.

Throughout the Western world, May 1, like November 1, is a day of deep traditional significance. In northern Europe, especially in the Harz mountains of Germany, and among some German Americans in the United States, April 30, the eve of May 1, is Walpurgis Night (*Walpurgisnacht*), named for Saint Walpurga, a martyred nun of the eighth century. Walpurga was the daughter of King Richard the Lion-Hearted; she moved to Germany and became the abbess of the monastery of Eichstatt. After her death she was canonized and became known as a protector against magic. Her day and its traditions almost certainly are traceable to pre-Christian celebrations that took place at this time. Walpurgis Night is in many ways similar to the American

Halloween, possibly due to the fact that May 1 and November 1 are two of the four major festival days of the Celtic peoples who once inhabited much of the European continent (the other two days being August 1 and February 1). Witches are believed to fly on Walpurgis Night, and they and the other supernatural creatures who are also active are mocked by people who wear costumes and hold parties for this special day. Bonfires are lit to ward off the evil creatures. In the German village of Bundheim, the townspeople have purposely and self-consciously injected aspects of their Germanic mythology of the wild hunt and elements from ancient spring festivals into Walpurgis Night. As part of the observation, young men dressed as demons and witches dance in ecstatic rituals to drive away evil. After the ecstatic dancing, the village has been purified and the villagers erect a maypole. This rejuvenation of the Walpurgis traditions was initiated in 1952, not to increase tourism, but as a means of reinstituting the town's traditions. In other areas, straw effigies of witches are paraded through the streets and burned in the fires. This tradition continues today in Sweden (see for example Russ 1982:56–59).

In many parts of the world May Day is more or less the equivalent of the American Labor Day. In the nineteenth century, American workers chose May 1 as the day from which eight hours of work would thereafter constitute a day's labor. Although the Knights of Labor had chosen the first Monday in September as Labor Day in 1882, many states observed it on May 1 throughout the 1880s. Internationally, during this time, May 1 was used as a date for labor strikes. Although the United States Congress officially ratified the first Monday of September as the American Labor Day observance, the International Labor Day was, and still is, observed on May 1. It is a public holiday in most European countries. The famous May Day celebrations in the former Soviet Union featured Russian women dressed in traditional peasant garb and adorned with flowers alongside the parades of missiles and military might. In South Africa in 1986, workers held a national strike in an effort to have May Day recognized as a national holiday. The strike, which became violent, began as a large traditional spring festival in honor of both May Day and workers' rights.

At first glance, one might wonder at the connection or continuity between May customs based on an ancient Roman flower festival, the nationalistic, militaristic displays in the Soviet Union, and labor demonstrations in other industrial countries. Perhaps it is the strike that is the link. May Day as an international Labor Day grew out of May labor strikes, among other things. Strikes and rallies are large public

May is Mary's month. Statue of the virgin crowned with flowers. Photo by Jack Santino, Holy Name Church, West Roxbury, Massachusetts, 1989.

events that, no matter how serious of purpose, take on many of the aspects of carnival and festivity. May 1 is a time of traditional festivity and a time when social rules can be turned upside down, when the weak become strong, the fool is seen to be wise, and the beggar becomes king—a heady time when the changing weather makes all things seem possible. The labor movement in the nineteenth century (and the more recent social movements of the 1960s also) plugged into this "feast of fools" phenomenon in an effort to realize social change. Those on the bottom of the social ladder took control, or at least tried to.

In the United States, the largest and most traditional May celebrations are religiously oriented, as the feast day of Mary, the mother of Jesus. The Catholic church of my childhood, Saint Peter's in Dorchester, Massachusetts, and its parochial school that I attended always had a May Procession, a spring extravaganza of bouquets and flowered tiaras worn by the young girl chosen as Queen of the May. In what is now apparent to me as a springtime celebration that is older than Christianity itself, this May parade featured flower symbolism similar to that of Easter, with the addition of the young girl who was named as its queen. The procession led into the church where the Queen of the May placed a crown of flowers on the statue of Mary.

The designation of May as the month of Mary's devotion probably has something to do with the goddess for whom the month is named: Maia, mother goddess of the earth. This is not to say that Mary of Galilee was not a real person, or that she did not historically give birth to Jesus. Rather it points to the fact we have seen throughout this book, that people invent new traditions from the ashes of the old, and reinterpret much of the preexisting symbolism they inherit, especially when it is so well suited to the time of the year.

As a religious feast day, May 1 is celebrated by the Roman Catholic Church with a ritual that, although dedicated to the mother of Jesus, shows clear and obvious affinity with spring festivals of the ancient world. This celebration, then, like so many others of our calendar, is rich with historical, symbolic, and psychological significance. Nevertheless, it is a Catholic religious parade and as such is not shared by all members of our society. Nor do our other summer holidays have the kind of significance and power we have seen in the celebrations of winter and spring. The one exception is the Fourth of July, which is one of the major holidays of the year, but even it is represented by the American flag rather than an organic item connected to the season.

For the national holidays of Memorial Day, Flag Day, Independence Day, and Labor Day, the flowers of summer are joined by the American flag as a major holiday symbol. The red, white, and blue motif joins the May baskets and the Memorial Day poppies of Flanders Field (in memory of a World War I battle) in May for Memorial Day, then reappears on Flag Day in June, Independence Day in July, and Labor Day in September. All of the national holidays of this period are civic. Each has its own *raison d'être,* but, it being summertime, each also is celebrated with backyard barbecues, outdoor picnics, and parades. In a way, the holidays celebrate *being* outside. Memorial Day, which began as a day of recognition of Civil War veterans, should be an American Day of the Dead, but Halloween is the holiday on which we recognize death as a *concept* (and give it its due), while small, local community–based grave-decoration-day rituals, sometimes called homecomings, held at various times throughout the country, are more significant to many people as rituals that mark *specific* deaths.

For instance, a 1953 report from Spring Hill, Kentucky, describes a Decoration Day held on the third Saturday of May. Family members gather at the family grave sites. The graveyard is cleaned and tended to in advance, so people can gather flowers to lay on the graves. In the account, Thelma Lynn Lamkin reports that the children were

Begun as a memorial for Civil War veterans, Memorial Day has become both a national Decoration Day of family graves, and the holiday that opens the summer season. Courtesy of the Center for Archival Collections, Bowling Green State University.

let loose to play in the graveyard. Decoration Day was also a day of courtship for the young people. Groups of girls and boys—young women and young men, I should say—reconnoiter. "The girls find a cute baby to play with. Then the timid boys who won't come to talk to us have an excuse—they come to play with the baby." After this period of warily scouting each other out, the boys and girls walk together in a tour of the cemetery. We can see in this Decoration Day an encapsulation of all the rites of passage of the family life cycle. The people are there to honor and commemorate the dead, but they set loose the youngest of the living to run through the grave markers, to play. If ever there was a better way of integrating life and death, and of helping young people to know and appreciate death as part of the life cycle, I have not yet come across it. The adolescents use the occasion as a time for courtship. By playing with a baby, they dramatize family roles, after which they pair off, foreshadowing future family units. Death, life, birth, marriage—all are here, combined into one ritualistic celebration of the life cycle (Lamkin 1953).

We place flowers on the graves of loved ones on Memorial Day, but other than that the day does not have the national impact that festivals which honor departed relatives and ancestors do in other countries. Waterloo, New York, has been recognized by President Lyndon Johnson and both houses of Congress as the birthplace of Memorial Day because the town decorated the graves of Civil War veterans as early as May 5, 1866. The claim is contested by Boalsburg, Pennsylvania, however, which claims to have begun the practice of decorating soldiers' graves two years earlier than Waterloo (Cerry 1969:739–54). General John A. Logan of the Grand Army of the Republic designated May 30, 1868, as a day "for strewing with flowers or otherwise decorating the graves of comrades" (Krythe 1962:141). Confederate states have felt that Memorial Day was a day of honor for Union soldiers, and so Florida in 1891 (later joined by nine other southern states), designated the birthday of Jefferson Davis, June 3, as Confederate Memorial Day.

Today, some states still do not officially recognize the May Memorial Day. However, most do, and over time the holiday has expanded to encompass our other national wars, including most recently the Vietnam conflict. Although Veterans' Day (formerly Armistice Day, noting the end of the First World War) is celebrated on November 11, Memorial Day has become the most important day of recognition of our armed forces.

There is no obvious connection between the backyard barbecue or trip to the beach and the deaths of our ancestors. However, it is ironic that more deaths occur due to automobile crashes during Memorial Day weekend than at any other comparable period of the year. Coincidentally, the Indianapolis 500 auto race is held on Memorial Day. While this particular race is going on, every year thousands of Americans are killed on the highways. On holiday weekends, especially Memorial Day weekend, we keep count. So we can see in the Indianapolis 500 a kind of symbolic exaggeration of our mechanized society and the kind of death it brings.

1986 saw the invention of a different kind of large-scale, ritualistic, celebratory event that was tied into Memorial Day. Hands Across America was held on the Sunday of Memorial Day weekend of that year. By looking at it closely, we can see how a symbolic, popular celebratory event was tied into a calendrical holiday. As a national event, Hands Across America was an effort to raise money for the nation's homeless by calling attention to the problem in a highly dramatic way. Originally, the vision was of millions of Americans holding hands for fifteen minutes, joined together in one unbroken chain across the United States. As the day approached, however, the success of the event began to appear doubtful. Not nearly enough people had pledged their participation for the line to be unbroken, and even worse, some doctors had publicly advised against people standing outside in the desert areas of the Southwest. For the final week before the event, the organizers made a last, major effort to attract people. The cause was taken up by the media, and it is interesting to look at the way it was handled.

First, some care was taken to distance Hands Across America from any of the other large-scale charity events, such as USA for Africa, that depended heavily on the participation of rock stars. Hands Across America was put forth as a patriotic "feel-good-America" event. The homeless, whom the event was originally intended to benefit, were not emphasized in the advertisements. Rather, people were urged simply to celebrate America, as if it were a kind of patriotic duty to participate. Hands Across America piggy-backed on the patriotic feelings engendered by Memorial Day. Flags were displayed on houses, parades scheduled to the tombs of veterans. Hands Across America channeled some of the energy of the holiday toward a particular goal, that of publicizing and alleviating hunger in America.

Some towns invent their own municipal events in May, using traditional imagery. Roslindale, Massachusetts, sponsored a spring cleaning it called the Big Sweep on May 10, 1989. The town had successfully incorporated the spring cleaning motif that seems so right at this time of renewal, with a community need, that of the revitalization of the image of the town and the spirit of the townspeople, by cleaning up the village center.

Throughout this book, I have been talking about the year in terms of quadrants, four segments divided by the solstices and equinoxes. The year's organization is not as simple as that, however. Not only do the holidays not correspond to those events in an exact manner (the Fourth of July, for instance, is the chief festival of summer, but it occurs fully two weeks after the summer solstice), but people also tend to perceive the year in many different ways. If we look at the year only in terms of the holidays, we find three periods. Fall to winter is one, winter to spring is a second, and summer is a third. For agriculturally based communities, the spring is the planting time and late summer the harvest. For the rest of us summer is one long season from May until September. In the first two periods, the process of the gradual lengthening and shortening of the days is apparent. Summer, on the other hand, seems to be an eternal present. We do not have the same kind of buildup through a series of holidays from the spring equinox, or from Easter and Passover, to June 21 or July 4, nor do we from midsummer to September 21. The buildup is the spring itself, or at least that portion of it from Easter on, and the wind down is the autumnal days of September and October.

If Memorial Day acts as an opening frame for summer, so does the end of the school year. Graduations especially are traditional symbolic events that function as summer openings. Likewise, the opening of school at the other end of the season is a kind of transition marker. As always, endings and beginnings are the same: summer ends, but school and autumn begin. Moreover, these celebrations are also participated in by friends and family, making them more than simply private affairs. Such personal events take on national and even international significance when the individuals are of a certain stature. For instance, the wedding of Prince Charles and Lady Diana of Britain was watched, enjoyed, and celebrated by people all over the world, and became a kind of one-time-only holiday in America. Likewise, the death and funeral of John F. Kennedy was a ritual that was participated in nationally. The death of Elvis Presley on August 16 is commemorated annually by thousands of fans who travel to the singer's home in Memphis, Tennessee. Regularly recurring social holidays are often based on life-cycle incidents, as when we celebrate the birthdays of George Washington, Abraham Lincoln, or Martin Luther King. For that matter, religious calendars are based on the life-cycle events of their prophets and deities. The most significant popular observations of the Christian calendar are commemorations of the birth, death, and resurrection of Jesus.

Returning to school and advancing to the next grade are rites of passage for schoolchildren, while high school and college graduations mark passage into adulthood. In this way, the rituals of the life cycle correspond to the seasonal year. For instance, June remains a favorite month for weddings, perhaps because it follows graduation. People finish their careers as students and begin a new stage of life in marriage. In fact, graduation, or commencement—a rite of passage in a very real sense, since it marks the end of one phase of life and the beginning of another—is a more intrinsically fitting ceremony with which to open the summer season than the civic holidays of this time of the year.

Before returning to work in September, after Labor Day, however, we enjoy summer. Baseball is of course the summer game, and the baseball season is yet another grid that we use to reckon time. Spring training begins in February, just about the time people are weary of winter. Like the holidays of February, spring training assures us of the eventual arrival of a long-awaited season. The actual playing season is initiated by the rites of opening day, which often features the President of the United States throwing out the ceremonial first ball at a game. As the season progresses, we watch the fortunes of our favorite team ebb and flow, until the mid-season All-Star break in July. I was once asked, in jest, if the All-Star game qualified as a holiday. I answered yes, then thought about it for a minute. I realized that while the All-Star game is not a holiday in any official or even unofficial sense, it *is* a festive occasion for many. It marks a midpoint of this particular grid, this interpretation of the year. Falling in mid-July, it is close to an actual midpoint in our contemporary American summer which begins on Memorial Day and ends on Labor Day. Like all the other grids we have for interpreting yearly flow, the baseball season has its own dynamics, its own logic. The baseball year builds to a series of elimination games that take us into the fall, and which culminate with the "October Classic," the World Series.

Music festivals such as polka, bluegrass, and rock festivals (like Woodstock and others over the years) are another modern, open-air, peculiarly summer entertainment, reminiscent of the evangelical camp meetings of the eighteenth and nineteenth centuries. Recent attempts by rock fans to hold a festival on the summer solstice at Stonehenge, in England, is a melding of several ideas: a recognition of the summer solstice as a special time; a recognition of the rock festival as a summer night's event, well-suited to midsummer and solstice rituals; and a recognition of Stonehenge, legendary site of druidical astronomical observations, as an appropriate place for such a festival. The permit was denied, but the attempt is something of a statement about the melding of the ancient and the modern: rock music takes its place as a celebratory sacrament alongside revered monuments and significant days.

Summer is identified above all with sunlight. It is a period that contains the longest day of the year. We even try to improve on the naturally long days by changing our time frame for a few months with daylight savings time. In effect, summer is one long season in sharp contrast to the rest of the year. For many occupations, summer is a period of intense activity, especially for outdoor work such as construction, landscaping, and farming. Some jobs are seasonal, such as anything having to do with tourism. When I was in high school, a very resourceful friend of mine was looking for a summer job. He thought to himself, "What kind of occupation will be hiring now?" He thought for a bit, then got the Yellow Pages, called an air conditioning installation company, and got a job.

Interestingly, these summer holidays are all civic holidays. Perhaps that is why the season dominates them. Although they have taken on some of the trappings of more traditional folk celebrations, they are primarily political and institutional in nature. In September, Labor Day honors work and those who perform it, and this is good, but such a celebration is not derived organically out of the seasons or the solar cycle or the agricultural cycle or the life-death cycle. These events could be held at any time of the year. Mother's Day in May could be said to be related to fertility, and further, to the fact that for Catholics May is devoted to a mother "deity," the Immaculate Mother of Christ, and before that, to an ancient Earth-mother goddess. However, most of these connections are unexploited during Mother's Day. Nothing about the day ever suggests these symbolic possibilities. Father's Day in June is even less connected to the season, while the Fourth of July commemorates a political event, the signing of the Declaration of Independence and the establishment of the United States of America as a national entity. However, of all of these, the Fourth of July has tapped most successfully into the ebb and flow of the natural year, because of its place on the calendar and the importance of the event it commemorates. We need a summer festival, just as we need fall, winter, and spring festivals. The founding of the nation in July serves nicely as a hook to hang one on. Rather than being derived from the seasons in which they occur, these holidays are imposed upon them. Eventually, the graft takes, and we relate to them in seasonal ways, so that Memorial Day is said to be the opening of summer and Labor Day its close.

Scholars have suggested that the United States has a "civil religion," distinct from other sects of Christianity, which includes the Enlightenment concepts (as set forth in Rousseau's *The Social Contract*) of belief in the existence of God, an afterlife, and the rewarding of good and the punishment of evil, along with a public disavowal of religious discrimination and an endorsement of religious tolerance (see Bellah 1967). Also a part of this civil religion is the tenet that "all men are created equal" and that human rights are created by God and therefore inherent in humanity, rather than merely granted by benevolent rulers. These ideas, combined with that of the separation of church and state, underlie American attitudes about democracy, manifest destiny, and the United States as a model for the world, a "city on a hill." Presidents Kennedy and Lincoln are seen as martyrs in this civil religion; indeed, it was Lincoln who institutionalized Thanksgiving Day as an annual day of prayer as well as giving thanks.

In a somewhat similar way, I would term many of our annual holidays civic holidays. Some, like Flag Day, are civic holidays exclusively. Others, like Thanksgiving, are political, seasonal, and religious. While not all civic holidays occur in the summertime, all the national (as opposed to regional, ethnic, or occupational) holidays of the summer are civic.

Flag Day in Bowling Green, Ohio, for instance, is a celebration of small business, carried out outdoors beneath unfurled American flags. In fact, Main Street is lined with flags overhanging the street. Underneath these flags are stalls selling various items, some of which are homemade, most of which are commercially manufactured. Bowling Green has its Arts and Crafts Fair on Flag Day, June 14. Looking down Main Street, one sees a statement of patriotism combined with the American ideal of individual, small-scale enterpreneurship and capitalism. This is a community event, no mistake. The people all know each other; they look forward to Flag Day and consider it a festive, enjoyable time for socializing. The small booths that line the streets are individual commercial ventures that are implicitly in competition with each other, but which combine to create an effect similar to a marketplace or bazaar in the Middle East. The goods, of course, differ from those offered in more traditional marketplaces. Often they emphasize the playful nature of the event and the playful aspects of summer as well: beach balls, lawn chairs, and outdoor grills are lined up on Main Street. Articles of clothing include lightweight thong sandals, imitation Hawaiian shirts, and shorts. Like the other holidays of summer, Memorial Day, Labor Day, and the Fourth of July, Flag Day is a civil holiday conducted oudoors. It is a secular ritual that celebrates summer and the dual civil religions of patriotism and capitalism. The acts of buying and selling are blessed by the sacred American flag flying above. Flag Day here is as much about selling as it is about patriotism, as much about capitalism as about democracy. The material objects of the day, the lawn chairs and grills and beach balls, celebrate the leisure activities of summer. Work is seen as a means to an end, that of leisure. One works so that one can play. Work is selling things, not making things. We are a consumer nation. Work is individualistic and competitive, but in a larger way it is cooperative. If the fair is largely a mercantile event that serves as an advertisement for the downtown shopping area, it depends on the participation of each of the shopkeepers in order to make it work. This is a small-town event in mid-America, one that is found in small towns throughout America, and it celebrates small-town ideals, beneath the unfurled flags.

## Witchcraft on the Summer Solstice

There can be a darker side to traditional belief, in small towns and larger cities alike. Flag Day may represent certain ideals, but fears of the outside and of the unfamiliar are also expressed traditionally. For instance, despite the efforts of the early Puritans to rid our customary holidays of all "superstition" and "pagan idolatry," the old dates of ancient celebration continue to have their appeal, especially to people who want to celebrate an alternative festival cycle. Many of the contemporary witchcraft cults have adopted a combination of the Celtic calendar, with its four great holidays on the first of November, February, May, and August, and the solstices and the equinoxes as more fundamental occasions for revelry, undiluted by centuries of Christianity and politics. These celebrations are said to be more natural, directly tied into the earth and its magic. As a result, these dates are sometimes greeted with fear of the satanic and the evil, much as in past times.

For example, on June 21, 1985, in Spencer Township outside of Toledo, Ohio, there was a major satanism scare. A police official announced to the press that he had inside information that a satanic cult was operating in a nearby area. Several bodies of sacrificial victims were supposedly buried in the countryside outside the cult's "headquarters," and, more importantly, the sheriff was told that there would likely be an orgy of human sacrifice that night. The sheriff went in with bulldozers, which turned up no bodies at all, not even traces. Police found only a headless doll, which they described to the press as "decapitated," and a rusty knife, which they claimed as evidence that indeed there had been some diabolical activities going on. At first, the sheriff announced that he had it on reliable authority that this day was one of the high holy days in the satanic calendar, but he did not connect it to the summer solstice until various members of the academic community pointed it out. No further evidence of any satanic or witchcraft activity ever emerged, and the incident was forgotten.

But on February 2, 1986, an almost identical incident occurred about fifty miles away, in Carleton, Michigan. I received a breathless phone call from a Toledo television reporter, who told me of the breaking story: a fifteen-year-old boy had shot his seventeen-year-old brother with a shotgun, and the murder was thought to be related to satanic cult activity. The police were entering the high schools and going through students' lockers in search of ritual objects or cult-related items, and school officials were pulling record albums and books from the library that they felt were influenced by satanism. On February 20, 1986, the front page of the *Toledo Blade* reported, "The date of the slaying corresponded with Witches' Sabbath, one of eight sacrificial days on the satanic calendar." A university professor (not myself) appeared on television commenting that February 2 is Candlemas and that this is a traditional "pagan" holiday, which would explain why February 2 was chosen as a day for witchcraft activity. Later, a "cult expert" said that "the use of a gun was 'somewhat bizaare and unusual,' indicating the murderer probably acted alone and was in an experimental stage of satanism." One student was quoted as saying, "I know he was into that Satan stuff, but I don't think that had anything to do with the shooting." Once again, as time passed, no further witchcraft or satanic cult activity turned up.

There have been regular reports of Satanism and witchcraft in northwest Ohio and southern Michigan, and they invariably arise at the solstices, equinoxes, or on the holidays at the beginnings of the four months of the Celtic festival calendar. These are the "eight sacrificial days" the newspaper referred to. Most of the fear and misunderstanding of these events is consistent with witchcraft scares of the past, in New England in 1692, and throughout Europe in the late Middle Ages and early-modern era. In the Michigan case, the boy seems to have been disturbed, and his interest in satanism was more a symptom of that than a cause of the killing. Still, we need to understand the irrational, so we plug these kinds of acts into a framework we can understand, and condemn.

Perhaps the most truly traditional behavior is that which is not self-conscious. These eruptions of cult fear are really a kind of solstice belief. The satanists who are high school students and the contemporary witchcraft cults have no direct historical continuity with the witches of the late-medieval or Enlightenment witchcraft movements. The new satanism and witchcraft cults are not identical; many witch groups do not recognize Satan as anything other than a part of the mythology of Christianity that they claim witchcraft predates. Nevertheless, these groups today are reviving traditions, not continuing them in an unbroken line. They take their knowledge of witchcraft and Satanic rituals from spurious authorities, books written with little or no knowledge of how human beings have actually perceived evil, or what they have believed about magic. But when the sheriff of a small midwestern town orders the exhumation of supposed sacrifices of ritual murders on the eve of the summer solstice (his sources told him there would be more killings on June 20 or 21), we are witnessing behavior motivated by folk belief surrounding the longest day of the year, a day traditionally associated with magic. A week earlier, a mass murder had been discovered in California, unrelated to either witchcraft or the solstice. Fifteen to twenty bodies were found buried in a rural area: they were the bodies of women tortured, raped, and killed by a pair of madmen who styled themselves "survivalists." Heavily armed, they spurned modern society. In a classic example of the folk process, this kind of bizarre, horrifying behavior became connected with a day that attracts belief in the unusual. So a rumor of a similar kind of mass murder surfaced in Ohio and was said to be connected to the solstice, a pivotal, transitional turning point in the passage of the year. True to form, a new body of legend and belief, and perhaps, if any of the rumors are true, a grisly and malconceived ritual, has attached itself to it (see for example Ellis 1989).

## Picking Cherries on the Summer Solstice

Ironically, while all of these gruesome events were going on, I was looking for something significant to do to mark the summer solstice personally. In between the phone calls from television people, I found it. A colleague had posted an announcement: *Come Pick Cherries.* So I did, fully aware of the seasonal nature of this harvest, and of the use of the cherry as a sexual metaphor throughout Anglo-American folklore and folk song. Standing on a ladder in a rural backyard, I thought about the alleged slayings, my face buried in the leaves of branches laden with cherries redder and riper than any I'd ever seen. The distance between the witchcraft fright and picking cherries on that warm and breezy day highlighted for me the two sides of our holiday occasions, which mirror the two sides of life: light and darkness, love and fear, good and evil, growth and death. The twenty-first of June, another annual point of endings and beginnings, was more meaningful with the picking of cherries than it might have been otherwise. In the autumn, people go to farms and orchards to pick apples and to buy pumpkins. At Christmas, a lot of people prefer to cut their own tree. To celebrate the solstice of summer (the beginning, by our calendar, but the midpoint by many other calendars) another kind of harvesting helps. The summer is celebrated on the beach, in the backyard, in the mountains, with picnics and clambakes and barbeques. But I found picking cherries in the afternoon sun, and later baking a cherry pie with my hand-picked harvest, a deeply satisfying and deeply symbolic act.

Summer stands by itself. Workers try to get away to the beach on weekends. Some people must take their vacations during the summer. Students are out of classes, businesses close for weeks at a time. At other times of the year, the seasons are defined by their holidays. During summer it is the other way around. The sun dominates everything else, including the holidays. A Washington, D.C., family who decorated their house for each holiday put a vase with a stylized image of the sun on their porch during the summer. In October they had Halloween images, jack-o'-lanterns, witches, black cats, and so forth, which were replaced by Thanksgiving images in November. Then came the Christmas wreath and the candles of December, followed in time by a heart, then by an Easter bunny and eggs. Although there are a lot of organic things in this sequence, they are all tied specifically to a holiday of the season. Not so the sun. It is not a symbol of the Fourth of July. July 4 is certainly an important annual holiday, but it does not dominate the summer the way Christmas dominates the winter. There are no Independence Day greeting cards in the stores, for instance.

That is not to say that the Fourth of July is not a holiday of major significance in the United States. That it *is* is borne out by the major celebration of Liberty Weekend in 1986, during which the centennial of the erection of the Statue of Liberty in New York harbor was (imprecisely) celebrated on the Fourth of July (the actual hundred-year anniversary was in October of that year). Liberty Weekend was a culmination of two hundred and ten years of Independence Days. The fireworks were more spectacular, and the celebration grander, than any that had gone before. In many ways, the Statue of Liberty Centennial was a more successful national celebration of this country than the Bicentennial celebration of 1976, ten years earlier, had been. The mood of the country in the 1980s was more conducive to such large-scale patriotic outbursts than it had been in the 1970s. The 1980s was a decade of large-scale public celebrations, with everything from Live Aid to Hands Across America. The Statue of Liberty celebration drew equally from the success of those events and the opening and closing ceremonies of the 1984 Olympics. During Liberty Weekend, Americans ritualistically celebrated themselves and all previous Fourth of July celebrations. Along with all the Hollywood-generated theatrics in New York, there were some genuinely touching moments. The statue enshrines the same values of freedom and justice that Americans feel their country embodies. It was an easy addition to traditional Fourth celebrations to honor Liberty on Independence Day. The process was similar to the Hands Across America event that preceded it by six weeks, but it was much easier to connect the events of 1776 to the arrival of the statue in 1886 in the commemoration of the two combined in 1986.

People of all ages attended the Liberty Weekend festivities in New York, but many of them were of the same generation that had attended the Woodstock music festival of 1969. The contrast between the two events is telling. As at Woodstock, there was certainly a feeling of solidarity, festivity, and community at Liberty Weekend. One incident, typical of the celebration, involved a man who approached a group of five policemen and sprayed them with a container that emitted confetti. The police all went for their holsters, in what looked to be an ugly incident in the making. From each holster came a spray can, and the police confettied the man in return.

If indeed Liberty Weekend did involve many of the same people that attended the great hippie celebration of Woodstock a generation earlier, it graphically represents the change in the attitude of the country. This festival was done in colors of red, white, and blue, worn proudly rather than sarcastically, as was the case in the 1960s. The participants celebrated their American citizenship, rather than attempting to create their own "Woodstock nation." Woodstock was about creating a separate community because the larger, more powerful and conventional one was felt to be inadequate and unacceptable. In 1986, people of the Woodstock age group, perhaps Woodstock participants themselves, celebrated the larger society. Patriotism was in style in the 1980s, as was dramatically made manifest at this Fourth of July celebration to top all previous Fourth of July celebrations.

The large-scale, celebratory event now universally refered to as Woodstock surprised virtually everyone connected with it at the time, including the organizers, the participants, and the musicians. No one had expected a crowd of several hundred thousand people to attend the rock music festival in August, 1969. To accommodate the crowd (to appease them, actually) the fences came down and admission prices were done away with. These decisions were made spontaneously. Liberty Weekend, on the other hand, was the result of massive long-range planning. The festive qualities, the *communitas* that Woodstock has become famous for, all developed on the spot.

The fact that Woodstock was held on a farm in the country was also significant: going to Woodstock (where popular musicians Bob Dylan and the Band had recently lived in seclusion for a number of years) was part of the back-to-nature movement of the time. By extension, so was the skinny-dipping and reveling in the mud that went on throughout the festival. The Woodstock generation saw themselves as a generation reborn, innocent like babies. The celebrated nudity apparent throughout the event was felt to be a sign of innocence, not sexuality. Liberty Weekend, on the other hand, was a necessarily urban event due to the location of the statue it celebrated, but it certainly carried with it none of the generational self-identification that Woodstock had.

People did not just sit at home and watch Liberty Weekend events on television, however. Some built their own Statues of Liberty. In Battle Creek, Michigan, an artist held a party on the banks of the Battle Creek river. Throughout the day of the Fourth, guests canoed on the water, foraging for driftwood to use in a sculpture. At the end of the day, some twenty people built a handsome, ten-foot replica of the famous statue. Similar homemade statues went up in cities and towns across America.

Along with the beach parties and backyard barbecues that dot the summer months, the Fourth of July is marked by fireworks, bonfires, and vacation trips to favorite spots. Independence Day is an example of the particular history of a society being a determinant in changing the date and nature of a traditional celebration. June 24, Midsummer Day (like Christmas, just a few days after a solstice) was traditionally celebrated with bonfires the eve prior to it, and, as on Halloween, fairies were believed to roam. The Catholic Church renamed it Saint John's Day, after John the Baptist, and sure enough, St John's Eve became the night of fairies and bonfires throughout Europe. One custom has people jumping over fires as part of the midsummer celebration, which supposedly parallels the sun crossing past the midpoint of the solar year. Peter Burke, in his *Popular Culture in Early Modern Europe*, points out that "just as the midwinter festival on 25 December came to be celebrated as the birthday of Christ, so the midsummer festival on 24 June came to be celebrated as the birth-day of the forerunner of Christ [John the Baptist]." (1978:180). It is also another holiday of rejuvenation, with the baptism of Christ, im-mersed in water, a ready symbol. It was once thought that the bon-fires of the day were magic rituals that mimicked the sun in its glory in the sky and helped give it strength for another year as the days began to grow shorter. The bonfires were lit in later centuries to re-member a baptism by water, so the symbolic weight of fire and wa-ter are combined. Further, it falls exactly six months after Christmas, on the opposite side of the year, just as the summer and winter sol-stices mirror each other.

Midsummer was based on the solstice and cleaved the season from May 1 (the end of spring) to August 1 (the beginning of harvest) in half. It too was a time for the sprites, as described in Shakespeare's *Midsummer Night's Dream*. Fairy beliefs of Midsummer Day never took root in the United States, but the bonfire tradition continues among Swedes, Finns, and Lithuanians, and is often found in conjunction with the celebration of Independence Day among other people. When I was a child, my family spent the Fourth of July in Bristol, New Hampshire. A carnival was set up on the town field that week, and my favorite memories of the holiday are the great bonfire the evening of July 3, the parade the next morning, and the fireworks that night.

Another Fourth of July custom that has the old midsummer tradi-tion at its root is that of pranking on the eve of the Fourth. In ways very reminiscent of Halloween pranking, residents of the state of Maine recall removing people's front steps from their porch then ring-ing the bell and running off, or hoisting wagons onto trees, or steal-ing outhouses. Curiously these same tricks were customarily played on May Eve as well.

A resident of Alna, Maine, in a 1985 interview by a folklore student from the Northeast Archives at the University of Maine at Orono, says, "Doing tricks as they ordinarily do on Halloween now, that was done in my area, where I grew up on the first of May. That's the way it was." He continues, "The young folk, they would, they'd haul off old wag-ons. If there'd happen to be one sitting in your yard they might haul it off and put it in a field or something like that. I can remember a next door neighbor, we went out, a bunch of us, one May night, and he had left his sulky plow out beside the barn, beside his yard there. The build-ing was up on a little hill and down below was a brook, a fair size brook. The boys took that sulky plow, there was enough of them, it didn't haul too hard. They hauled it down the hill and parked it in the brook. I was part of the crew, yes. The night of May 1."

His wife followed up: "The stunts that they did on May first, in

June contains the summer solstice and the traditional Midsummer's Eve. This interesting magazine cover showcases the fairies that roam on that night. June 1916. Courtesy of the *American Printer* magazine.

Fourth of July cover, *Ladies Home Journal,* 1942. Women attend to the flag while the men are off to war. Even though women joined the work force in large numbers during World War II, here they are depicted primarily as ritual specialists. © 1942, Meredith Corporation. All rights reserved. Reprinted from *Ladies' Home Journal* magazine.

his area, were done on the Fourth of July in my area. That's when they might get the sled up on somebody's store, or they'd do something crazy, how about that? On the Fourth of July, the night before the Fourth. That was mischief night. May, for us, that was to hang May baskets, we would hang May baskets on May 1. And we would keep hanging May baskets all during May, as far as that's concerned."

Draping trees and houses with toilet paper is a favorite Halloween prank currently in vogue. It is also popular during other special days of social transition such as graduation and the end of the school year. The following account is of a Fourth of July prank, of a sort, that combines the Halloween toilet paper with the explosives that are generic to the Fourth: "My father sold fireworks during the Fourth of July. And I can distinctly remember a guy, he was quite a joker. He came into the drugstore and bought a whole case of toilet paper and a whole bunch of cherry bombs. And another guy, a friend of his, bought a case at another store and some cherry bombs. And they stood up on the corners, put the cherry bombs into the toilet paper and threw it up and let the confetti come down!"

Summer is also the season for a great many ethnic and religious celebrations. Saints' days, blessings of the fleets, and other local and regional festivities fill the weeks. For instance, in many Black communities in America, especially in Texas and Oklahoma, Emancipation Day celebrations are as important as, if not more important than, Fourth of July festivities. As a kind of Black Independence Day, Emancipation Day celebrates the actual freeing of the slaves, which occurred after the end of the Civil War. Susan G. Davis has noted a tradition of alternative Black Fourth of July celebrations in Philadelphia in the nineteenth century. These might be held on the fifth of July, for instance, to irritate the white population, and also to underscore the celebrants' position as separate from the larger society (Davis 1986:46). C. L. Dellums, a long time labor union activist who was born in Texas over eighty years ago, told me that he was only a generation removed from slavery: "My father was actually born in slavery. Now generally, January 1 was looked upon as the liberation of the slaves. But there wasn't slave one freed January 1, 1863, not one. Abraham Lincoln's proclamation didn't free anybody. Slaves weren't freed in Texas until June 19, 1865. And my dad was born in April 1865. So he was a slave baby, you know for about two and a half months. So when I say I'm the son of a slave, I am the son of a slave. And then I was born only thirty-five years later. So, you see, I was born pretty close to slavery itself" (Santino 1989:9).

The Emancipation Day celebration in Texas and Oklahoma is called Juneteenth. According to folklorist William Wiggins, the day had its legendary beginnings when a Black former soldier for the Union rode a mule into the Southwest to announce to the Black people there that they were free. He arrived in Oklahoma on June 19. As the stories have it, many slaves stopped their work immediately upon hearing the news. The commemoration of that day has since become like a "second Christmas" in terms of its importance to Black people in the area. The celebration's components, however, are similar to those of the Fourth of July; that is, the day is celebrated with parades, floats, marching bands, picnics, and baseball games. Freedom, a theme found in the Fourth of July holiday in the aspect of "independence," is a much more immediate aspect of Juneteenth celebrations. Many of the floats and banners depict scenes of the Blacks' struggle against slavery, and in earlier years, former slaves marched in the parades. Wiggins points out that the folk history of the origin of the event uses two images of slavery, the mule and the slave himself, and recasts them into heroic symbols of freedom. "The mule, formerly used as a field beast of burden, now carries a messenger of freedom; the slaves stop being passive victims of the system and proclaim their new status. They do not simply say they are free, they start *being* free" (Wiggins 1982:287).

Although Juneteenth is primarily a Black celebration, its baseball games, bull-riding contests, and pit-barbecue picnics are integrated. Politicians might sponsor the barbecue, then attend it in order to campaign for public office. In the town that Wiggins studied, the Juneteenth baseball games were the only time that whites and Blacks intermingled on an equal basis. Despite the inherent competition of a sporting event, the baseball games helped foster mutual respect, as does the celebration of the day itself, a celebration of Black ethnicity and culture. For over a hundred years, Juneteenth was celebrated as a major but unofficial holiday among Black people; in some cases people risked losing their jobs if they took the day off to participate in the events. But participate they did, and in 1972 two Black congressmen introduced a bill in the Texas state legislature that recognized Juneteenth as an "annual, though unofficial holiday of significance to all Texans, and particularly, to the Blacks of Texas, for whom this date symbolizes freedom from slavery." Finally, in 1979, Juneteenth was recognized as an official state holiday (Wiggins 1982:292–93; see also Wiggins 1987).

### The Laotian-American Rocket Festival

Of course, there are other ethnic celebrations throughout the summer that are unrelated to European tradition. A great Laotian festival in

May is the *Boun Bang Fai,* or the Rocket Festival. Like many Lao traditions, this festival has been brought to the United States by Laotians who came in the 1970s and 1980s. In Laos, the Rocket Festival marks the coming of the rainy season. It provides people with a chance to gather together and enjoy festivities for the short time during which the weather makes it impossible to work.

On the morning of the Rocket Festival, a religious commemoration of the birth and death of the great Buddha is held. On this day, new monks are taken into monastic communities and people give special offerings to the monks. Although the Rocket Festival was once a religious holiday, it has now become open to and enjoyed by people of all faiths. After the religious ceremony, the people dress up in special traditonal costumes and gather outdoors. Monks provide handmade rockets: bamboo poles filled with a special mixture of gunpowder. These rockets are beautifully decorated with mythical dragons and colored streamers, and may be up to twenty feet in length. In Laos, the Rocket Festival includes a competitive event in which rockets from many villages are judged according to how well they are decorated and how far they fly when they are launched. A group from each village, playing music and carrying their rocket, parades by a panel of judges, hoping they will be judged the best.

The Rocket Festival is said to date to the time when the Lao people believed in many gods, and sent up rockets to them in hopes of securing rains for a good rice harvest. Although the festival has been conducted in the Washington, D.C., area, which is home to many Lao people, the conditions in America are so different that it may not continue to be relevant. There is no real rainy season, and there is no rice harvest. The *Boun Bang Fai* has been continued for nostalgic purposes, and as a way of introducing long-time residents of the United States to the Laotian culture. In the United States the Rocket Festival celebrates ethnicity, but the day may come when it is no longer seen in this country.

## Community Festivals

Community festivals, state and county fairs (said to be the *real* harvest festivals of our society), religious celebrations of many different ethnic groups, and occupational rituals are plentiful during the summer and, for many people, provide some of the most important celebratory events of the entire year. A Blessing of the Fleet, for instance, is held in many fishing villages. Perhaps the most famous takes place in the old New England town of Gloucester, Masssachusetts, for several days surrounding the feast day of Saint Peter, the patron saint of fishermen. The blessing is done publicly, often by the cardinal of the archdiocese of Boston. The town celebrates for days before and after, tourists come to observe, a mass is celebrated at the statue of an old fisherman, and after a procession to the harbor where the fleet is docked, the ships are blessed. This event combines all aspects of festival, ritual, and celebration. The ritual of the Roman Catholic mass and a special blessing is at its center. Prior to the day of the blessing, the townspeople wear costumes, the men sometimes dress as women as they parade through the narrow streets, crowd the taverns, spill out into the streets, make noise, and generally engage in typically festive behavior. Near the docks, another kind of carnival takes place: a midway is set up with rides and food concessions that cater mostly to the tourists. The Blessing of the Fleet is a religious event. It is also an ethnic event (the men who make up the fishing crews are largely Portuguese). It is an occupational event: these are real, working boats, and the economy of the townspeople is dependent on good catches. The work is hard, unpredictable, and dangerous, and the fishermen take the blessing quite seriously. Moreover, it celebrates the saint's day. A statue of Saint Peter is carried through the town while people eagerly attach money to it as an offering of thanks and to help ensure a healthy and prosperous future. And the event celebrates Gloucester herself, a town that is synonymous with fishing and with Portuguese immigrants. Undoubtedly, the three-day celebration is one of the most important festival or ritual days to the residents of this town.

We find in Gloucester a dichotomy between festival and ritual (see Abrahams 1987). The Blessing of the Fleet, along with the attendant festive behavior (transvestite costume, partying, public drinking, and licentiousness) and the statue of Saint Peter, attracts tourism and is written up as a "weekend getaway" in the "What To Do for the Weekend" section of urban newspapers. However, a visit to Gloucester reveals that the town is still very much a real working town with a working fishing fleet, and that the events are very important and have real power for the townspeople participating in them. For the tourists who come to observe, it is all spectacle; for the members of the local regional and occupational community, it is ritual. They participate in the activities, they are engaged by them, their lives are affected. It is their boats that are being blessed by the cardinal of the archdiocese of Boston. They're the ones who face the dangers of the sea and the uncertainties of the catch and who need the blessing. Granted, attention spans vary throughout the course of the events, but the quality of participation, as anthropologist John MacAloon has suggested—engaged and active participation rather than detached and passive—may be a means by which we can distinguish ritual from spectacle (1984:241–80). The Blessing of the Fleet is ritual for the members of the in-group, the community; it is spectacle for the tourists, the visitors. It is festival for both.

Similar kinds of saints' days are found all over the country, and each celebrates its own particular community and the ethnic groups that make up that community. Likewise, blessings of fishing fleets occur in communities on both coasts, and the Gulf Coast and the Great Lakes as well. These are festivals in which occupational identity is as important as ethnic or regional identity. A blessing of the fleet in Ohio is held at Put-In-Bay in April. Unlike the ceremony at Gloucester, the blessing at Put-In-Bay does not involve a homogeneous ethnic population or a working fishing fleet. Boats partaking in this rite include ferryboats, water taxis, private craft, and an oil tanker.

Other occupations also have blessings. In an age when fewer and fewer families maintain small farms, we have lost much of our agrarian-based folklore. This is ironic, because many of our oldest folk customs and beliefs, including the very concept of harvest festivals and fertility festivals that has been so central to the understanding of our many calendrical holidays, were agriculturally based. Today, however, agribusiness has replaced the self-sufficient, independent farmer to the point where a self-conscious revival is necessary in order to re-establish some of the old traditions.

## Labor Day

Since 1969, a church in Fairfax, Virginia, has held an annual Labor Day Blessing of the Tools, followed by a picnic. In 1984, the Washington *Post* reported, "blessed in this symbolic commemoration of Labor Day were, among other things, a Casio pocket calculator, a meat thermometer, a pink feather duster and a bottle of Clorox, a green Dunlop 3 tennis ball, a Spaulding football and a red plastic lacrosse stick." Only one farming tool, a hoe, was brought to be blessed, even though the area had not too many years previously been entirely farmland. Instead, the "tools" reflect contemporary life, including a recognition that housework is real work and as noble as any labor. After the blessing, the 123-year-old church holds a picnic, which is as important in its way to the people who attend as the religious services. The whole event, although of recent origin, seems old and traditional, and right, to the participants. The church has been holding a Labor Day picnic since "before there was even a Labor Day." The addition of the Blessing of the Tools as a ritual act of specific relevance to Labor Day, an act intended to make Labor Day personally meaningful, is a perfect example of the contemporary development of holiday rituals. It gives the holiday a sacred aspect that then takes on a festive atmosphere: the picnic after the Blessing is held in a carnival-like atmosphere, surrounded by hamburger stands and dunking booths (Washington *Post* 8 Sept. 1981: B1).

September, like May, is a transitional month. When the first Labor Day was celebrated in New York on September 5, 1882, the idea had been proffered by a labor activist named Peter J. McGuire, president and founder of the United Brotherhood of Carpenters and Joiners of America, who suggested the date in September because it was halfway between the Fourth of July and Thanksgiving, "a most pleasant season of the year, . . . and [it] would fill a gap in the chronlogy of our legal holidays." Oregon in 1887 was the first state to establish it as an official observance, and Congress instituted it in the District of Columbia in 1894. Originally, the day's rituals included, along with picnics, fireworks, and speechmaking, a parade of workingmen, but this aspect has been lost to the summer's-end activities of today. In its Labor Day edition of 1984, *USA Today* reported that 70 million people would be traveling by automobile that weekend, then went on to say that the airlines and Amtrak rail services were temporarily expanding service to deal with the increase in travelers. The same story mentioned that the National Football League season began that weekend, as did the college football season. An adjacent story on the same page noted, "Saturday [of Labor Day weekend] begins baseball's very own season, sandwiched between summer and the fall: the September Stretch Run," when competition between teams in contention for their division championship heats up.

Labor Day is also the weekend that initiates the political cycle of presidential politics in earnest during election years. In 1984, in Fountain Valley, California, Ronald Reagan officially began his reelection campaign. In New York, Democratic candidates Walter Mondale and Geraldine Ferraro led a parade of union workers up Fifth Avenue. Joan Mondale led a similar parade in Detroit. Four years earlier, on Labor Day, 1980, President Jimmy Carter held a picnic on the White House lawn for labor leaders, as he began his own reelection campaign. In both cases, the democratic party was using the Labor Day celebration of work as a symbolic springboard for its presidential candidates.

In Cleveland, Ohio, where a parade down Euclid Avenue, followed by a rally, a party, and fireworks mark the Labor Day festivities, a headline in the *Plain Dealer* screamed "Labor Day Hype Cheats Us of Summer." Rick Horowitz, the author of the story wrote,

August has run its course; September is perched on the doorstep. With September comes Labor Day, which the newspaper and television folks keep calling "the unofficial end of summer." . . . Garbage. Check the calendar, ladies and gentlemen: it won't be autumn for nearly a month. If it's not yet autumn, then it has to be . . . summer! . . . Signalling an end to summer pleasures [was not] exactly what the Knights of Labor had in mind when they celebrated the first Labor Day in New York back in 1882. No indeed. The idea back then was to honor working people, not to make them put away the sailboat and lawn chairs for another year. . . . I've heard the arguments. There's a time to play and a time to work, a time to wear shorts and a time to wear shoes, a time for the beach and a time to shut down the beach house. All true; summer can't run all year long. But you can't blame a person for trying.

By mid-August, while the summer heat is still heavy upon us, the growth cycle of the land has begun its decline. A monastery in Connecticut holds its Blessing of the Fields on August 6, the Feast of the Assumption of the Virgin Mary, and I was told by a member of that monastery that the ritual is regarded as a celebration of the harvest. Where I live, despite the usual humidity of late summer days, the average daily temperature begins to drop on August 15. Although there is summer heat and sunshine in August and September, the fields are beginning to suggest, with their bounty and their faded colors, that we are entering another phase of the year.

# 5

## Autumn into Winter: Celebrating Death and Life

Try as we might to hold on to summer, the world will not stand still. After Labor Day, the heat will eventually ease up, and soon we begin to see the results of our summer efforts in the gardens, displayed on porches and railings as symbols of the harvest and the coming fall. Folklife scholar Don Yoder says that the Pennsylvania Dutch Harvest Home tradition looks as if "the farm and the forest came to church" (1990 [1958]:235). Unlike the Puritan New Englanders, for whom Thanksgiving became a major festival in place of the forbidden Christmas holiday, Pennsylvania's "Gay Dutch"—the Lutheran and Reformed—celebrated Harvest Home in summer or early autumn. The country churches were decorated with cornstalks, sheaves of wheat, loaves of bread, and the fruits and vegetables of the harvest.

In a similar way, other people today decorate their houses with the fruits and vegetables of the fields after Labor Day. In cities and towns, people mark the transition from summer to fall by placing pumpkins, corn, and scarecrow-like dummies on their front porches and stairs. These harvest figures on the doorstep look somewhat out of place in the city. But if the crops are being brought from the fields into the town, city, or home, or, as Yoder suggests, the field and forest comes into the church, why not the scarecrows as well? The scarecrows or harvest dummies decorate the public spaces of otherwise private places: doorways, front porches, walkways, stairways, even mailboxes. All of these are transitional areas between inside and outside, between public and private. The mailbox is the place through which commerce and communication between the home and the outside takes place, and with the increasing tendency to decorate for the holidays we also see an increase in the number of decorated mailboxes. The harvest is a taking of things from the outside to the inside. The crops of the fields are brought in and transformed into meals, the pumpkins are transformed into jack-o'-lanterns, and corn is transformed into decorations that signal the seasonal change. Figuratively speaking, the scarecrows too are transformed from summer guardians of the growing crops to autumn guardians of the domestic home.

The actual transition is gradual. The harvest of the summer fruits and their eventual decorative display mark this change, as do the important Jewish holidays of September. Labor Day seems to be a transitional point in the occupational and academic aspects of our lives. However, the warm days continue long after Labor Day. I have also suggested that we might look to the period of daylight savings time as one indication of when we, as a society, really perceive the summer to begin and end; but in terms of the actual weather, the autumnal equinox (September 21) is pretty much the point when the humidity comes down, the days begin to be noticeably shorter, and the nights become cooler.

## Jewish New Year and Autumn Festivals

The middle of September brings the greatest of the Jewish holy days, Rosh Hashanah and Yom Kippur, which are followed by the related harvest festival of Sukkoth. Rosh Hashanah and Yom Kippur are year's-end festivals in the Jewish calendar. Jews traditionally begin the year in the autumn near the equinox, and like the new year festivals of all peoples, these days celebrate both endings and beginnings. Rosh Hashanah is New Year's Day, and it is the first of the ten Days of Penitence that culminate with the holiest day of the year, the Day of Atonement, Yom Kippur. During these ten days, people do everything they can to right old wrongs, to make amends for any transgressions they have made against God and against other people. Also during this time, individuals are allowed to release themselves of any vow taken during the year that they might later regret, provided no one else is affected.

People are judged and their fates are sealed for the coming year at this time: on Rosh Hashanah they are judged; on Yom Kippur their names are inscribed by God in the sacred Book of Life. Based on their actions of the previous year, they are judged to be wicked, blessed, or somewhere in between. The Ten Days allow those who are in between to make up for the wrongs they have done. For Gentiles, it can sometimes be a confusing time of year. One woman wondered why a Jewish friend called her each year in the fall to tell her how sorry he was for all these things he had done. She never understood until she learned about the Days of Penitence.

On Rosh Hashanah, the book is opened. On Yom Kippur, fates are inscribed and sealed. At the end of Yom Kippur services in the temple, after the final, intricate sounding of the ram's horn, known as the shofar, the highest holy day is completed and the gates of heaven closed. During the intervening days, possibilities are open. People can affect their own fate by making amends for their sins.

Rosh Hashanah is not celebrated in the same way as the nationally celebrated New Year's Eve parties in December. Rather, it marks the beginning of a solemn and holy time. The Sabbath that falls during these ten days is likewise considered special, while Yom Kippur is the highest holy day of the Jewish year. Both days—Rosh Hashanah and Yom Kippur—are spent at the temple. Yom Kippur services last all day, and people must fast from sundown to sundown. Still, these year's-end holidays have in them the quality of transition that we find in other festivals of the new year, no matter when they are celebrated. Yom Kippur marks the end of the solemn days and the beginning of the regular days of the new year. The Ten Days, during which the gates of heaven are open, are a time out of time, a period of liminality during which people can shape their destinies, retract vows, and right wrongs. In short, one can make oneself over for the new year, in a way that recalls, however dimly, the custom of New Year's resolutions or the Vietnamese custom of dissolving unwanted entanglements.

Rosh Hashanah and Yom Kippur fall near the autumnal equinox, somewhere between early September and early October. So the turning of the year is tied to the turning of the seasons. The first festival of the new year is Sukkoth, a harvest festival that is celebrated a few days after Yom Kippur. In fact, some people begin to prepare for Sukkoth immediately after the completion of Yom Kippur services, and before enjoying a good meal to break the Yom Kippur fast.

Once, these three festivals may have been one great harvest festival that time and circumstance have split into three different celebrations, much as the Lupercalia gave rise over the centuries to several different holidays of spring. Today, however, they are distinct. Sukkoth is not one of the Days of Penitence, although it is felt to be part of the season in a festive way. The primary tradition for Sukkoth is the building of the sukkah, or booth, or tabernacle, in the backyard. No nails can be used. The booth must have at least two standing walls, and the roof is built of leaves and twigs. Whereas the holy days of Rosh Hashanah and Yom Kippur are celebrated in the temple, Sukkoth takes place at home. For eight days, all meals are eaten in the sukkah. "Living in the twentieth century, some of these rituals just seem weird. Probably a thousand years ago they made more sense," says one man I interviewed. He told me of how he and his father and brother built the sukkah each year, and of the rituals of eating the *es-rog*, a lemon-like fruit, and shaking the *lulov*, a branch of palm leaves, while saying prayers. The holiday is a favorite of his. He associates it with the compelling early autumn weather, and the smells of the branches and leaves of the hut. "It was really pretty pleasant inside. It smelled like what it was made out of. It was nice to sit in it at sundown and eat."

## *Halloween*

Among the seasons of the year, autumn is my favorite, and among the months of the year, September is the most beautiful. Once, when I was about twelve years old, standing in a cow pasture in New Hampshire, I noticed for the first time in my life that the milkweed had opened and was sending out its silky spores. The long, familiar green grass that I had played in during the summer was fading, both in color and in strength. Some orange flowers that I had not seen before were in bloom, and the sun was setting. It was warm, but the colors of the countryside were different in some way that I could not articulate. Somehow it was golden, and I knew that it was golden in more ways than one. This, I realized, was the beginning of the fall.

Because November ends autumn with a cold, slate grey, Thanksgiving straddles the line as both a fall and a winter holiday. November, though I love it, is a bleak month, more bleak than the winter months that follow it, once the snows come, more bleak even than long-suffered and apparently endless February. The winter, at its best, is fun, refreshing. The fresh snow is bright, sports abound, we can get out into the winter. The winter holidays are designed to overcome the short days and the cold temperatures. Christmas and New Year's and Valentine's Day dazzle with colors and candles. But the fall is a steady progression down, deep into the darkest days and longest nights of the year. Halloween may be the central holiday of the autumn.

The most vivid childhood memories I have of any holiday are of Halloween. Even more than the thrill of waking up early on Christmas morning to rush to the tree, I remember the excitement of that magical evening in latest October, walking the neighborhood streets of Boston with my two older sisters, carrying the treats we would collect in a cardboard jack-o'-lantern. My "pumpkin," as I called it, always filled up quickly, so we would have to return home to empty

The pumpkin, which stands for the harvest, is transformed into a jack-o'-lantern that represents Halloween.

it and go out again. But by this time, streets were beginning to emp-ty, and we had already been to most of the houses in the immediate neighborhood, so the choice was either to return home and stay in, or venture further afield. In the earliest years, the tough-looking "big kids" who were out for a night's mischief were scary enough to keep me in.

At home, however, the night continued to be special. We dumped our bags of candy on the kitchen table, and among the three children, there was more candy than I had ever imagined or could possibly believe. Somehow, there was never as much candy the next day; whether my parents had hidden some of it or the size shrank in the light of day I have never found out.

On Halloween night, I could stay up late, perhaps until 8:30 P.M., and watch television with my father in the small front room that I slept in. The flickering candlelight of the jack-o'-lantern that he had shown me how to carve hours earlier mesmerized me. I was tired but still filled with the sound of the crispy leaves that I had been crunching under-foot all night, invigorated with the sounds and smells of the cold black night decorated with candles and pumpkins and jack-o'-lanterns with dancing eyes, dazzled by the masks and costumes of all the children wandering the streets, and amazed that adults would give us candy simply because we rang their doorbells and said "Trick or treat." There was mystery here; there was mystery in the black cats and walking skeletons and living scarecrows that we saw decorating school win-dows, mystery in the grinning gargoyles and jack-o'-lanterns on all the porches. I loved Halloween.

The day after Halloween is All Saints' Day, which is a holy day of obligation in the Catholic calendar, a day when one must attend mass. That morning would inevitably be grey and rainy, and I invariably thought it a good way to begin November. On the way to Saint Pe-ter's Church, I noticed the debris of the night before: the streets were littered with candy wrappers, torn bags, and smashed pumpkins, and the windows of the crowded variety store I stopped into along the way were covered with soap. Once I was in the store, I could always count on finding the first of the special Christmas issues of my fa-vorite comic books.

Although I never thought too much about it at the time, I instinc-tively realized the place of Halloween in the seasonal cycle. I vague-ly intuited its organic relationship to the church calendar and its holy days, and though I only half understood it, I fully felt the potency of its symbolism.

The customs I have been referring to can be traced directly to the ancient Celtic day of Samhain. Halloween was born in the fires of pre-Christian new year's festivals, and fathered by the Celtic peoples of England, Ireland, and Scotland. The Catholic Church is its stepmother. The holiday we enjoy today is an amalgam of Celtic druidical ritual, Christian theology, and northern European folk belief. Halloween is about death, and it involves people's attempts to understand death and control it. During Halloween, people play with death, mock it, and fear it.

The Celtic peoples once inhabited much of the European continent but were, by the time of Christ, pushed largely to the hinterlands. Today, their descendants include the Irish, Welsh, Scots, and Bretons, who inhabit Brittany in the northern part of France. The first day of the new year in the Celtic calendar was celebrated on November 1 and was known as Samhain (pronounced "Sahwen"). Along with Samhain on November 1, the Celts celebrated major festivals on February 1 (Imbolc), May 1 (Beltane), and August 1 (Lughnasa). Most of what we know of the Celtic Samhain is contained in four Irish sagas that were written down sometime between the ninth and twelfth centuries, and which necessarily reflect the Christianization of the festival that had been going on for some centuries. The traditions and practices described are much older than the records themselves. From them, we know that Samhain was the New Year's Day of the Celts. Throughout the old stories, Samhain is the focal point: battles were fought then, journeys begun, wars decided. Samhain was apparently the most important of the four major Celtic feast days. Samhain, a transitional day from the old year to the new, was also believed to be a day of the dead and a night of wandering souls. It was believed that at the time of transition to the new year, the souls of those who had died during the previous year assembled to travel into the land of the dead. The living lit bonfires and sacrificed fruits and vegetables to honor the dead and expiate their sins.

The festival of Samhain was begun at sundown the evening prior, that is, October 31, and was associated with the harvest. Many chores were measured against this day. Kevin Danaher, in *The Year in Ireland* describes the work associated with Samhain:

Samhain, 1 November, was the first day of winter and the end of the farmer's year. All his crops, all his livestock had to be secure for the hard season to come. Corn of all sorts, hay, potatoes, turnips, apples, must by now be harvested and stored with ricks well made and well thatched and tied. Dry cattle and sheep were moved from distant moorland and mountain pastures and brought to the fields near the farmstead. Milking cows were brought into the byre for the winter and hand-feeding with stored fodder began. In the South-east of Ireland, where this crop was grown, winter wheat had to be in the ground by this date. (1972:206)

Among the Celts, and throughout the tribal peoples of northern Europe, what we today consider as late autumn was counted as early winter. It was a time to slaughter livestock, because there was not food enough to provide for all the animals through the long, cold season, and the slaughtered animals provided great stores of supplies for the people. This time of year, then, was a time for feasting. Along with the natural aspects of the day (the harvest of organic crops), Samhain was also filled with the supernatural. In one of the old tales, a hero named Nera is sent begging from door to door on Samhain, and he enters the fairy world through a cave. Although the development of fairy mythology is probably post-Christian, entering the fairy world on Samhain points to one of the beliefs about this day, that the doors and gates to the otherworld were open, and that, while the souls of the dead were passing from this world to the other, the spirits and creatures of that world could just as easily find access into ours. The bonfires not only lit the way for the wandering dead; they helped scare away these creatures as well. The offerings of food might appease them. Because the barriers between the worlds were down, the night was dangerous: as it says in the saga of the hero Nera, "Great was the darkness of that night, and demons would appear on that night always" (Cross and Slover 1936:248).

In another saga, known as the Second Book of Invasions, a race of supernatural beings known as Fomorians demand tribute from the native people. The people become accustomed to delivering goods and harvest fruits to the Formorians at Samhain, although they eventually rebel. It is the paying of tribute that interests me here. It parallels the folk custom of setting out food and gifts to appease wandering spirits, which in turn parallels the folk practice of giving gifts of food and drink to maskers who imitate those spirits. In the case of Samhain, the stories and legends explain the custom but are probably not the real causes of it. The Celts probably had a happy tradition of mumming associated with Samhain for longer than anyone could remember, and if asked why, they could tell of the wandering spirits and creatures they emulated, as an etiological myth, one that explains the origin of something. American Halloween trick-or-treating is a version of this practice. It is a long road from the saga literature of the middle ages to children in masks trick-or-treating door-to-door, a road with many intersections and forks and sideroads and curves, but one on which we can see the beginnings of traditions still practiced today. We see the idea of the dead wandering the earth begging food, and the giving of food and drink as payment to these spirits. Thus our children dress as skeletons and ghosts: the signs of the walking dead. The other creatures, such as witches and goblins, date from the period of the Christianization of the festival.

## Holiday Mumming

Mumming, from the Danish word *mumme*, meaning to parade in masks, consists of dressing in costume and performing from house to house in return for a gift of food and drink. Mumming in one form or another is associated with holidays at different times and places all over the world. For instance, mumming continues in Newfoundland at Christmas, and our Christmas caroling is similar to it. Christmas caroling, now on the wane, retains two of the features of mumming: (1) a performance, in return for (2) a reward: food and drink taken inside a person's home. After the caroling, the singers are invited in for egg nog, or wassail, or hot chocolate and coffee.

Halloween trick-or-treating is closely analogous to mumming. Mummers in the British and Irish traditions ask permission to enter the house; in some parts of the United States, trick-or-treaters do the same. Although there is no dramatic performance involved, there is a verbal formula (albeit a short one). Actually, the wearing of a costume, and possibly the making of one, constitute a kind of performance, especially since the trick-or-treaters are children and their costumes are scrutinized—perhaps I should say fawned over—by the adults whose houses they visit.

Our children's custom of dressing in disguise and processing from house to house demanding treats is a recent one. Although most people recall that it gained popularity in the early 1950s, the earliest memory of it that I have located dates it as early as the 1930s. No one knows exactly how it began, but it is clearly a contemporary version of the British "guising" (from "disguise"), meaning to wear costumes or disguises and roam the community. Many people today can recall their first encounter with trick-or-treating as it is now known: "The youngsters came around. I think they were about sixth grade, perhaps. They said to me, 'Trick or treat!' And I said, 'What?' And this youngster said, 'You give us something, or we'll wax your windows.' Yes, a choice was given. And I found something!"

In the years prior to the advent of trick-or-treating, children wore homemade costumes and paraded around carrying candlelit jack-o'-

Children in New York, ca. 1900. Photo by Brown Brothers.

lanterns. Sometimes they would ring bells, then hold the candlelit face to the door in an effort to scare the resident. Halloween is a night of inversion, when regular rules of society are suspended. So children can play tricks on adults and demand treats from them. Although some people today view trick-or-treating as begging and therefore consider it a bad precedent for children to be exposed to, actually it is not begging at all. Taken literally, it is a threat: give me something or I'll punish you with a prank, such as soaping your windows. Thus we see that Halloween allows for a reversal of regular roles. The child engages in a relationship with an adult that mirrors the adult-child relationship. Adults are told how to behave, told what to do, and threatened with punishment if they do not do what they are told.

Furthermore, trick-or-treating is a social convention. Not only is it not real begging, it is not really blackmail either. Parents and children agree to this ritualistic exchange. No one is truly threatened by it. Adults teach their children how to do it, and go with them when they do it. Normal rules of society are suspended, but within bounds. Halloween is a night for pranks and mischief, but these are carried out, usually by older children, independently of trick-or-treating (often as an alternative to it), and are generally directed against marginal people, such as the "neighborhood grouch."

The true reversal of ordinary rules and social roles occurs when adults play tricks on children. Rex Lowe says,

> I figure that kids ought to earn their treats when they come to the house. Normally, we try to scare them a bit, so Chris and I got upstairs, and when they came to knock on the door, we had this wig on a string, and we'd lower it out the window and dangle it up and down in front of their faces and pull it up, and they'd scream a little bit. And the next year I was out on the roof overlooking the porch, I was out on the peak and I was going to scare kids by hanging down and growling at them as they came over. I noticed this little kid coming down the street in costume with his mother's hand in his. Actually, my wife got a little angry over me at this because the kid said, "Oh, let's go up here to this house and get a treat," and his mother said, "Oh no, remember, that's the bad house!" She took the kid on down the street. I guess we were getting a horrible reputation in the neighborhood!

This is an inversion of an inversion. Frightening children is precisely the opposite of the everyday norm regarding adult-child relationships. For an adult to intentionally scare a child is in fact a deeply-held taboo in our society, but one that is allowed, within limits, on Halloween.

Trick-or-treating continues to evolve, not always pleasantly. People are afraid of poisoned candy and apples with razor blades in them, and so only take their children to the homes of friends. Moreover, neighborhoods themselves are changing. Many people live in large apartment buildings, condominiums, and housing developments where they do not always know their neighbors. Because they do not know each other, people do not trust each other. Indeed, the entire razor-blade-in-the-apple scare may reflect this increasing sense of anonymity and the fear of the unknown that results (see Grider 1984; and Best and Horiuchi 1985). I have watched groups of children pass by our house, which had a light on the porch and a burning jack-o'-lantern, and ring the bells of only a prearranged few.

The custom continues to evolve in other ways. College students go "trick-or-drinking" on campus! As one student puts it, "You go around to dorms. You can dress up if you want to, and knock on the door and say 'Trick or drink!' Generally, people would give you a drink or get really ticked off at you!" Another student comments that she stopped trick-or-treating as a child when she was about eleven, because "it wasn't cool. In college, people start trick-or-treating, or trick-or-drinking again." Why in college? Like childhood, the college years are a transitional stage. Students are somewhat isolated on campus, with a large number of peers. Everyone is more or less the same age. During this stage of passage to adulthood, students often enjoy a reversion to childhood. Such a symbolic reversion is typical in rites of passage, since one is learning to be a new person and so must be born again.

Throughout this book, we have seen that our holidays are derived from old celebrations that predate the establishment of Christianity, and that many, if not most of the customs and symbols of our holidays can be explained only in the context of their histories. Halloween is no exception, although it is derived primarily from a Celtic rather than a Roman festival. The Romans did have their influence as well, however, through their harvest festival of the goddess Pomona. Most American Halloween traditions are inherited from the Irish, however, who came to this country in large numbers in the nineteenth century, especially during the middle years of that century in order to escape the potato famine that was devastating their country. The Irish are Celtic descendants, and Ireland was the one place the Romans did not conquer. But the principle is the same as we have seen for Valentine's Day and the spring festivals. In A.D. 601, Pope Gregory I, known as Gregory the Great, issued a now-famous edict to his missionaries concerning the native customs and beliefs of the peoples he hoped to convert. Rather than try to obliterate native peoples' customs and beliefs, he instructed, use them. If a group of prople worship a tree, rather than cut it down, consecrate it to Christ and allow them to continue their worship. Following this principle, Catholic holy days and feast days were set at the times of native holy days, festivals, and celebrations.

Samhain, with its attention to the supernatural, was perceived by the church as particularly objectionable. So while missionaries identified Christian holy days with native holy days, and their God and saints with local deities, they branded the other supernatural personages recognized by the native people, in this case the Celts, as apparitions and manifestations of the devil. The missionaries taught that, while people were correct in their understanding that they had experienced supernatural presences, these were in fact delusions sent by the (Christian) devil. In this way, the creatures who roamed on Samhain were defined as more than just powerfully dangerous tricksters. They were deliberately evil and malevolent. Moreover, the representatives of the traditional religion, in this case the priestly caste known as the druids, were declared evil devil worshipers, since they worshiped so-called false gods. Finally, the Celtic underworld inevitably became associated with the Christian hell.

The effects of this policy were to diminish but not totally dispel belief in the traditional gods. Many scholars think that this accounts for the origin of fairy belief, that the old gods and races of divine beings "shrank" as they were eclipsed by Christianity. A common folk belief is that the fairies were fallen angels who followed Lucifer into rebellion. Priests taught that, as a result, they were banished to the hills and hollows, rivers and streams of earth. Thus the fairies were associated with devils in Catholic theology.

The Feast of All Saints was assigned to November 1, in an attempt to replace Samhain. The feast was in honor of all Christian saints, particularly those who did not otherwise have a special day assigned to them. This saints' day was meant to draw off from Samhain the devotion of the Celtic peoples, and to replace it forever. In this it failed. The old beliefs never really died out. The very powerful symbolism of the traveling dead was too strong, and perhaps too basic to the human psyche, to be satisfied by this new, more abstract Catholic feast day. In the ninth century the church established November 2 as All Souls' Day. On this day, the living pray for the souls of the dead. This was closer to the original idea of Samhain. But once again, the practice of retaining traditional customs while attempting to redefine them had an opposite result: the traditional beliefs and customs lived on. All Saints' Day is also known as All Hallows. The word "hallow" means "saint" and was commonly used in the Middle Ages, from the Middle English *halwe*, and we still use the word "hallowed" to mean "sanctified" or "holy." As it was during the era of Samhain, the evening prior to the day was the time of the most intense activity, both human and supernatural. People continued to celebrate the occasion, known variously as Hallow Even or All Hallows Eve, as a time of the wandering dead, but the supernatural beings were now associated with evil. The folk continued to propitiate those spirits and their costumed, masked representatives with gifts of food and drink. Consequently, All Hallows Even, known today as Halloween, is an ancient Celtic New Year's Day in modern dress.

Because the church celebrates All Saints' and All Souls' days, Halloween has an analogue in many predominantly Catholic countries. One such analogue is the Mexican Day of the Dead on November 2, All Souls' Day. A blending of European and Indian beliefs and customs concerning the souls of the dead, this day is a major celebration in Mexico. As in the United States at Halloween, symbolic images of death are everywhere to be found during this time. By far the most popular of these is the skeleton or the human skull. Toy skeletons dancing with lively young maidens, laughing skeletons on horseback playing guitar, and candies in the shape of skulls are sold all over Mexico. In a way similar to the celebration of Halloween in the

Day of the Dead skeleton rising from the grave. Photo by David Hampshire, Instructional Media Services, Bowling Green State University.

United States, death is played with, mocked, but accepted and incorporated into life during this festival of the dead. Unlike Halloween, however, the Day of the Dead is an occasion for people to visit the graves of their ancestors and decorate them with flowers. The Day of the Dead recognizes death as a force in life generally, and is a time to pay respect to those who have died.

The Day of the Dead also balances the religious with the social. Altars with candles, flowers, crucifixes, skulls, holy cards, and all manner of other symbols and icons are set up in the home. Prayers are said at the graves; then people sit down and have picnics at the gravesites. Dancing, partying, and feasting with friends follow. The

celebration seamlessly combines the sacred and the secular, and unlike Halloween, functions fully as a day of the dead. Hispanic Americans from Mexico and other Central and South American countries
who now live in the United States celebrate the Day of the Dead with
fiestas throughout the country, especially in California, Louisiana,
Texas, and Washington, D.C. In other areas with large Hispanic populations, the observation of the Day of the Dead may involve church
services only. In Bowling Green, Ohio, for instance, the Catholic
church conducts a special mass in Spanish for All Souls' Day. A woman explained to me that grave visitation and decoration is not done,
because most of the earlier generations of the family were buried back
in Texas (see Turner 1982; and Carmichael and Sayer 1991).

Many people in America today believe that it is wrong to celebrate
Halloween, because they feel that it glorifies witches and evil spirits
and celebrates Satan himself. Sometimes it is denounced as pagan.
However, both the holy day of All Saints and the customs and beliefs involving supernatural creatures have common sources, and so
some people are making efforts to recombine the divergent traditions.
Some churches ask both children and adults to come to mass on the
first of November, or its eve, dressed as saints. A priest in Maine actually places jack-o'-lanterns on the altar. For several years, he has
been inviting people to dress in costume for the mass, in a somewhat
controversial attempt to interweave the religious significance of the
folk customs with the universal meanings inherent in the religious
rituals.

Other holidays, such as Easter, combine pre-Christian or nonreligious
symbols with sacred ceremony. People do not complain about Easter
eggs and rabbits as pagan symbols, for instance. But Halloween is pe-
culiar because its "evil" symbols are *not* non-Christian. The devil, witches, and even ghosts all have specific meanings within a Christian context, and this is why this holiday stirs up so much resentment.

Most Americans do not know that in Great Britain, Jack O'Lantern
is a legendary folk figure who has many tales told about him. Moreover, in Ireland and Great Britain, jack-o'-lanterns are carved from
large turnips, known as swedes, which are actually a different type
of vegetable from the smaller, garden turnip. The pumpkin is native
to the new world, but carving large, pulpy vegetables to represent
the legendary wandering trickster is not. Jack O'Lantern is said to be
the spirit of a blacksmith named Jack who was too evil to get into
heaven but, because he had outwitted the devil, was not allowed into
hell. Turned away, he scoops up a glowing coal with the vegetable
he happens to be eating, and uses it as a lantern to light his way as

he wanders the earth. A marginal figure, he fits uneasily into a rigid, dualistic Christian cosmology. In fact, the same is true of the other creatures of Halloween, such as witches and (in Great Britain) fairies, who are also said to be most active on the eve of All Hallows. As a traditional story, the origin of Jack O'Lantern exists in many variants, and is essentially the same as the story of Will o' the Wisp, a man named Will who snatches a handful of burning straw from hell as he is refused entry. We saw a similar story with the fairies who are said to be fallen angels. In some of these tales, it is said that the angels chose, at the last minute, not to enter hell with Lucifer (now called Satan) but, because they had followed his rebellion, were not able to return to heaven. Thus they became magical creatures of this middle earth. Fairy lore is contradictory in places: in two old folk ballads about Halloween, fairies are portrayed differently. In "Tam Lin," the fairy queen is evil and malevolent, while in "Allison Gross," it is the queen of fairies who rescues a knight from a witch's spell. Like the wandering spirits, fairies ride on Halloween, stealing men, women, and children.

Though witches have an entirely different origin and history, they are often identified and confused with fairies in the folk imagination, especially in Scotland and Ireland. It is sometimes said, for instance, that witches steal babies and sell them to the fairies on Halloween. In some of the witch trials, self-confessed witches testified that they had trafficked with the fairies. One such instance involves one Isabel Gowdie, who said that she went with the fairies "under the hills." There she met "the broad faced man who was king of the fairies, ... and the woman in white who was their queen" (Briggs 1967:90; see also Wentz 1973 [1911]:109).

Some people claim that Western European witchcraft is simply a continuation (oftentimes suppressed and driven underground) of ancient nature and fertility cults. Indeed, there is a continuity between medieval witchcraft and the ancient fertility cults of the Greek and Roman gods and goddesses, especially those of Pan, Dionysus, and Diana, or Hecate. Moreover, the Greek nature god Pan, with his horns, his cloven hooves, his goat-like, bestial nature, as well as the passionate ecstasy of his female devotees, was the most direct influence on the image of the devil in Christianity. All those attributes—the horns, the hooves, the appearance as a goat-man—became attributes of the devil.

Nevertheless, there is no evedence that there was a direct line or a hidden underground movement to keep the old fertility cults alive. Rather, these cults contributed ideas and provided models for later movements to follow. In the medieval context, true witchcraft is a statement about Christianity, made in its terms. While it is a rejection of Christ, it is a recognition of the Christian devil (not Pan) and a conscious embracing of evil, not simply of nature (Russell 1972:48).

During the ninth century, the idea of the formal pact with the devil had entered into witchcraft tradition. All magic, it was thought, must require the aid of some supernatural beings. Since this could not come from the Lord or his angels for maleficent purposes, it must be of the devil. In a perversion of the baptismal vows, witches allegedly renounced Christ and embraced—literally—the devil. Practices once associated with pre-Christian and non-Christian festivals and religions, such as dancing and revelry, and belief in shapeshifting and nocturnal flight were by the ninth century being condemned as attributes of witchcraft. In the tenth century, the list of such attributes grew to include the formalized pact, cannibalism, orgiastic sex, and the adoration of the devil. A document from this time, called *The Corrector*, contains the first known reference to the ability of witches to fly through the air on broomsticks (Russell 1972:79).

However, the greatest witch crazes swept Europe largely after the Middle Ages had begun to wane. Some historians feel that the changes going on in society, a rising middle class and a population shift into the cities, led to a stress that erupted with the witch accusations and executions. Whatever the reasons, it has been conservatively estimated that as many as half a million people were put to death in Europe and Great Britain over the course of the sixteenth and seventeenth centuries.

The American colonists of this period knew of Halloween chiefly as a day by which yearly tasks and seasonal chores were measured. In an English almanac in use at the time, Halloween is referred to, like Samhain before it, as a day when certain husbandly jobs must be done:

> At Hallowtide, slaughter time entereth in,
> and then doth the husbandman's feasting begin.
> From thence unto Shrovetide kill now and then some
> their offal for household the better will come.

This verse contains the pastoral and agricultural aspects of the day in the yearly cycle, but it does not refer to any supernatural beliefs. Of course, the Puritans and colonists of the seventeenth century shared the witchcraft beliefs of the European continent, since it was in 1692 that the famous Salem witchcraft trials took place. In all, only about thirty people were hung as a result of these, and eight more throughout New England, a small number in comparison to the estimated hundreds of thousands in Europe. But the belief in witches was present and resulted in people's deaths. In the nineteenth century, when the great wave of Irish immigration to this country took place (first the Ulster Protestants in the early part of the century, followed by Catholics), the newly arrived immigrants found a body of fully formed witchcraft belief waiting for them. In turn, they brought their Halloween customs and beliefs from the old country, and these were established here. The merging of these cultures provided the basis of the American Halloween.

Because of their allegiance to the devil and their evil nature generally, witches, like fairies, were said to be most active on Halloween, meeting then and flying through the night searching for hapless souls to steal. The belief in Halloween as a night of activity for dangerous supernatural creatures is one context for understanding the pranks of today's mischief-makers. Halloween is sometimes called Mischief Night in Indiana and the midwest, or Cabbage Night in New England, from the days when youngsters roamed the towns wielding cabbage stumps to smear on people's doors and windows. Alternatively, October 30 is sometimes known as Mischief Night, or, in Detroit, Devil's Night, when fires are lit throughout the city (supposedly recalling the fires of hell). The Halloween period is a time when youths play pranks on adults, when adults sometimes scare children, and when authority figures and unpopular people in the community awake to find their houses bombarded with rotten eggs. A good tale of such a trick comes from Eastport, Maine:

> One of the worst things we ever did was, there was a guy who came into Eastport, must have been around 1939, just before World War II. Nobody knew where he came from. We used to call him the Tattooed Man because he had tattoos on his arm. He came in there on an old boat. Probably a thirty-eight-foot peapod. A peapod, a double-ended boat. He tied up to the little wharf that we used to use as our clubhouse. Nobody used that little wharf, and we used to fish off it. The bait shack we used as our clubhouse. Well, he got permission from the factory owner to tie up to that wharf. Of course, he had permission, all right, but we didn't like that at all.
>
> So we went down there one Halloween. That's when things always happen, on Halloween. As I remember, there's about a twenty-four or twenty-five-foot tide in Eastport. At low tide, your boat is setting on the beach; high tide, it's about twenty to twenty-two feet up [on the water]. So, he wouldn't let us fish off that wharf anymore, he claimed that it was his wharf now.
>
> So, anyway, we went down there one Halloween. He was in his lit-

tle boat there, little fire going in his little stove. Low tide. We got a
bunch of ropes and tied his stern down to the piling, right on the bottom of the ground on the beach. And the tide come up. And we all sat
back and watched.

The tide come up and the tide come up and the bow started coming up and the stern stayed down and the first thing you know he come
screeching out of there, because the damned stove got upset because
the boat tipped. Smoke rolled out of the cabin. There he is: his boat's
tied down and he can't move. Water coming over the stern of his boat.
Swamped him. We're all setting there roaring. We didn't get in any trouble for that, because most of the guys, the fishermen in town, didn't
like him either. Everyone thought that was a big joke.

Then one day he just sailed away. Don't know where he went to.
The Tattooed Man, no one knew where he came from, but one day he
just sailed out of there with an old, leaky boat. Oh yes, it was real soon
after this Halloween incident. He'd had enough of us. He didn't want
to spend anymore Halloweens in Eastport. (Folklore Archives, University of Maine, Orono)

More recently, an event in Bowling Green, Ohio, demonstrated the
ways in which the traditions associated with a single holiday can
clash. In this case, a family displayed Halloween decorations on their
front porch, including an elaborately built witch. The witch was so
much a part of the family, she even had a name: Maleficent. Named
for the witch in the Walt Disney version of *Sleeping Beauty*, she was
six feet tall and sported elaborate horns. As might be expected, she
attracted a lot of attention from passersby. Smiling pedestrians stoped
to look, while traffic slowed down on the street. One week before
Halloween, 1987, she disappeared.

Sandy Wray was devastated. She had spent over forty hours creating Maleficent, which she described as a labor of love. So she posted a sign on her porch where the witch had been, saying WE LOVED
OUR WITCH! PLEASE RETURN HER TO US. She contacted the local newspaper, which carried the story on the front page, and she distributed
pictures of the witch in case anyone might see it at a party. "We hope
that maybe someone just wants to use her for the holiday and then
will bring her back. I'd be forever grateful even if they just left her in
a heap on the porch." Her husband Kelly complained that stealing
the witch also stole the magic for the little kids. "It also makes it hard
to keep your own spirit." The Wrays vowed that in the future their
decorations would be as cheap and disposable as possible.

A few days later, the witch was returned. The Wrays were delight-
ed, thankful for the help the newspaper and their neighbors had giv-
en them (one neighbor went on a door-to-door search), and charita-

ble toward the thieves, who turned out to be students at the university. In a letter to the Bowling Green *Sentinel Tribune*, Mrs. Wray said, "Confronted with the results of his 'prank,' the Bowling Green State University student felt guilt and regret. Maleficent was returned to us amid squeals of delight late Tuesday afternoon. . . . To the young people who stole our 'spirits': It was an error in judgment; no more, no less. Thoughtless, yes, but not intentionally malicious. And, to take responsbility for your actions and correct your mistakes shows the maturity and compassion for other people that everyone told me *not* to expect. Well, I believed in you, and, by golly, you came through. Thank you."

One of the most common of all Halloween tricks is smashing pumpkins and jack-o'-lanterns that decorate porches. Both the decorating and the destruction are traditional to Halloween. As the decorating tradition grows more elaborate, so do the targets grow more tempting. The two clashing traditions represent different age groups and different stages of life: the domestic, family tradition of making the decorations, and the subversive, peer group tradition of destroying, or at least stealing, them. In fact, many of the customary behaviors associated with Halloween can be seen as age-specific: trick-or-treating at a young age accompanied by a family member, then trick-or-treating with other children, then, as one grows into adolescence, going out on Halloween with one's friends not to trick-or-treat, but perhaps to engage in some mischief. The changes in activities continue through the life-cycle: in college and as young adults we might attend masquerade parties, until, if we become parents, we begin to engage in the cycle from the other side. We become the providers of treats, the escorts of young children.

Not only does the movement through these behaviors correspond to different stages of life; they are also informal rites of passage that actually mark the transitions. Many people can remember the point in their life when they began to wish their parents would allow them to go out on their own. I have found that many of my students regret that they are too old to trick-or-treat any longer, which is, I think, another sign that the movement through these stages is something that people are consciously aware of. For myself, the transitional nature of these various roles became very apparent to me the year my first child was able to fully grasp Halloween as a night of free candy and outdoor excitement. I was never so aware of myself as a parent or as an adult than I was that night, watching my son Ian run ahead of me, calling to him to be careful.

Another important, though informal, rite of passage occurred when

I demonstrated to my children the art of jack-o'-lantern carving. I vividly remember my father teaching me, and now I was passing the tradition on. As the primary symbol of Halloween, the jack-o'-lantern is the most ubiquitous motif in home displays. The full, standing figures very often are jack-o'-lanterns given bodily form. Even Halloween costume disguises are based on the jack-o'-lantern, and we can see that there is a direct continuity between the jack-o'-lantern and the so-called harvest figure on the one hand, both of which are decorations of the home, and the Halloween costumes on the other, which are decorations of the self. People draw from the same well of symbols to create either, so masqueraders are often Halloween figures come to life.

The Indian corn, or standing corn shocks, or the pumpkins when left uncarved, can be displayed throughout the season, through Thanksgiving, and sometimes through the winter. The unworked vegetable or organic item carries the general seasonal symbolism. For Halloween specifically, though, the vegetables are worked. The pumpkin is carved and given a face. Lit by a candle within, it takes on an eerie, ambivalent, frightening demeanor, which reminds us of its original status as one of the creatures of death and the underworld who inhabit All Hallows.

We can see here a dichotomy of rural and urban, natural and built, and ultimately, of nature and culture. The tasteful, aesthetic arranging and displaying of these fruits and vegetables is in itself a cultural act. Usually, though, a cultural act is performed *upon* the vegetable: it is carved into a jack-o'-lantern and given an identity, thus connecting it to the otherworld and the supernatural. So the nature-versus-culture dichotomy, defined and eased by bringing the pumpkin into the built environment, becomes a life-versus-death dichotomy by virtue of transforming the pumpkin into a manufactured object that represents the world of spirits.

A comparison with some of the organic items used as Christmas decorations is interesting. We buy a pumpkin much like a Christmas tree, and in turn decorate it to render it more than simply a tree. Just as the unworked vegetable, such as the corn hung on the door, comes to represent the harvest and the season in general, so does the wreath survive the Christmas season and stay up through the entire winter. Taking down the evergreen wreath is one of the signs of the end of winter. The Halloween decorations are of the harvest and speak to us of the *coming* death that is winter, while the Christmas-winter decorations are evergreen and suggest life eternally present *through* the dead of winter.

Halloween masqueraders, 1980s style. Halloween has become an adult holiday. Photo by Jack Santino, Washington, D.C., 1983.

The other major component of our contemporary Halloween celebrations is the costumed parading in the streets of towns and cities throughout the country that is by now a standard feature of the evening's events. The evil creatures stir on the eve of All Saints' Day, as if they are enjoying a final revel before the day that establishes the primacy of the Christian religion, a day that acknowledges the victory of Christianity over the indigenous religion, as it were. It is almost like Mardi Gras in miniature: a day of festivity and revelry as a prelude to the solemn Christian holy day. Not only are traditional ideas of death and evil represented in costumes of witches and skeletons, but contemporary fears and plagues of modern life are also seen in the costumes worn in the Halloween parades of today, costumes such as poisoned Tylenol packages, Rely tampons (which caused toxic shock syndrome), and nuclear waste. In fact, at the level of rumor and legend, stories of axe murderers and candy poisoners and people who put razor blades in apples have joined, if not replaced, the fear of ghosts and witches, but the dread of the unknown and the uncontrollable continues to be addressed in both cases.

### Halloween and Seasonal Time

In the old Celtic calendar, the harvest season began on August 1, and today a resident of north central Maine comments, "It was almost like the first celebration of harvest would be the apples in people's backyards. . . . Even though for a large extent my holidays were really tied up with religious ritual, they were really fun because they signified the passing of the season. And Halloween was always the real end of fall and the beginning of winter. Because sometimes there was snow when we went trick-or-treating. It was always really cold. You'd sweat inside your mask, but it was cold out. You'd carry apples around with you, and they'd be real crisp and cold, and when you were thirsty, that's what you'd take. . . . One of the things I noticed this year was that they were putting up stuff for Christmas on Halloween night."

Halloween is closely linked with Thanksgiving and Christmas. Like Thanksgiving, it is, at least in part, a harvest holiday, and like Christmas, it is related to old new year celebrations of ancient cultures, though not the same ones. Historically, beliefs about mythic Norse spirits and deities who flew through the air to gather souls and reward heroes influenced the Celtic fairy lore and witch lore that became a part of Halloween, and they also contributed to the development of the flying Father Christmas figure we know as Santa Claus, with his furs and his northern European reindeer.

There are other relationships as well, and to understand these, first we have to understand something about the British holiday on November 5 known as Guy Fawkes Day. This is a commemoration of the execution of a papist—a Roman Catholic—who planned to blow up the Protestant House of Parliament of King James I on November 5, 1605. He was apprehended, hung, drawn, and quartered. In 1606, November 5 was declared by the same parliament as a day of public thanksgiving. Since then, his day has been celebrated in Great Britain and in other countries with historical links to England such as New Zealand. Children build dummies known as Guys several days

"One Holiday After Another," reads the inside of this card. The seasonal symbols—a witch, a turkey wearing a pilgrim's hat, and Santa—each punch the calendrical time clock as it approaches 12—midnight on New Year's Eve? © Kerston Brothers Company.

in advance of the holiday. These they display rather prominently on some street corner and entreat passersby for "a penny for the Guy." November 4 is known as Mischief Night, when children are free to play pranks on adults and on each other as well. Finally, on the night of November 5, the Guys are burned in glorious bonfires. Some say this marks the execution of the real Guy Fawkes, even though he was in fact not burned at the stake.

The celebration of Guy Fawkes Day was brought to North America with the British colonists. It is no longer celebrated here, although there is an annual society gathering at the Cranbrook Academy of Art in Bloomfield, Michigan, on November 5 called a Guy Fawkes Ball. In Newfoundland, November 5 is still celebrated as Bonfire Day. We have reports of it in the United States as late as 1893, when it was called Pope's Day, and this may explain a number of November customs celebrated in and around New York City. Election Day bonfires might be descended from the November fires of Guy Fawkes Day. So might Thanksgiving begging. In Manhattan, until about the Second World War, children dressed in rags on Thanksgiving morning and went in groups from house to house asking for "anything for the poor," or "anything for Thanksgiving." They received, usually, a piece of fruit or some nuts. Jenny Fasano lived as a child on East 104th Street in Manhattan, and she remembers the Thanksgiving begging of the early part of this century very well:

> We were all very disappointed if it didn't *snow* on Thanksgiving. Because it usually *snowed* on Thanksgiving. Now we're lucky if it snows for Easter, maybe!
>
> I remember this one particular day it was snowing. I guess I was about seven years old and we wanted to go out and my mother said, "It's snowing." She said, "If it stops you can go out." But it didn't stop and she let us go out anyway, because she was cooking dinner and we were getting under her feet or something. So she let us go out anyway. But we dressed up before we went out. We dressed up, not in our own ordinary clothes, but as a clown, or anything we could grab, a pair of long trousers rolled up, or, I used to dress up in my sister's clothes—of course they came down to my ankles—and her high heels. Then we would have a paper bag, that we would go around asking for—I imagine it came about from the cornucopia, right, the pilgrims had the cornucopia?—and we used to get food. Not candy, well, I guess people couldn't afford candy, but thank God we always had plenty of food. But we still went out, and we'd get maybe a piece of cake, or a cookie, or a piece of fruit, or nuts. Nuts are what we usually got, all kinds of nuts, because nuts you could get at that time.

Mrs. Fasano says that the custom died in her neighborhood with the American entry into the First World War. Another woman, however, about ten years younger than Mrs. Fasano, told me of the Thanksgiving begging in her childhood neighborhood in Brooklyn, which she dates to around 1927 and 1928. Celeste Schamel told me,

> You didn't dress up in "costumes," you dressed up in beggars' clothes. I would wear my brothers' old suits and pants and sometimes they would wear a beat-up dress. But usually it was old, raggedy knickers.
>
> I remember once, running down the street, I was the last one to get ready. You put dirt all over your face, with, you know, an old cap, your hair was all up under the cap. I was running down the street to join my brothers and right away up comes the fist ready for a fight. He thought I was a little kid from around the corner looking for a fight. He never lived that down.
>
> We would go out of our neighborhood, which was lower-middle-class, all working people, you wouldn't get much there. So we would go to the other side of Prospect Park, which was known as Park Row and is still a very beautiful place. It was usually all doctors. Brownstone houses, three or four floors, all gorgeous. We would go *there* and bang on the door. Now, you never took money. You took fruit or food, some kind of cookies or fruit. And the thing was, you would say, "Got anything for Thanksgiving?"

The custom, so reminiscent of Halloween, predates trick-or-treating. I was told about it first by an Italian woman who had lived in Manhattan when she was growing up. Since then, I have found that it was carried out by members of the various European peoples who settled in New York during the nineteenth century, and that these same people did not practice a parallel Halloween activity in their neighborhoods. When I wondered if the fruits and other treats were brought home and contributed to the Thanksgiving feast, I was told they were not. Some people did share them with those less well off than they. Others hoarded their booty and ate it as they pleased.

This Thanksgiving Day begging was described in a nineteenth-century book as "the importunate begging . . . of ragged fantastics, usually children of Roman Catholic parents." If this custom is descended from begging on Guy Fawkes Day, how did it become connected to an anti-Roman, anti-pope, anti-Catholic holiday? We might speculate that in New York the name Pope's Day remained after the original meaning was lost, so that Catholics thought it *appropriate* to celebrate the day. The British Guy Fawkes traditions are similar to those of Halloween, both then and now, in regard to the making of dummies, the begging by children, and the bonfires. But England is neither a Roman Catholic nor a Celtic country, and so Halloween, based on the Roman Catholic feast of All Saints, does not enjoy widespread popularity. Guy Fawkes Day is in many ways a British analogue to Halloween, and it continues many of the Celtic customs associated with Samhain. These in turn were established in America by the British, and as the United States declared her independence and gradually grew more distant from her parent country, those same traditions shifted once again, to events such as Election Day and Thanksgiving, while being adopted by the newer populations of that city in the 1800s.

## Thanksgiving

As Halloween passes, rotting jack-o'-lanterns are discarded. Witches and ghosts are removed. The pumpkins, Indian corn, and sheaves from the fields stay, representing the harvest season and signaling the approach of Thanksgiving, an "official," that is, a legal, governmentally decreed harvest holiday. Unlike Thanksgiving, Halloween is much more of a folk holiday. We are given no day off, but people celebrate it anyway. All Hallows Day, or All Saints' Day, is a holy day of obligation in the Catholic church, but this is the closest that the Eve of All Hallows, the Eve of All Saints, comes to official institutionalization. Thanksgiving, on the other hand, has been a part of our national mythology since the seventeenth century, and has been formally sponsored by presidential decrees since the time of Abraham Lincoln.

The likely forerunner of our Thanksgiving holiday is the English Harvest Home tradition, which included feasting as part of the celebration of the bringing in of the last crops of the field. As Englishmen, the Pilgrims were certainly aware of these practices, but as Puritans, they condemned the custom as pagan and idolatrous. For Harvest Home, and other European harvest festivals as well, carried with them customs that referred to corn (or grain) goddesses, including Ceres, the Roman goddess of wheat. The Roman harvest festival named in her honor, the Cerelia, was held in October in the ancient world, and although belief in the Roman gods has long since disappeared, English countrymen from the Middle Ages to modern times have named village girls for the Corn Maiden, actually calling her Ceres in some places, adorning her with a wreath made from the cuttings of the last sheaf of grain, and parading with her through the fields and the town. In the words of an anonymous verse,

> The last in-gathering of the crop
> Is loaded, and they climb to the top
> And there huzza with all their force
> while Ceres mounts the foremost horse:
> "Gee up!" the rustic goddess cries,
> And shouts more long and loud arise;
> The swagging cart, with motion slow,
> Reels careless on, and off they go!
> (Linton 1949:37)

The last sheaf of grain left standing in the field was said to house the spirit of the Corn Mother. Of course, the word corn when used in reference to Britain and Europe refers to any grain; the Indian maize we know as corn in America was unknown in Europe before the contact with the North American Indians. The last cartload of the gathered crop was decorated, the last cuttings from the last sheaf made into decorative weavings called corn dollies. In some regions, a girl might be the Corn Maiden, as in the poem. These customs varied greatly throughout England and Scotland, but all of the Harvest Home festivities led to feasting, drinking, singing, storytelling, music making, and much merriment. Sometimes the reaper who cut the last sheaf of grain was then the Lord of the Harvest and hosted the festivities. As the Lord, he was entitled to collect fees from his guests.

Such customs are found throughout Europe, especially those that place great emphasis on the last standing sheaf and the last load of the crops. In Austria, the last sheaf is called the cock sheaf, and he who cuts it is the cock of the harvest. Here we have the spirit of the harvest symbolized in masculine rather than feminine terms; the last load of grain would be decorated with a fanciful, beribboned cock, or even a live one. The Romans, as we have seen, had their grain harvest festival in October, as did the Greeks. In the Bible, the Jewish Sukkoth, or Feast of the Tabernacles, held in September or October, is established in the book of Deuteronomy: Moses instructs the Hebrews, "Thou shalt keep the Feast of Tabernacles seven days, after that thou hast gathered in from thy threshing floor and from thy wine press, and thou shalt rejoice in thy feast" (17:13–14). References to other non-Hebraic harvest festivals are also found in the Bible. The Puritans who settled Plymouth did not approve of festival and ritual celebrations that they considered idolatrous, but when they feasted in communion and fellowship in 1621 after the harvest had been brought in, they either consciously or unconsciously operated within a tradition that their British heritage had prepared them for, and that peoples everywhere had felt it right to do.

The history of Thanksgiving reveals that this holiday combines religion, politics, and seasonal activities in its celebration. We all know the story of how the Pilgrims landed their ship the *Mayflower* in the new world in 1620, fleeing religious oppression in England. They were members of a strict reformist group known as Puritans, who sailed first to Holland, then to America. Arriving here, they established "Plimoth Plantation" (as it was then spelled) in the Massachusetts Bay Colony. Winter was cold and harsh, and the newly arrived religious sojourners survived largely through the largesse and good grace of the inhabitants of this new land, the natives they called Indians. Upon surviving that first rough winter (actually, only fifty of the original one hundred people survived), two things happened. First, a feast was held. Later, in July of 1623, a day of thanksgiving was called for as well. This was a religious day of prayer, fasting, and somber reflection. The feast of 1621 in Plymouth Plantation was most likely inspired by the British Harvest Home tradition, but public days of thanksgiving were, unlike the revelry of the first feast, religious days of fast. In fact, the Pilgrims called for this day of thanksgiving two years after the feast we today call the first Thanksgiving. This feast that was shared with the area Indians was a harvest celebration; the Thanksgiving of 1623 was a religious fast day. Before the end of the seventeenth century, however, the two concepts had mingled, so that a public day with a large family feast commemorating the meal at Plymouth was proclaimed in Connecticut in 1665: "This court doth appoint a solemn day of Thanksgiving to be kept throughout this colony on the last Wednesday of October . . . for the blessing of the fruits of the earth and the general health of the plantations" (Linton 1949: 72). Our national Thanksgiving holiday combines aspects of both of these events.

A Fast Day is still observed in New Hampshire on the fourth Monday of April as a statewide holiday. On March 17, 1681, the General Assembly of that state called for a day of "public fasting, humiliation, and prayer" for the health of one of its leading citizens, first governor John Cutt, who had been taken ill. To make matters worse, the comet that would become known as Halley's was blazing in the night sky, and this "awful, portentuous . . . star" was felt to signal calamity of some sort. John Cutt died on April 1. The fast day in his honor persisted over the centuries, and in 1949 was regularized as the fourth Monday of April, where it remains to this day. Known simply as Fast Day, it is a descendant of the days of the Puritan colonies.

As Ralph and Adele Linton point out in their good book on Thanksgiving, *We Gather Together* (1949), such Thanksgiving celebrations, although common, were regional matters. The date of each Thanksgiving varied from colony to colony. For one thing, the Puritan Pilgrims objected to fixed dates for festivals on the basis that fixed dates do not exist in nature, and that the Providence of God was likely to be made manifest at unlikely times. One could not comfortably predict them and so should not presume to set calendrical dates to express thanks for them. The fixed dates of Easter and Christmas were denounced as nonbiblical, as was the celebration of those days generally. Christmas Day 1620 went unrecognized and uncelebrated in Plymouth by the Pilgrims, but the following October saw the festive celebration of the first successful harvest. Thanksgiving remained the primary holiday celebration of New England for two centuries. Linton reports from a diary of 1779, by Julianna Smith of Massachusetts, in which the author comments, "Then there were six of the Livingston family next door. They had never seen a Thanksgiving dinner before, having been used to keep Christmas Day instead, as is the wont in New York and Province."

President George Washington issued a proclamation that established Thursday, November 26, 1789, as a national Thanksgiving holiday. This was done as much to thank God for the recent victory in the War of Independence as it was to commemorate the Pilgrims of a century and a half earlier. By late November, harvest is well past, so

United We Stand. Thanksgiving Day, November 24, 1864. Holiday celebrations always reflect the contemporary issues and events of the day, while they commemorate historical and mythic events. Photo by David Hampshire, Instructional Media Services, Bowling Green State University.

these events were not harvest feasts in any direct way. From their very beginnings the national Thanksgiving holidays were civic and political. Washington's proclamation read in part: "Now therefore I do recommend and assign Thursday, the twenty-sixth of November next, to be devoted to the service of that great and glorious Being ... for the kind care and protection of the people of this country, previous to their becoming a nation; for the signal manifold mercies, and the favorable interpositions of his providence, in the course and conclusion of the late war ... for the peacable and rational manner in which we have been enabled to establish Constitutions of Government for our safety and happiness, and particularly the national one now lately instituted."

The holiday continued to grow in importance, but as a day celebrated at different times in different places by different people. It was not until October 3, 1863, that President Abraham Lincoln issued a presidential National Thanksgiving Proclamation, naming the last Thursday of November as the official day of celebration. Like Washington's, this proclamation too was framed by a national war, in this case the Civil War; but, unlike the occasion of the first presidential proclamation, this decree came in the middle of a war which had an uncertain outcome. Perhaps Lincoln saw the political advantages inherent in the celebration of the common history of all the nation at a time when the nation had divided in two and attacked itself.

Lincoln was convinced to establish Thanksgiving as a national holiday by Sarah Josepha Hale, who had been working ceaselessly toward this end since at least 1827. In her novel of that year, *Northwood,* she recognized the political and nationalistic nature of the Thanksgiving celebration by comparing the day to the Fourth of July. She later became editor of a national magazine, *Godey's Lady's Book,* which she used as a vehicle for her unflagging effort to see Thanksgiving established as a national day of remembrance and celebration. According to Linton, it is "highly probable" that she met with Lincoln personally and influenced him toward his decision of 1863. The institutionalization of Thanksgiving was probably inevitable, but it would not have happened when and how it did without Mrs. Hale's efforts. In an editorial in the *Godey's Lady's Book* of 1865, she wrote of the then just-established national holiday:

> Our Thanksgiving Day, becoming the focus, as it were, of the private life and virtues of the people, should be hallowed and exalted, and made the day of generous deeds and innocent enjoyments, of noble aspirations and heavenly hopes.
>
> What themes and opportunities are here for our reverend clergy! A holy day is added to our days of rest from worldly labors; a third joyful anniversary is sealed for the American Republic.
>
> The Twenty-second of February is sacred to the memory of Washington and patriotic duties.
>
> The Fourth of July is the Jubilee of National Independence.
>
> The *last Thursday in November,* let it be consecrated now to our Father in heaven, for His bounteous blessing bestowed upon us, as the perpetual Day of Thanksgiving for the American people.

An accurate portrayal of Thanksgiving. The turkey is the primary symbol. It is a patriotic day, thus the American shields. The crossed knives and forks allude to the feast. Ca. 1910. Courtesy of the Center for Archival Collections, Bowling Green State University.

The harvest that we give thanks for is one of great bounty. It reflects that sense the colonists had of America as a new Eden, eternally fertile, with an almost endless amount of game and produce. A long-standing Thanksgiving symbol is the cornucopia, the horn of plenty, from which fruits and vegetables tumble forth endlessly. Likewise, the turkey has become today's central Thanksgiving symbol. In fact, many people call the day "Turkey Day." The turkey is a large bird, now raised domestically for consumption, bigger and fatter than the bird the Pilgrims knew, a "Butterball" as one commercial brand is known. The turkey is a symbol of deep, almost maternal nourishment. In our American tall tales, animals are giant. Game abounds. Hunters fire a single shot into a tree and birds fall for twenty-four hours. In the early years of the republic, America seemed to have everything, and more of it than anywhere else. The belief that God has especially favored this land is deeply embedded in Thanksgiving. We act it out within the Thanksgiving meal as we give thanks to the Lord for all his blessings. The blessings are manifested in the food itself:

its quantity, its voluminousness. We eat until we can eat no more, and still there is food left to be eaten. The big, round, fat turkey in the center of the table serves all seated around it, inexhaustibly, and then continues to feed us through the holiday weekend.

Alan Gevinson is a film historian who works for the American Film Institute in Los Angeles. He is also a vegetarian. At my request, he wrote to me about a Thanksgiving celebration he celebrated with other vegetarians who support animals' rights. This is his description of that meal, which featured a live turkey:

> I was impressed by the genuine feeling of the participants, for the love, concern, respect, sanctity, wonder of life—including turkeys. I don't think most Thanksgivings are really about anything other than getting together with family and/or friends, eating big meals, and watching football. Because this gathering was held to some extent to make a point—that one need not celebrate or give thanks for life by slaughtering other life—it probably was more focused than traditional meals. It was given by the Vegetarian Society of Los Angeles and was the tenth such dinner given. After the meal, which was in a vegetarian restaurant, speakers talked about various things, and singers sang some less than entertaining songs. . . . Most of the speakers were from different animal rights groups and spoke fairly eloquently and movingly about issues they hoped those at the dinner would get involved in. TV cameras came and took shots of the turkey walking around the stage. I had a good feeling about the night, which really was Thanksgiving Eve, because it was nice to be with a group of people who felt the way I did.
>
> It has struck me recently how the animal rights movement has in some ways developed itself into a group with various unifying "ways of life." That interests me because it is so recent and is still developing. Eating, dressing, grooming have all changed because of the prohibition against using slaughterhouse products. It reminds me of the way Orthodox Judaism limits these areas and, in limiting them, makes those who accept the limitations feel part of the group. Also, language is affected (some people will, to make the act more visual and thus more repulsive, speak of eating meat as eating "flesh"; slogans are formed that become popular). Certain books and magazines are read and talked about, and events in the news become a focus for letter writing and demonstrating, and leisure time is devoted to activities that will help the cause.

In his perceptive and eloquent letter, Alan sees the way groups are formed around common interests and shared experiences, and the ways these affect the entirety of the group's life style. This group of animal rights activists and vegetarians has taken the traditional

Thanksgiving turkey and turned it into a symbol of the animal rights movement. They have particularized the basic symbol of the holiday by inverting it. They have maintained tradition by adapting it to their special situation.

Although we think of April Fools' Day when we think of sending someone after a nonexistent item, many occupations routinely send new workers on such fools' errands. In the National Football League, holiday traditions and occupational traditions merge. Thanksgiving is a time to send rookie players to collect a (nonexistent) free turkey. *USA Today* reported a 1984 incident when Pittsburgh Steeler rookie Tony Dungy was set up by teammates Franco Harris and Mel Blount: "They got me good. . . . They got me going with plans to cook the turkey, first at Franco's house, then at Mel's. . . . The manager [of the store] told me that [Steeler president] Dan Rooney had it."

"Dan told me he had just given the last one to Coach Chuck Noll and that I could go ask Chuck for it." Because he was afraid to go to Noll, Dungy went back to the locker room and said, "Mel, we've got no turkey." Then, Dungy recounted, "everyone broke out laughing."

Along with the turkey, the Pilgrims are primary symbols of Thanksgiving. Indeed, the image of the "first Thanksgiving" is one of great power in American society. Miles Standish, John Alden, and Priscilla Mullens were the principal characters in the Longfellow poem that has immortalized the events of those early years, *The Courtship of Miles Standish*. The images of Pilgrims we see today may refer to those people specifically, at least in some people's minds, but most of the Thanksgiving Pilgrims are generic. So are the Indians. We have no "Chief Massasoit" candles on sale at the department stores. Rather, we have cute Indians and nameless Pilgrims, usually a man and a woman. The first Thanksgiving, the Pilgrims, the fellowship with the Indians, all these have become mythic events in the American consciousness. Historically, there has been a bias toward England as the cultural parent of the United States, and toward New England as the geographical place of origin, despite the fact that it is not the oldest or first area settled, nor were Englishmen the first or only settlers. Nevertheless, the Thanksgiving story has become a kind of origin myth for the United States. It is felt to be the first truly *American* event, and we call the Pilgrims our forefathers. It is not surprising, then, that we portray them as a male and female pair. They are our distant parents.

*Native* Americans, on the other hand, take an opposing view to the traditional interpretation of Thanksgiving, emphasizing the darker aspects of colonialism and the establishment of European hegemony. Many Native peoples in the United States today, in fact, hold alter-

ICE CREAM

FOR THE W LE W LE HOLIDAYS

This 1983 menu from Friendly Restaurants is a nice illustration of the period of the year known as "the Holidays." Pilgrims and Indians represent Thanksgiving, Santa is there from Christmas, and Father Time represents New Year's. Note also the falling star that dots the *i* in the Friendly logo. This could be a subtle reference to the star that led the magi to Bethlehem. If one follows this star, it leads to the restaurant. Photo by David Hampshire, Instructional Media Services, Bowling Green State University.

native events at Thanksgiving in order to emphasize and publicize the Indian experience and understanding of this holiday.

Thanksgiving opens that period of the year we call "the holidays," which include Christmas and New Year's, and, increasingly, Hanukkah as well. But of all of them, Thanksgiving is the most heavily traveled holiday of the year, the one holiday for which travel is the most essential. No doubt this is in part due to timing. Since Thanksgiving is always on a Thursday, it creates a four-day weekend holiday. People must be at their destinations by Thursday and back again by the following Monday. However, the important point is that so many of us feel the need to travel for Thanksgiving. Where are we all going? The answer: home. Home for the holidays. And where is home? At Thanksgiving, home means the home of one's youth, or the home where one's parents live, or one's grandparents. Very often, Thanksgiving dinner is held at the home of the eldest members of the family, as immortalized in Lydia Maria Child's famous lines, "Over the river and through the wood, to grandmother's house we go." The family patriarch or matriarch is seated at the head of the table. The focus of this feast is on them. That is why we have traveled so far, in honor of them and of family values of togetherness, solidarity, communality. The family is celebrated, and specifically it is the eldest generation of the family who is honored. Our Thanksgiving symbols are of the eldest generation of "Americans," a kind of mythic American Adam and Eve, the male and female Pilgrims. We honor them as we honor our parents and grandparents. The focus of this holiday is on tradition and continuity. It is on the past, and our place in it as Americans and as family members. We honor our family elders, surrounded by images of our "forefathers," our American cultural elders.

The day after Thanksgiving unofficially marks the opening of the Christmas shopping season, and even though there have been advertising campaigns going on for weeks, newspapers on that Friday often feature a front-page photo of downtown city streets crowded with Christmas shoppers. In Detroit, the finale of the Thanksgiving Day Parade is the arrival of Santa Claus, and in other cities and towns, Santa arrives by helicopter in shopping malls on that Friday after the Thanksgiving meal. Thanksgiving is its own holiday, but it is also a part of what is probably the most important and coherent festival period of the contemporary American year. It is the first of a sequence of winter holidays that take us through the darkest days of the year.

Halloween and Thanksgiving share harvest symbolism, Thanksgiving and Christmas share the family feast, and Christmas and New Year's share midwinter symbolism and the use of a baby as a symbol of rebirth and renewal. Halloween has images of death in anticipation of sustaining life through the coming winter; Christmas and New Year's have images of life that remain through the winter. Thanksgiving is about the life of the family unit; its focus is on past generations. Christmas is about new life, and its attention is devoted to children and future generations. Also, the progression of the holidays in the fall quadrant is very much tied into the changing seasons; the holidays of October, November, and December are each at the end of a month that has become fully identified with the holiday at its end.

The holiday symbols not only tell us where we are in the year; they tell us what has passed, because many of them are organic. The dry and dying Christmas trees that line the sidewalks after the turn of the year are public statements about the passing of the holidays, just as decorating them was a statement about approaching festival. This is also true of the rotting pumpkins on November porches and smashed jack-o'-lanterns in November streets.


## Christmas

With no disrespect intended to anyone's beliefs, it is important to realize that no one knows the date of the birth of Christ. When, in the fourth century A.D., the church fathers of Rome settled on a day to celebrate this event, the decision was based on a variety of factors, not the least of which was the fact that December 25 had been the date of popular observance for centuries. Also, the establishment of this date may well have been influnced by the Roman Saturnalia celebrations that stretched from the solstice to the first of January, perhaps also by the numerous winter solstice celebrations of other peoples in Europe, and most definitely by the Persian celebration of the birth of Mithra, *Sol Invictus,* the Unconquerable Sun, which was also held on December 25. The Mithraic religion was popular throughout the Mediterranean area and the Middle East and was the faith of many of the Roman legionnaires. Undoubtedly, this festival too developed from an earlier solstice festival, but in recorded historical times it was a major influence on the early Christians. Along with the northern European Yule, all of these festivals were midwinter festivals that marked the winter solstice. The twelve days of Christmas may be an inheritence of the twelve days of the Saturnalia, and of the Babylonian festival before it, the previously mentioned Zagmuk. These twelve days of the festival of the winter solstice, the point of the solar new year, were believed to correspond to the twelve months of the coming year. The English people of the eighteenth century felt this to be true, as did the Romans and the Babylonians. In A.D. 567, the Council of Tours proclaimed the twelve days from Christmas to Epiphany as a holy and festive season. In a sense, then, in its furthest, dimmest past, Christmas may have a now-forgotten, prehistoric ritual of the sun as one of its ancestors. Although Christmas is a religious commemoration of the birth of Jesus, it may well be celebrated on December 25 because of the winter solstice that actually occurs a few days earlier. Ultimately, we find that the fundamental events of the natural order such as the solstices underlie our most precious holidays, which in turn are shaped by history and human hands.

The first mention of December 25 as the date of the Feast of the Holy Birth is contained in a Roman document called the Philocalian Calendar. This dates to A.D. 354, but contains sections that are believed

Christmas Greeting

Sometimes holiday cards from earlier days seem strange to us today. At the turn of the century, summer scenes were commonly used for Christmas and New Year's cards, with verses such as "May your every day be filled with summer sunshine." Courtesy of the Center for Archival Collections, Bowling Green State University.

to have been written a bit earlier, in 336. The reference to the Nativity celebration may be as old as that, and is at least as old as the document itself. The first recorded use of the name *Cristes Maesse* dates from the year 1038. The December 25 date had been accepted by the Christian world since about A.D. 400, although the Greek churches, which did not change to the Gregorian reformed calendar, celebrate it thirteen days later, on January 6. Our contemporary style of counting by days adds a bit of confusion to the famous concept of the twelve days of Christmas. These are actually thirteen days. Originally, the peoples of Europe counted by nights, and so they correctly referred to the twelve nights from December 25 to January 6.

Advent, the four-week period of reverent expectation that precedes Christmas, much as Lent is a period of solemnity that precedes Easter, was established by the Church shortly after the establishment of the date of the Feast of the Nativity. By the ninth century, it had become universally observed. Today in America people complain that we begin the Christmas season too early, and that this is done for

We have extended the use of evergreens to the decoration of our vehicles, our second homes. Photo by Jack Santino, Boston, 1989.

mercantile purposes, but in Europe for the past several hundred years, we find that the season began as early as November 11, Saint Martin's Day, or Martinmas. Contemporary Advent begins on the Sunday nearest Saint Andrew's Day, November 30.

Throughout this winter season, foliage and evergreens are so important that they have achieved primary symbolic significance. The Christmas tree, of course, is central to American Christmas celebrations, but holly and mistletoe and the poinsettia from Mexico (known there as the flower of the Holy Night) also beautify the festival. Evergreen decorations were common in ancient Rome during the Saturnalia, as were trees hung with burning candles. Early Christians kept up the custom by decorating their homes with laurel.

In Scandinavian countries today, Yule, or *Jul,* is the word for Christmas. Originally, a carol was a song that was danced to, and people in Sweden still dance around the tree to *"Nu ar det Jul igen,"* or "Now it is Christmas again":

> Now Christmas is here again,
> And Christmas is here again,
> And Christmas we'll have till Easter.

Then Easter is here again,
And Easter is here again,
And Easter we'll have till Christmas.

Now this will not be so,
And this will not be so,
For in between comes Lenten fasting.

The simple lyrics point to the seasonal relationships between holidays and a folk recognition that the holidays mark the turning of the world. In fact, the word *Yule* may come from the old Germanic word *Iol* (or, variously, *Iul, Giul,* etc.) which means "a turning wheel" and might refer to the turning sun after the winter solstice. Another possible explanation for the origin of the word is found in the Old English *geol,* which means "feast." The entire month of December was known as *geola,* or feast-month, in the times before Christianity, because of the great solstice celebration. This name later was retained to refer to the Christmas feast as Yule in England and *Jul* in Scandinavia. The old custom of the Yule log (midwinter fire, midwinter light) became a Christmas custom. Poet Robert Herrick wrote of it in 1648 as the Christmas "brand," which must be burned until sunset, after which "Part must be kept, wherewith to tend, the Christmas log next year." At its fullest or most elaborate realization, the Yule log is the whole trunk of a tree that was selected and felled on the preceding Candlemas and dried through the year. So once again, one ritual looks ahead to another. Candlemas is for many the end of the Christmas season, but the tradition is to end the season by preparing for the next, and to carry a part of it through the year.

Holly, ivy, and mistletoe were all believed to have special power by the north Europeans. In fact, the mistletoe was held so sacred in the religion of the druids that enemies who met each other under it in the forest were required to lay down their arms, exchange friendly greetings, and keep a truce until the following day. From this our custom of kissing underneath mistletoe may have descended. Until recently, the English decorated with a kissing bough. But now the tree dominates, the evergreen tree that Charles Dickens called "a new German toy" in 1850, but by 1891 was considered "old-fashioned" by President Harrison when he told reporters, "We shall have an old-fashioned Christmas tree for the grandchildren upstairs" (Weiser 1952:121).

The earliest reference to a Christmas tree comes from a forest ordinance in Alsace (now part of France) in 1561 that prohibits taking for Christmas "more than one bush of more than eight shoes' length." A travel book from 1605 records that "At Christmas time in Strassburg they set up fir trees in the rooms, and they hang on them roses cut of many colored paper, apples, wafers, gilt, sugar, and so on" (Snyder 1983:13). As early as 1710, German immigrants from the upper Rhine area may have set up the first Christmas tree in the United States, and certainly the custom was strengthened by the wave of German immigration that started around 1830. This German custom in turn probably sprang from two sources: the Paradise trees of the medieval mystery plays, and the decorated wooden pyramid known as the *Weihnachtspyramide*.

In the Middle Ages, throughout Europe, folk plays that recounted stories from the Bible (often humorously), were performed in the churches during liturgical celebrations of the holy days of the church calendar. One such play was that of Adam and Eve, which featured as part of its staging a fir tree, decorated with apples and surrounded by candles, which represented the tree of life. Later, these plays ceased being performed in church, but the Paradise tree was taken up by people as a domestic custom. Along with the apples, wafers that represented the sacred host of the mass were used as decorations, later to be joined by Christmas cookies and other decorations. In the meantime, the German people had been celebrating Christmas by setting up a wooden structure shaped like a pyramid that was covered with boughs of evergreen fir and laurel. The Paradise tree and the *Weihnachtspyramide* combined to become the modern Christmas tree. Today in Bavaria, the branches and trees decorated with apples and Christmas lights are still called *Paradeis*.

Christmas symbolism, so much of it derived from solstice-midwinter rituals, festivals, and celebrations, is appropriate for the late-December, year's-end period in ways that transcend any particular religion. The lights and candles, the evergreens, the eternal circle of the wreath all remind us of promised new beginnings at apparent endings, of life ongoing during the death-sleep of winter. December 21 has the least amount of daylight of any day of the year, and peoples over the world celebrate with a festival of lights at this time. Hanukkah, while not the "Jewish Christmas" as it is sometimes erroneously and arrogantly called, is a day that marks a period of miraculous light, eight days when a lamp's flame burned without fuel. The menorah, which holds eight candles, commemorates this event and is a central symbol of Hanukkah: the lighting of each candle on eight successive days is one of its central customs. Not mentioned in any of the books of the Bible, Hanukkah was never a major Jewish holy day. It has received its greatest elaboration in the United States in modern times, in part as a response to the Christian festival. As such, it can be said to be a largely American holiday.

Chanukah, or Hanukkah, is a festival of lights at the darkest time of the year. Photo by David Hampshire, Instructional Media Services, Bowling Green State University.

Peoples everywhere use flaming light at this darkest day of the year. The candles familiar to the Christian Christmas holiday are probably Roman in origin. The Romans used candles prominently in their rituals and festivals and the early Church, based in Rome, followed this custom. In Scandinavia, a log was burned through the night during the midwinter festival of Yule. Some peoples consciously saw in the solstice the birth of the sun, in that the solstice also is the point when the days begin to get longer again. The ancient celebration of the birth of Mithra was called the Birth of the Unconquerable Sun. For Christians, the holiday at this time of year marks not the birth of the sun but the birth of the Son, who is believed to be the Way, the Truth, and the Light. The early church recognized that they were likely to be suspected of trying to co-opt other religious celebrations, and were sensitive to the criticism. They countered by insisting that they had set the time for the celebration of Christ's birth at the time of the solstice so as to divert people from pagan practices by giving them a truly miraculous, Christian event to focus on. Nevertheless, saints writing in the first centuries of the establishment of Christianity were aware of the irony involved, and felt it to be divinely inspired. In A.D. 258, for instance, Saint Cyprian wrote, "O, how wonderfully acted

Divine Providence that on the day which the Sun was born . . . Christ should be born!" And Saint John Chrysostom, in A.D. 407, wrote, "They call December 25th the Birthday of the Unconquered: Who is indeed so unconquered as our Lord? . . . or, if they say that it is the birthday of the Sun: *He* is the Sun of Justice."

## *Kwanzaa*

Initiated in 1966 by Dr. Maulana "Ron" Karenga, a professor at UCLA at the time, Kwanzaa reflects the ways various groups of people celebrate the midwinter holidays in ways that are specific to their own cultural, religious, or ethnic backgrounds. Karenga is from Nigeria. During the holiday period, he found that it was very difficult for him and his fellow students to celebrate, since they felt the American traditions were foreign to them. As a result of this need, and also as a sign of his increasing sense of black nationalism, Karenga invented an American ritual, based on African traditions, called *Kwanzaa*, Swahili for "First Fruits." Derived from African harvest celebrations, Kwanzaa partakes of the Western festivals of light traditions that mark both Hanukkah and Christmas. On each day during Kwanzaa, which is celebrated for seven days beginning on December 26 and culminating on January 1, a candle on a seven-branched candlabra is lit. Each candle honors one of seven principles: *umoja* (unity); *kujichagulia* (self-determination); *ujima* (collective work and responsibilty); *ujamma* (cooperative economics); *nia* (purpose); *kuumba* (creativity); and *imani* (faith). A child asks a parent about each of these principles before lighting the candle.

Although Kwanzaa is felt to be an alternative to the commercialized aspects of Christmas, it is not intended to replace it. Often, in fact, Kwanzaa celebrations are conducted in churches and parochial schools. Rather, it is more an ethnic celebration than a religious one, although it is very spiritual in its celebration of family and the seven principles, which are known collectively as the *nguzo saba*. A Kwanzaa celebration includes a basket of fruit to reflect its nature as a harvest festival, along with a unity cup from which everyone drinks, and a straw mat on which the items are placed. The ritual culminates in the *karamu*, or feast.

Although begun recently, the celebration of Kwanzaa has grown rapidly. One source says that over 18 million Americans currently observe it (Reidy 1992:27). Kwanzaa has joined the increasingly pluralistic collection of holidays and celebrations that, together, reflect a growing recognition of our rich cultural diversity.

## Festivals of Light

The midwinter festival of lights takes a special form in West Texas and New Mexico. *Luminarias,* or little lights, also known as *farolitos,* or little lanterns, in Santa Fe, are a Christmas Eve tradition said to date from the times of the Spanish conquistadors. The luminarias are simply small candles burned inside brown paper bags that are filled with sand to weight the bags and moor the candles. These are lit and placed along driveways and roadsides, so as to light the way for the coming Christ Child. Originally, the luminarias were small bonfires, about three feet high. Today's luminarias evolved from several sources, including the Mexican custom of hanging lanterns for festive occasions. The first small paper lanterns were made from decorative, colored wrapping paper, but when traders from the United States introduced the brown paper bag, these were quickly adapted because they were inexpensive and made the tradition more accessible to everyone. The luminarias are too fragile to be hung, so are instead placed on the ground at sundown on Christmas Eve. All house and street lights are turned off, and motorists are asked to dim their headlights as they tour residential areas to look at the lights. The effect is a shimmering sea of amber, slowly burning through the Christmas Eve night. The custom, which is three centuries old, is growing throughout the Southwest and across the nation. The Toledo Zoo lined its roadways with luminarias in 1987.

Bonfires have been a part of almost every holiday we have looked at, and Christmas is no exception. This should come as no surprise, especially because of the fundamental symbolism of light that is everywhere found in celebrations held at the time of the winter solstice. In Louisiana, along the Mississippi River, large crowds gather to light bonfires on Christmas Eve. As many as twenty to a mile, the fires are made of logs, cane reed, old rubber tires, and bamboo. The tradition is a French one; it was brought to Louisiana after the Civil War by Marist priests. In France, bonfires known as *feux de joie* (fires of joy) were burned on the eve of Epiphany, the eve of Ash Wednesday, various saints' days, and New Year's Eve. The Marist fathers continued the New Year's bonfire custom in Louisiana, but as Christmas grew more important as a winter holiday in the late nineteenth century, the bonfire tradition was moved to Christmas Eve. Today, groups of families begin to construct the bonfires shortly before Thanksgiving. The work continues until Christmas Eve, when the lighting of the fires provides a spectacular fireworks display for the hundreds of onlookers gathered on the levees. These Christmas bonfires are considered the focal point of the Christmas celebrations, along with midnight mass and, afterward, a gumbo dinner.

Along with the Christmas bonfires in Louisiana and the luminarias of the Southwest are the absolutely amazing displays of lights and decorations that Americans all over the country put up on their houses and build in their yards. From Fort Worth, Texas, to Maine, the decorations grow more elaborate every year. A South Philadelphia family says it is a German tradition. The neighborhood has been particularly famous for its Christmas lights since the 1930s, and whatever its origin, it is now a neighborhood tradition. In much the same way, families all over the country are involved in what is an essentially American popular display of lights at midwinter.

### The Creche Controversy

In the seventeenth century, the Puritans made an organized and institutionalized effort to stamp out all observances of Christmas in the colonies. They passed laws against any celebratory activities on December 25 and proudly boasted when the day came and went with no suspension of work. Today, such laws against the celebration of Christmas are unthinkable, because they would infringe upon people's rights to freedom of religion. Yet the fact that Christmas is a Christian holy day raises problems precisely in regard to freedom of religion and freedom of expression, and nowhere is this more evident than in the annual round of controversies surrounding the public displays of Christmas creches.

Saint Francis of Assisi is said to have created the first creche in 1224, when he used real people and live animals to reconstruct the Nativity scene in a cave near the Italian village of Greccio. His purpose was to teach by illustration the humble beginnings of Jesus. These living pantomimes of the birth of Christ soon became an Italian custom, before spreading throughout the entire Christian world. The tradition that the animals are given the power of speech on Christmas Eve is supposed to stem from this practice of using live animals. In some churches today, the custom continues, as in the Living Nativity of the Highland Park United Methodist Church of Topeka, Kansas. More commonly, however, statues are used. From the Middle Ages through the seventeenth and eighteenth centuries, hand-carved wooden figures became increasingly elaborate. Often these included caricatures of local townspeople and were costumed in the styles of their day.

Originally, creches were restricted to churches. Today, however, in towns and cities throughout the United States, objections have been raised to publicly funded nativity scenes being erected on public areas, such as in front of town halls, on the basis that these displays violate the principle of separation of church and state. Although the Supreme Court has ruled that there need not be "a complete separation of church and state," U.S. District Court judges have ruled against such displays in Concord, New Hampshire, and Dearborn, Michican. The U.S. Supreme Court allowed city officials in Pawtucket, Rhode Island, to include a creche as part of a display on private land in the middle of the city; a similar issue remains undecided in Scarsdale, New York. Churches, of course, are allowed to display creches on church property, but agencies of state and local government have been warned either to make their displays nondenominational by adding other symbolic elements, or to do away with them altogether. In Dearborn, a large menorah was added to the display, which pleased some people but angered others. In Washington, D.C., the National Christmas Tree has been joined on the National Mall by a menorah, but here again this angers many people, both Jewish and Christian, not to mention atheists and Buddhists and members of other religious groups that make up an increasing proportion of our society.

The issue is a complicated one. Christmas is, by definition, Christian, and thus, an official endorsement of it constitutes a violation of the doctrine of separation of church and state. On the other side is the issue of freedom of religious expression. Moreover, the other familiar symbols of Christmas, such as Santa Claus, although often referred to as secular, are still symbols of a Christian holiday. The solution of adding the menorah to Christmas displays is seen by many as an insult to Judaism because it effectively reduces Hanukkah to an adjunct of Christmas. For instance, an elaborately decorated home in Hollywood, Florida, includes in its display of seventy animated objects and more than forty-five thousand lights a boy lighting a menorah. This is alongside a mechanical manger scene, elves making toys, two Santas holding a *Merry Christmas* sign, and an Eskimo petting a polar bear. The effect is to render all of these symbolic elements—Santas, polar bears, the Christ child, and the menorah—as being of the same order, when in fact they derive from different traditions, and people feel quite differently about each of them.

As America grows more pluralistic and more aware of its pluralism, the problems of defining our national holidays, many of which are Christian, will grow. Easter falls on a Sunday, so the question of suspending work is avoided. Saint Patrick's Day is celebrated in Boston as Evacuation Day, a legal holiday. What we are seeing with the

Christmas creche controversies is a recognition of the problem and an attempt to deal with it rather than avoid it. In effect, we are in the process once again of redefining our holidays to conform to contemporary situations. It is a process that we have seen throughout history and back into prehistory.

There was a time in our history when New Year's was the day of the winter celebration. During the nineteenth century, people exchanged gifts on New Year's, and they went visiting. This is in part a legacy of the Puritans, and in part an inheritance from the German settlers who brought with them the evergreen Christmas tree and many of the New Year's customs as well. In old "Dutch" New York, Santa Claus came on New Year's, for instance. New Year's cards of the past featured all the midwinter symbols such as holly and candles that we now associate with Christmas. Today we are finding that there are an increasing number of cards devoted to New Year's, and while many of these depict celebratory images such as party hats and noisemakers, many more are featuring winter scenes, holly, and decorated houses, and are done in red and green; in short, they look like Christmas cards, except they make no reference to either the religious images of the Christ Child and the stable in Bethlehem, nor do they show Santa Claus. The contemporary New Year's cards have reclaimed the midwinter symbolism they once owned. And today New Year's is beginning to absorb some of the midwinter imagery of Christmas and be identified by evergreens and wreathes and snowmen, along with party hats, noisemakers, and champagne. In the nineteenth century, New Year's cards were quite popular. They were eclipsed by Christmas cards for most of the twentieth century but are now making a comeback, and are joined by Hanukkah cards, including some that address the fact that Christmas dominates American society in December (for instance, a Hanukkah card depicts a line of bearded Jews in traditional garb joining hands. One man is in Santa Claus costume. "Happy Hanukkah," the card reads, "to an unorthodox kind of guy!")

These greeting cards reflect the increasing awareness of cultural pluralism and religious and ethnic diversity in our country. Not everyone is Christian, nor is everyone religious. Yet Christmas is an undeniable, overpowering, and attractive holiday. Much of its attraction lies in the perfect psychological and symbolic "fit" between it and the time of year. Since the evergreens, holly, snowmen, and even the brightly shining star are not intrinsically religious symbols and in fact were associated with midwinter festivals that predate the Christmas feast historically, these can be separated from the Christmas holiday

Christmas cards are increasingly becoming ecumenical. This one recognizes the symbol of the candle and light at the darkest time of the year, common to both Hanukkah and Christmas. The card is especially appropriate for couples of different religious faiths. © Recycled Paper Products, Inc. All rights reserved. Original design by Hadley Robertson. Reprinted by permission.

and used to represent the season through the New Year. This is one strategy for including a wide range of people in the celebration of the holiday spirit.

We see the adaptation on the greeting-card racks. The New Year's cards referred to above are one way around the dilemma. We still celebrate the season, but focus the greeting on the secular New Year's Day rather than the problematic Christmas. Solstice cards have begun to appear, and we also notice a growing number of Hanukkah cards. These point to the creation and development of holidays in December other than Christmas. Many of these cards reflect humorously on the Christmas season and thus show a recognition of the fact that Christmas is an inescapable fact of American life.

Santa Claus, even though he is frequently referred to as an example of the secular or pagan aspects of the contemporary Christmas celebration, refers specifically to Christmas, and is a part of Christmas, and is therefore inappropriate for a nondenominational celebration. His name is derived from Saint Nicholas, although that fact is receding from public memory. L. Frank Baum, the author of *The Wizard of Oz*, wrote a book entitled *The Life and Adventures of Santa Claus*, wherein he created a non-Christian origin for the figure. Likewise, the 1986 film *Santa Claus—The Movie* took great pains to establish a mag-

Santa paying obeisance to the Baby Jesus. This homemade display reflects the maker's feelings about the centrality of the Nativity in the Christmas festivities. Interestingly, it pairs an old man and a baby, just as New Year's symbolism does. Photo by Jack Santino, Bowling Green, Ohio, 1992.

ical origin for him, conveniently overlooking the obvious derivation of *Santa* from *Saint* and *Claus* from *Nicholas*. The evolution from the original Saint Nicholas, patron saint of fishermen, bishop of Myra, to the jolly old elf of Clement Moore's poem is a long one, and many non-Christian elements were adapted along the way. Sometimes, some Christian groups negotiate this problem by combining the figure of Santa with that of the Christ Child, depicting Santa kneeling before the Divine Baby and praying, for instance, thus suggesting not only that Santa is correctly seen in a Christian context, but also that he is secondary to the Baby Jesus.

So the problem is this: how does one live in the United States fully as a citizen and a member of the American culture today and not partake in the major holiday of the year? The answer: with great difficulty. We cannot deny that Christmas is, at its heart, a religious celebration. At the same time, it is a general midwinter holiday. When the more general aspects are elaborated, some Christians complain that the day is becoming too commercialized, that it is losing its true meaning. "Put Christ back in Christmas," the billboards read. When the emphasis is on the birth of Christ, non-believers legitimately complain that their rights are being violated. So we now have the Supreme Court facing decisions as to whether towns can use public moneys to pay for displays of creches on town property during Christmastime. These cases represent nothing less than the American people as a society deciding how it will celebrate this festival. These cases are us as a nation adapting to social changes.

We are seeing the development of two—or actually several—Christmases: the privately religious and ethnic, and the publicly national. The religious celebrations vary according to group, like ethnic holidays, and are sacred. This religious aspect is becoming one component out of many, and is interpreted by religious groups as they consider appropriate. In this way, Hanukkah becomes absorbed as the Jewish religious component, not to be confused with Christmas, entirely unrelated historically, but functioning as the ethnic midwinter celebration during a national holiday period. Black people have developed Kwanzaa, December 26, as an ethnic celebration; atheists celebrate Solstice Day. Meanwhile, the national and international media focus on the less obviously religious aspects of Christmas in their holiday campaigns, or ignore them altogether. The values of peace, good will, cheer, generosity, and self-sacrifice are embodied in secular tales of Scrooge and the Grinch, leaving people to devote themselves to religious and ethnic rituals as they see fit.

I think of this as a nationalization of Christmas. Along this line, we may continue to see the development of New Year's Day as the central public day of the season. This nationalization of holidays is nothing new: it has happened before with Thanksgiving and might just happen in the future with Mardi Gras. When I use the term *nationalization*, I do not mean the invention and establishment of an official "tradition" or civic holiday by a government. Instead, I mean the growth of a holiday, celebrated by people on a grass-roots level, to national magnitude, and elastic enough to be inclusive rather than exclusive. For instance, although the celebration of Thanksgiving was officially established by presidential decree, this really was a ratification of a folk holiday commemorating the Pilgrims' feast at Plymouth that had been celebrated more or less continuously since 1684. Today Christmas is "stretching" so as to accomodate the contours of the changing American profile.

## Santa Claus

Santa Claus derives his name from Nicholas, the legendary saint who was bishop of Myra, in Turkey, in the fourth century. He is said to have died on December 6, A.D. 342. December 6 is celebrated as his feast day, and in many countries this is the day he arrives with his presents and punishments. As a Christian saint, he was believed to have worked many miracles. A patron saint of fishermen, he calms the raging seas during times of storm. The most famous legend, however, concerns a more down-to-earth kind of "miracle," the time Nicholas saved three young women from selling themselves into prostitution. As the story goes, a man had fallen into extreme poverty. In order to raise money to help their father, his three daughters had decided to become prostitutes, the only avenue they saw open to them. Nicholas, still a young man and himself quite wealthy, long before becoming a bishop, heard of these three desperate young women and their poor father. Moved by the tale, he secretly visited their house in the dark of three successive nights, and on each visit tossed through an open window a ball of gold. His gift saved the girls from a life of sin and their father from economic hardship. Eventually, his secret became well known.

Like all folk legends, this story exists in many variations. In some versions of the tale (probably later ones) the three gold balls landed in the stockings the girls had hung by the chimney to dry. The skeleton narrative, however—that Nicholas secretly left gifts under cover of night—is the same from tale to tale. Although he is credited with many other miracles, and his three gold balls have become the symbol for pawnbrokers, this particular legend of Nicholas as gift bearer was important in the later development of the legend of Saint Nicholas as a midwinter deity who punishes the bad and rewards the good with gifts.

Because he had calmed the storms at sea, Nicholas became a patron saint of fishermen, who carried his legends to ports in Europe and Asia. Nicholas became the patron saint of Russia when its tsar, Vladimir, converted to Christianity in the tenth century. In this way, the legends of Saint Nicholas entered into northern Europe, including Lapland and all of Scandinavia. There, Christianity blended with Germanic religion and its native beliefs of divinities who rode the

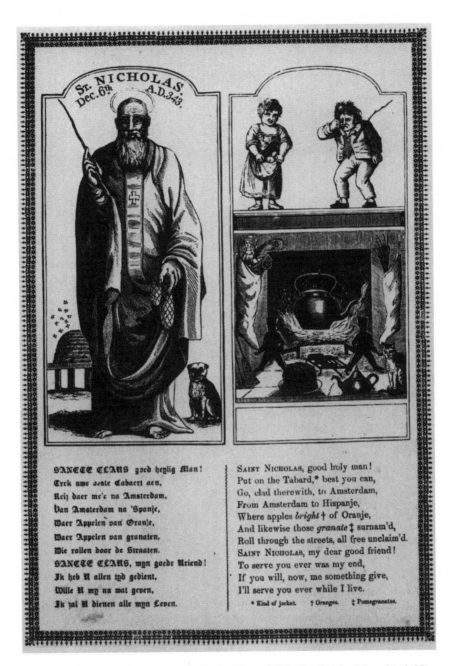

"The First Celebration of the Festival of Saint Nicholas by the New-York Historical Society, December 6, 1810." Wood engraving by Alexander Anderson, reprint 1864. Courtesy of the New-York Historical Society, New York City.

*Harper's Weekly,* 1869.

night skies to reward the valorous and punish the evil. The chief god of the north European pantheon, Woden, or Odin, was believed to ride his eight-legged white horse through our world, along with the famous Valkyries, warrior women who rode the winds to gather the souls of heroes who had fallen in battle. Many supernatural beings are descended from these mythic beliefs, including the night riders

"The Doings of Kriss Kringle" include watching the children of the world by telescope and recording the names of all the good children, along with filling their stockings. A series of illustrations from childrens' books, 1897. Courtesy of the Popular Culture Library, Bowling Green State University.

through the European skies today. In Holland, Saint Nicholas, known there as Sinter Klaas, rides a white horse, as did Woden before him. Like Woden, he has become a hairy old man, known in some places as Pelznichol, or Hairy Nicholas. In some parts of Germany, Nicholas is accompanied by a hairy, shaggy, frightening figure with horns, a black face, and red eyes, carrying chains. This monster is known by many different names. In various places he is called Bartel, Klaubauf, or Krampus. In some places, Nicholas is combined with this figure and is known as Knect Ruprecht, who rides about dressed in animal skins and straw. Or he is known as Aschenklas, Nicholas who brings ashes for the bad, or Pelznickol, Hairy Nicholas. In Austria, Nicholas still wears his bishop's robes and mitre when he brings gifts on December 6, his feast day, but in northern Europe he has combined more completely with the ancient gods to become a spirit of winter. The American Santa Claus carries the Turkish bishop's name—he is Old Saint Nick—but he rides the reindeer of northern Europe and is said to live in the frozen north, the North Pole. His bishop's robes

*St. Nicholas,* by Robert Weir, 1837, National Museum of American Art. St. Nick as a clean-shaven, mischievous sprite. This nineteenth-century rendition predates the later influential drawings of Thomas Nast. Courtesy of the National-al Museum of American Art, Smithsonian Institution, Washington, D.C.

have become the furs one needs to live in permanent winter, but they still bear a distant visual similarity to the red and white robes of the cleric. As Earl Count says, "this is how a god turns into a saint. Both Woden and St. Nicholas are travellers on the road; they wander afoot and on horseback, inspecting the deeds of mankind, making sure that right and order prevail. They do this when the days of the year are the shortest, when a new year is on its way, when the fortunes of the future are being cast. Both of them ride the storm; they can subdue it or they can rouse it. They have ended up by becoming the same person" (1953:86).

A Santa Claus clad in white who resembles a winter deity travels with the Baby Jesus and a single reindeer on a turn-of-the-century card. They can be seen as an old man and a baby, paralleling the old year and baby new year symbols of January 1. Today we do not usually picture these two primary figures of Christmas together. Courtesy of the Center for Archival Collections, Bowling Green State University.

The Pennsylvania Germans call him Belsnichel, and he carries a switch to punish those children who have been bad. Today, we have lost most of the punitive aspects of this Christmas gift bringer. The threat of receiving a lump of coal from Santa Claus in the stocking on Christmas Eve is about the only remnant of this belief we have left (see Jones 1978).

In Europe, after the Reformation of the seventeenth century, the feast and veneration of Saint Nicholas were abolished in many places, including England, where a figure known as Father Christmas was substituted. Father Christmas is a winter deity, white-haired and bearded, who wears a crown of holly. The German settlers brought their beliefs and stories about Saint Nicholas with them to this country during two great waves of immigration, in the early 1700s and the middle 1800s, and Hollanders brought their Sinter Klaas to their settlement of New Amsterdam. As the English colonized New York, they adapted their Father Christmas, who did not bring gifts, to these traditions, and Santa Claus as we know him today was born. Washington Irving, in *A History of New York*, published in 1809, helped cre-

ate the Americanized version of this mythic figure when he described
the saint as "laying a finger beside his nose" and dropping gifts down
chimneys. Then Clement Moore's "An Account of a Visit from St.
Nicholas" (popularly known as "The Night Before Christmas") was
published on December 23, 1823. Some scholars think that this poem
was actually written by Henry Livingston, Jr., and there is compelling evidence to support this point of view. Perhaps Livingston had
written a poem that Moore adapted (Coffin 1973:87–91). Whatever the
case, in the now-famous poem, Santa is described as a "jolly old elf,"
with a team of eight reindeer, who comes to children on Christmas
Eve Day, rather than December 6 or New Year's Day. As with Washington Irving, it is difficult to know how much these authors invented themselves and how much they reported from what they had
heard in tradition. Some of the published versions of the "Visit," for
instance, called it "The Night Before New Year's," bowing to the customs of their audiences.

Thomas Nast is another contributor to the American development
of Santa Claus. Although he was born in Bavaria in 1840, he came to
the United States when he was six years old. He grew up to become
an editorial cartoonist and illustrator of some note; he is credited with
creating and popularizing the Republican elephant and the Democratic donkey, the symbols of the two major political parties. He is also
considered the primary source for the way we picture Santa Claus
because of a series of drawings he did for *Harper's Weekly* between
1863 and 1886. Together, Irving, Moore, and Nast are largely responsible for the way we in America envision Santa Claus. There has not
always been such a standardized representation, however. Some
Christmas cards from the turn of the century still show Santa as a
winter divinity, or traveling with the Christ child in a sleigh pulled
by a solitary reindeer.

Throughout Europe, traditions vary as to who doles out the midwinter largesse, and when. Nicholas and the Christ Child are the most
popular gift bringers: Nicholas on his saint's day, December 6; and
the Christ Child, *el Niño Jesus* in Spain, on the eve of his birth. Martin Luther substituted the Christ Child for Saint Nicholas as the bearer
of gifts, and the day of the giving from Nicholas's feast day to Christmas, as part of his effort to remove vestiges of paganism and idolatry from the Church. In many parts of Europe, it is the Christ Child
who is the gift bringer, and it is from him that Santa derives another
of his names, Kris Kringle, from the German *Christkindl*. Saint Lucy
(Santa Lucia) provides breakfast on her day, December 13, which is
an important part of the Christmas season in Sweden. Other saints

In Sweden, on the feast of Santa Lucia, December 13, a girl dressed in white and wearing a crown of burning candles awakes the family with gifts of cake and coffee. She may also visit workers at their jobs during the day. Illustration by Ake Gustavsson, from *Swedish Christmas,* compiled by E. Cagner. Gothenburg, 1955. Courtesy of the Popular Culture Library, Bowling Green State University.

known as gift bringers include Saint Martin, whose feast day of November 11 is considered to be the start of the round of Christmas holidays in Europe, a season that can stretch to Candlemas, February 2. The twelve days of Christmas are at the center, in a constellation of winter holidays that corresponds to the old manner of reckoning winter, from November to February, with the solstice as the midpoint.

In Germany, the *Christkindl* is represented by a female angel who carries with her candles and a tree. Although called *Christkindl*, she is not the Holy Child, but rather his messenger. Iconographically, she is closely related to Saint Lucy. In Sweden, Santa Lucia's, or Saint Lucy's, Day is known as "little Yule." A young girl customarily dresses in a white robe with a red sash and wears in her hair a crown of nine candles. Interestingly, *Lucia* means "light," and when this day was celebrated according to the Old Style (Julian) calendar, it fell on the winter solstice. So it is another candlelit festival of lights tied to the shortest days of the year, and perhaps this has something to do with its appellation as little Yule. In Sicily they light bonfires on Saint Lucy's Day, and in Tyrol, it is Lucy who brings gifts for the girls, because Nicholas brings presents to boys only.

In Russia, Kolyada is the name for Christmas. The word is derived from the old Roman Kalends, the celebration of the new year at the first of January. Kolyada is also the name of the white-robed woman who rides a sled drawn by a single white horse from house to house on Christmas Eve to brings gifts to the children. She is joined by Kolya (Nicholas), who leaves wheat cakes on the windowsills. In some parts of Russia, the mythic figure is called Babushka, or Grandmother, and there are also tales of Grandfather Frost, a Father Christmas or winter spirit figure. In Rome and other parts of Italy, we find another scary figure, this time a woman known as Lady Befana. Like the bestial, hairy figures in central Europe, she too is wild and frightening to behold. Like them, she brings punishment as well as rewards. She rides on January 6, the Feast of the Epiphany, and it is from this feast that she derives her name.

Today, we see the development, perhaps a bit playfully, of newer mythic embodiments of the season. A greeting card parodies Clement Moore's "Visit From St. Nicholas" with a verse that announces a visit from the Hanukkah Man. Another card, in a return to a more pagan spirit, features a winter sprite unrelated to any Christian bishop, while a card that directly responds to the growing recognition of cultural pluralism and religious diversity in this country features a Jewish Santa. Another sign of the times is found in the efforts to create a new set of mythic gift givers, again Jewish rather than Christian in origin. An enterprising couple have created the mythic grandparents Bubbe and Zede (names Jewish children traditionally call their grandparents). They live in Nome, Alaska, and, if you write to them and tell them your wishes, they will, like Santa Claus, bring gifts to satisfy you. According to a magazine report, the concept is a runaway success. Bubbe and Zede are receiving mail from all over the country, and from children of all backgrounds. This is another example of tradition reinventing itself to suit the society. Bubbe and Zede are obviously derived from Jewish familly traditions, but are also based on Santa Claus, who in turn was derived from saints' legends and northern European mythic deities.

## Saint Nick in Indiana

Saint Nicholas's feast day is a major holiday in northern Europe, a vital part of the Christmas season, and still celebrated as such among some families in the United States. In fact, in some cases it is being revitalized.

Rose Lindberg, born in 1903 in St. John, Indiana, remembers Saint Nicholas as a fearsome figure who visited her home on December 5, the eve of St. Nicholas's Day:

> We were too scared to celebrate. We were so good that they didn't even know we were around. When he came and knocked at the kitchen door and threw in a big bunch from the willow tree—whips—we knew we had to be good because they'd be used on us if we weren't. He stuck his head in the kitchen door. Then he'd have a bag with candy and popcorn and apples and oranges and that was it.
>
> He had a helper named Hans Drop. And from then on, you'd think that he'd be spying on us and seeing if we were good or bad and Christmas would depend on that. We believed that Saint Nicholas and Santa Claus were different, and that Saint Nicholas reported to Santa. That's what they had us believing. We were dummies! The living room was locked for a week. Nobody could go in there and we didn't have the least idea what was going on behind the doors. But I suppose the older ones were working on the tree and what not. And then the night before Christmas we'd all go in there and they'd have the organ and my sister, Til, would play the organ and we'd sing *O Heilige Nacht. Stille Nacht.* German songs. Then we had a China doll. Oh, we'd get to look at it a couple of times during the year. We really didn't get to play with it because, you know, they were expensive. And we put that by the door. I think Saint Nicholas would pick that up and it would come back all dressed up in new clothes, so that was always something to look forward to.
>
> On Christmas, Santa Claus, he came with switches and my brothers, they got it good. And I even remember, I don't even know how old I was, my brothers, they ran out of the door and went down to the apple orchard and whoever Santa was in those days, God only knows. Maybe one of the hired hands, somebody that tried to scare the dickens out of the boys. We'd be lucky to get an orange or just a cap or a sweater. Santa would decorate the tree with candy and we'd get to eat that after the tree came down.

Rose's daughter, Jeanette (Lindberg) Vail, was born in 1934 in Hammond, Indiana. She did not grow up with a Saint Nicholas's Day tradition, but remembers fondly special foods associated with the Christmas season: German molasses cookies, fruitcake, and

> Mom's famous Christmas pie. That was a homemade pie crust, and a layer of pineapple and bananas and marshmallows and on top of that whipped cream and a cherry. And we'd always have our good old standby pumpkin pie. On New Year's, one traditional thing my mom did was make *kuchen*. That's a German coffeecake. On New Year's it was special. She made wreaths out of the dough. She'd cut it into strips and braid it. She'd make a round circle with them and put them in cake plates and she'd bake them, let them cool, frost them. That's something we'd always do on New Year's Eve, make New Year's wreaths and have them for breakfast on New Year's Day. I remember staying up until midnight in my room, and wait for midnight and listen for the bells. They would ring the church bells then.

The next generation in this family, today all grown, have reintroduced Saint Nicholas's Day customs to their children's Christmas celebration, and have adopted the custom of baking the cookies and the New Year's wreaths. The traditions themselves continue as ethnic customs in this German-American family, but first and foremost they are family customs that derive from German ethnicity.

There are two levels of symbolism involved in Christmas: those specifically having to do with the birth of Christ, and those having to do with the season of the year. Often the two are intertwined. While Halloween, two months earlier, deals with death, Christmas deals with birth and new life, especially in the religious figure of the Christ child.

As with Thanksgiving, a meal is an important component of Christmas, although it is not of the singular importance the Thanksgiving feast is. The family gathers around the table again, to eat a meal, perhaps the identical meal of turkey with all the trimmings. However, unlike Thanksgiving, people with young children are less likely to travel to the home of the grandparents on Christmas day. Once the children are old enough to understand the Santa Claus story, parents want their children to have Christmas in their "own" homes. In this case, "home" now means the home of the youngest generation, rather than the eldest generation. The focus of Christmas is on children: Santa enters through the hearth, the symbolic center of the home, and leaves gifts for the children. As a mythic figure, Santa Claus is a parental substitute. The parents leave their children presents under the tree, then take photographs of the children opening them. The central religious symbol of Christmas, the creche, features a child—a sacred child—at the center, who is surrounded by doting parents (a mother and a surrogate father), and then by shepherds, animals, angels, and foreign kings. Essentially, it is a nuclear family surrounded by persons of increasingly more distant relationship to the child. While Thanksgiving honors the eldest generation of the family, Christmas honors the youngest. While Thanksgiving draws our attention to the past and the accomplishments of those who have gone before, Christmas emphasizes the future. The home of our youth contains our history. The home of our children contains their future. Thanksgiving's imagery includes pilgrims; Christmas, a sacred child. Thanksgiving takes place, metaphorically, at Grandmother's; the family focus is on the eldest family member. Christmas is held at the home of the children and its focus is on the youngest members of the family. Thanksgiving, in late November, symbolized in part by harvested wheat and corn, is the color of faded fields, while Christmas is evergreen. Thanksgiving relects the end of the harvest, while Christmas reflects the ending and beginning of new solar and calendrical years. Both days are family days, and both emphasize familial bonds and socially constructive values, but Thanksgiving does it in terms of recognition of the past while Christmas does it in terms of open-ended possibilities of the future.

## Las Posadas

The search of the Holy Family for a home is recreated annually in the Christmas custom known as *las posadas*. Another example of performing from house to house at holiday time, this Mexican tradition is growing throughout the United States, especially in Southern California and the Southwest. For nine nights prior to Christmas, groups of friends and neighbors arrange among themselves to visit each other's homes, carrying homemade candles that are also known as *las posadas*. The result is a candlelit procession through the city streets. The visits recreate the journey of Mary and Joseph as they searched for a place where Mary could give birth to the Baby Jesus, *el Niño Jesus*. Someone is dressed as Joseph, someone as Mary. Others come dressed as shepherds, villagers, and so forth. Each night they knock on someone's door and request lodging; each night they are refused, until *la Noche buena*, Christmas Eve, when they are given a place to rest. Once they are inside, the birth of Christ is reenacted.

*Las posadas* take place among friends, in their homes. Recently, larger, more public presentations of *las posadas*, open to community dwellers and tourists alike, have joined the home celebrations. For these, perhaps Mary will ride a real donkey, or a real goat might join in the procession. *El Niño Jesus* might be played by a real baby. In both cases, in the neighborhoods and at the larger events, the flow is from the procession, through the reenactment of the Nativity, to a fiesta. Children are very important in *las posadas*. Often they play the principal roles of Mary and Joseph. The fiesta is a party featuring holiday foods such as tamales, and children's games. Chief among the latter is the breaking of the *piñata*. Children compete with each other to smash papier-mâché dolls filled with candy and sweets and maybe even pennies. These elements of *las posadas* vary from place to place. Sometimes the processions are held for five nights, sometimes only three. They must be held only during the nine nights prior to Christmas. All the typical elements of the Christmas-midwinter celebrations are found in *las posadas*, but in forms unique to Hispanic tradition: the emphasis on candles and light, the parading and performing from house to house, the sacred and secular aspects of the celebration, the emphasis on the Holy Family, and the involvement of children as the chief beneficiaries of the fun and excitement.

For many, Christmas can be a difficult time. If a family has been through a divorce or a death, for instance, the old customs and family rituals may be more full of pain than pleasure. Many people who find themselves single parents for the first time have learned that the best way to deal with the pain and to recapture the Christmas joy is to create new traditions. Rather than stay in the old house for the holidays, with all its haunted memories, they may go someplace else, to a hotel, perhaps. They take their children to a place thay have never been; they do new things. Another way of redefining the holiday is to recreate the objects associated with it. People make new decorations, put the tree in a different room, vary the time when they exchange gifts (Christmas Eve instead of Christmas Day, for example, or vice versa). They invite new friends in for dinner, exchange gifts with new people. New experiences make new memories, and new memories can revitalize an old holiday. This kind of redefinition, of being creative with traditional holiday ideas, is what has been happening for the past several thousand years.

People have even begun to redefine the redefinitions. Madalyn Murray O'Hair, a renowned and outspoken atheist, celebrates December 21 as Solstice Day. Organizations such as O'Hair's American Atheist Center and the American Humanist Association try to pierce centuries of Christian tradition in order to get back to the pre-Christian foundation of the Christmas holidays. They celebrate the winter solstice on December 25 as an alternative to Christmas. Some celebrate more exactly on December 21. They retain those customs that they believe can be shown to predate Christianity, such as decorating a tree (they refer to it as a solstice tree), attending parties, and exchanging gifts.

Other examples of newly created traditions include the successful winter solstice celebrations known (and incorporated) as the Revels. These celebrations grew from performances held in New York in 1959 by John Langstaff. The first full performances known properly as Revels began in 1972 in Cambridge, Massachusetts, as an attempt to return to the more basic symbols and meanings of winter celebrations and to recreate these in a way that holds real meaning for participants. The intention is to involve the audiences in the performances, to turn them from spectators to participants, and to turn the presentations into participatory events, to make them into truly ritualistic celebrations. The Revels use material from medieval mystery plays, folk rituals, and religious traditions from around the world as sources, and they have been exceedingly well received. The response has been so strong that Langstaff has come to see that the Revels provide a kind of real ritual for people, that they fill a real need. Revels are now held in New York City, Washington, D.C., and in Vermont as well as in Cambridge. Langstaff and company have begun presenting Revels for the summer solstice as well.

## New Year's Eve and Day

In a sense the Revels as well as the contemporary New Year's Eve celebrations such as Boston's First Night are celebrations of midwinter, but the Revels are self-consciously traditional in content, so as to create a feeling of continuity with past Christmas and solstice celebrations the world over. First Night and the urban New Year's Eve celebrations elsewhere that feature contemporary music and dancing are deliberately modern. To some extent they probably appeal to different taste groups, but this pattern also parallels the change in mood from Christmas to New Year's. While Christmas focuses on the future in a solemn and sacred way, New Year's does it with abandon.

The image of the newborn baby at Christmas can be interpreted as a kind of new year symbol as well as a religious one, because it represents new life. New Year's is for Americans a more secular holiday (although it is a Christian feast day that commemorates the circumcision of the baby Jesus, a holy day of obligation in the Catholic church), but it too has its images of rebirth and renewal, including

Baby New Year for 1925 is tuned in to the events of the universe. Reprinted by permission of *The American Legion Magazine.* © 1924.

as part of its symbolism an image of a baby. I am referring to the Baby New Year, of course, shown entering while the Old Year, an old man who bears an uncanny resemblance to Father Time, exits. In a way, Santa Claus and the Christ Child are a Christmas parallel to the Old Year and Baby New Year, although at Christmas, the two figures are not linked together or specifically said to represent the passage of time. With the Old Year and Baby New Year symbols, the year is graphically rendered as a life. A comparison of the Christmas baby with the New Year baby illustrates the difference in the two holidays: the Christ Child is sacred, while the baby New Year is playful.

When Good King Wenceslaus looked out, it was "on the Feast of Stephen," or the day after Christmas, December 26. On Saint Stephen's Day in England and Ireland, it was and to some extent still is customary to "hunt the wren," wherein boys and young men dress in leaves and branches, hunt and capture or kill a bird, then troop from home to home with a decorated branch or small bush to collect money. December 26 is also known as Boxing Day. One folk etymology for Boxing Day is that the name derives from the practice of wrapping and boxing gifts for the poor, which were delivered the day after Christmas in England. Boxing Day is celebrated in Canada as a legal holiday. Other than Christmas Day, January 1, and January 6, the twelve days of Christmas are not celebrated with special custom or ritual in the United States. Indeed, the period between Christmas and New Year's has been termed by one journalist "days of malaise," a time out of time when the old year is over and the new one not yet begun (Washington *Post* 31 Dec. 1984: D7). But even though Christmas Day is past, something of the old twelve days remains: it is the Christmas season.

Toward the end of the week, though, the images we see all around us begin to change. Santas, stars, and angels give way to party hats, noisemakers, and champagne bottles. New Year's greetings cards feature these objects as the symbols of the New Year's Eve celebration, along with the traditional Old Year and Baby New Year. Sometimes, Baby New Year is seen wearing a party hat. These images are in keeping with the way we celebrate New Year's Eve and what we celebrate. We go to parties with our friends. We watch the clock until shortly before midnight, then begin a countdown. Probably the television is tuned to a broadcast from New York's Times Square, where a ball of lights will descend from a pole at the stroke of midnight to the cheers of thousands of people in the street.

New Year's Eve marks the instant of transition from the old year to the new, the old man to the new baby. In a way, it recapitulates

Although this 1900 card depicts little elves, the scene is centered on the moment of passage from the old year to the new. Note the sun on the bottom of the pendulum. Is this a reference to the solstice and the solar new year? Note also that the elves are making noise and celebrating. Courtesy of the Center for Archival Collections, Bowling Green State University.

the meanings of Thanksgiving and Christmas—first the consideration of the past, then a recognition of the future. We might make New Year's resolutions at this moment when the future is open and anything seems possible. We celebrate, not with family but with our friends, with our peer relations rather than our blood relations. We celebrate not the socially constuctive values of home and hearth, of tradition, or of peace on earth, goodwill toward men; rather, we celebrate with drunkenness and licentiousness. The champagne bottles on the cards, even the campaigns set up to encourage people not to drive on New Year's Eve emphasize that not only is it acceptable to drink, but one is expected to drink to excess. Thanksgiving and Christmas are indoor holidays: that is where the meal is taken, that is where the gifts are opened. New Year's Eve is celebrated on the street, even if only vicariously through the television.

Moments of transition are often considered times when the past and the future meet, when one can perhaps influence the future course of one's life, or learn what lies ahead. These junctures are sometimes dangerous. Midnight, for instance, the point between today and tomorrow, yesterday and today, is known as the witching hour. Such points of transition are often accompanied by magic beliefs, ritual, or the kinds of spontaneous, licentious, boisterous celebrations that mark New Year's Eve. Times such as these are also times of social leveling: if one happens to be standing next to the boss during the celebration, one might say and do things that would otherwise be unthinkable. At midnight, we might kiss someone we don't know, or take liberties that we simply would never think of trying during more "regular" time.

So. As we move through the quadrant of the year from the autumnal equinox to the winter solstice and the high festival week that takes us to the first of January, the leaves turn red and gold and yellow, then brown as they fall from the trees. The sky grows grey, the trees black and bare against it, and the landscape a dull and faded brown, before the snows arrive to cover it all with silver and white. The evergreens stand out. The three holidays at the end of the months of October, November, and December illustrate and document these changes. As the days gather darkness, we first enjoy a holiday that talks to us of the harvest and of death and of the necessary relation of the two. Then we move to a holiday that is also about the harvest, along with our place in the scheme of history and in the generations of our families. From these, we move to another family celebration, the emphasis of which is on youth and the future, and which is a candle lit in the darkness instead of a curse. There is a direct connection between death at Halloween (harvest signaling the seasonal death we know as winter) and the symbolism of rebirth and renewal at the point of midwinter, the baby born at Christmas and the baby New Year also. Thanksgiving and Christmas we celebrate with our family, in the home, and we celebrate family values. At New Year's we celebrate an instant of passage from the old year to the new, and we celebrate it out on the streets or at parties with our peers. Christmas leads us into a celebration of excess and ribaldry, as we kiss out the old year and make merry the new, exploring ourselves fully as free human beings before we accept again the necessary roles and rules of mundane life and begin the yearly cycle over again, looking forward, eternally optimistically, to spring.

# Epilogue:
# New Hearts Today

An old folk song asks, "Will the circle be unbroken, by and by, Lord, by and by?" The circular wreath, a symbol of unbroken time, seems to have joined us as a fellow traveler through the yearly round. The qualities that have made wreaths attractive symbols for midwinter have proven to be equally appealing the rest of the year as well. They aren't just for Christmas any more.

The traditional green wreath of winter is a familiar sight on homes and office buildings from December through January and into February. The custom of decorating the homestead with evergreens during the winter months is ancient. The Romans decorated for the Saturnalia by bringing in boughs of evergreens, while holly and mistletoe were important in the solstice celebrations of the northern European tribes. The circle has ever been a symbol of eternity, of unbrokenness. The evergreens manifest life in the dead of winter. Together, they make a powerful and centuries-old symbol, that of an unbroken circle of unending life, displayed proudly on the entrance to one's home at the time of the year's shortest days and coldest nights, but also the time of the beginning of the lengthening days and the hint of coming spring. The wreaths suggest that life continues, even through the adversity of winter. Hung on the doors of our homes, this message is of particular relevance to the families inside, who are born, grow, and die, generation after generation. The family too continues through life's adversities.

We use the circle to express eternity in the rituals of our lives: wedding rings show undying devotion and commitment, and wreaths of flowers send off those of our loved ones who have departed this world. Flowers of life blanket the casket and altar and, when waked at home, the living room of the deceased. Here too the wreath speaks of eternity and the place of death in the cycle of eternal life and rebirth.

Today, we are seeing wreaths all year round. Not the Christmas wreath left up to decay publicly, but different wreaths for different seasons, different holidays. No sooner are the Christmas holiday wreaths taken down than are they replaced with red and white ones for Valentine's Day, then green for Saint Patrick's Day. A year-round favorite is the wreath made of grape vines. Although its leafless, wiry brown strands give it a harvest-season feel, people add and subtract bits of ribbon, bows, flowers, hearts, shamrocks, or even eggs to render this all-purpose wreath suitable for the annual succession of calendrical holidays. Replacing a red and white bow with a green and white plaid ribbon suddenly transforms a Valentine's Day wreath into one for Saint Patrick's Day.

The Easter bonnet has also made a comeback, but now it too is worn on the home rather than on the head. Not a wreath, exactly, but still a circle when hung against a door, with purple, pink, and white flowers for Easter and spring. Wreaths of real flowers are also common. As we move through the year, the wreaths display the symbols of the special days of the seasons. Symbols of Christmas in December, red hearts in late January and early February, green shamrocks in March, rabbits and chicks in April, flowers in May and June, through the summer, until they are joined by pumpkins, Indian corn, and corn dollies at harvest time in the fall.

More recently, people have begun to adorn their homes with seasonal flags: Christmas flags with Santa on them, or a trumpet broadcasting "Joy," or a picture of a Christmas wreath. I first saw these in Boston, where they were replaced in February with flags featuring Valentine hearts, later in the spring with flags picturing bouquets of flowers, and in the summer with images of sun. Since then I have learned of a woman in Colorado who makes flags for these and many other seasons and holidays. Perhaps because of the church tradition of hanging flags and banners through the liturgical year, this secular custom of hanging holiday flags is gaining popularity.

The wheel of the year can be painted in colors, from the orange and yellows of October and Halloween (with black added to suggest the darker side of life); through the grey skies and brown landscape of November, reflected in the colors of the Pilgrims' garb and the roasted turkey; the red of holly berries and Santa's suit (once bishop's robes) and the (ever)green of December; the red and white of Valentine's Day with its suggestion of passion, blood, and new life in the winter snows of February; the spring green of Saint Patrick's Day and the flower pastels of Easter and spring; finally to the bright yellow sun and red, white, and blue flags of the summer holidays of

patriotism and beach parties. Each season and each holiday is dressed
in its own special colors. These come to stand for the holiday itself.

This verse from an old New Year's card recognizes this seasonal
progression of colors, and also the essentially regenerative nature of
New Year's Day. One need not necessarily accept its theology to appreciate its message:

> The earth was dress'd in dreary brown,
> in Winter brown, but yesternight;
> but Angels while we slept came down
> and turn'd her robes to shining white.
> For this they say, is New Year's Day,
> And so the Angels kind and true
> Have wiped the old earth's sins away,
> And made her pure again and new.
> So you and I, I think, must try
> to love each other, learn, and pray;
> Then God will bless us from the sky,
> And give us all new hearts today.

Like the year itself, we come round again to New Year's. The poem
captures the essence of all the holidays in the cycle of the year: the
progression toward rebirth and renewal. To be pure again and new:
this is what our holidays offer us, and what we, in the words of the
old Valentine, to love and custom owe.

# Source Notes

The studies of symbols and rituals by anthropologist Victor Turner have been most influential to the development of my own thinking on contemporary holiday celebrations. Turner's work, in turn, was developed out of the groundbreaking ideas put forth by French sociologist Arnold Van Gennep, whose *Les Rites de Passage* was published in 1908 but not translated into English until 1960 (by M. B. Vizedom and G. L. Caffee; introduction by Solon T. Kimball; Chicago: University of Chicago Press). Van Gennep analyzed the rituals of the life cycle and calendrical festivals as rites of passage from one stage of life to another, or from one season or other significant unit of time to another. He found that such rites usually comprise three stages: separation, transition, and reincorporation.

Turner's elaboration of Van Gennep's work concentrated on the middle stage of transition. He was enormously productive; here I can mention only the works that are of most importance to this book. *The Forest of Symbols: Aspects of Ndembu Ritual* (Ithaca, N.Y.: Cornell University Press, 1967) is a collection of essays which includes "Symbols in Ndembu Ritual" and "Betwixt and Between: The Liminal Period in *Rites de Passage*." Both essays are seminal. Equally important are *The Ritual Process: Structure and Anti-Structure* (Ithaca, N.Y.: Cornell University Press, 1969) and *Image and Pilgrimage in Christian Culture* (New York: Columbia University Press, 1978).

Turner served as guest curator for the *Celebration: A World of Art and Ritual* exhibit at the Smithsonian Institution, for which I coordinated the Living Celebrations component, a series of live presentations of traditional celebrations. Accompanying that exhibition is a book of essays edited by Turner, entitled *Celebration: Studies in Festivity and Ritual* (Washington, D.C.: Smithsonian Institution Press, 1982). Among its many important articles, those most relevant to this book include Roger D. Abrahams' "The Language of Festivals: Celebrating the Economy," in which the author, a noted folklorist, looks at festivals in terms of the seasonal round and also in terms of economic production. He also casts his scholarly eye on the modern festive events of contemporary mass culture. Another article I found quite moving is Barbara Myerhoff's "Rites of Passage: Process and Paradox," in which the author, an important anthropologist, recognizes the need for new rituals to mark social realities such as divorce. She suggests that we should consciously create them. I think she is right, and I think we *are* creating them, as I have tried to point out in this book. I would also mention as important Victor and Edith Turner's "Religious Celebrations"; and John J. MacAloon's "Sociation and Sociability in Political Celebrations."

In addition to the essays in this volume, each of these scholars has other works that I have found very useful. Barbara Myerhoff's *Number Our Days* (New York: Simon and Schuster, 1978) is an excellent study of the creation and adaptation of rituals by a group of elderly Jews in California. Sally Moore and Barbara Myerhoff, *Secular Ritual* (Assen, Netherlands: Van Gorcum, 1977) is an important study of rituals that are not specifically religious. John J. MacAloon has produced an excellent study of the modern Olympics entitled *This Great Symbol* (Chicago: University of Chicago Press, 1981), and he has edited a collection of essays called *Rite, Drama, Festival, and Spectacle: Rehearsals Toward a Theory of Cultural Performance* (Philadelphia: Institute for the Study of Human Issues, 1984). His article in that volume, "Olympic Games and the Theory of Spectacle in Modern Societies," distinguishes between ritual, festival, and spectacle and contributes a useful model for studying mass-mediated festive events. Likewise, Roger D. Abrahams' fieldwork and analysis of large-scale, public festive events is among the most thought-provoking work of its kind. His work with festival events on the island of St. Vincent is indispensable; this includes "Christmas and Carnival on Saint Vincent," in *Western Folklore* 31 (1972); and the collection of his articles on West Indian festive behavior, *The Man-of-Words in the West Indies* (Baltimore: Johns Hopkins University Press, 1983).

Other folklorists have also influenced my work, particularly those who have worked with ritual, festival, and celebration. Henry Glassie's beautiful *All Silver and No Brass: An Irish Christmas Mumming* (Bloomington: Indiana University Press, 1975) is one such work. Another is *La Terra in Piazza* by Alan Dundes and Alessandro Falassi (Berkeley: University of California Press, 1975). Falassi has also edited an important collection of essays entitled *Time Out of Time: Essays on the Festival* (Albuquerque: University of New Mexico Press, 1987). Don Yoder's descriptions of the Pennsylvania Dutch Harvest Home appeared in *Pennsylvania Folklife* 9, no. 4 (Fall 1958): 2–11, and 13, no. 4 (July 1964): 4, and is reprinted along with many important articles on festival customs in his *Discovering American Folklife* (Ann Arbor: UMI Research Press, 1990). Yvonne Hiipakka Lockwood has done field research with Finnish Americans in Michigan; I have relied upon her for information on St. Urho's Day. See her article "Immigrant to Ethnic: Symbols of Identity Among Finnish Americans" in the *Folklife Annual 1986* (Washington, D.C.: American Folklife Center, 1987). William Wiggins is the foremost authority on Juneteenth and other black emancipation celebrations. He has published his research in *O Freedom! Afro-American Emancipation Celebrations* (Nashville: University of Tennessee Press, 1987). Willard Moore has studied Julebukking in Minnesota. See his "Ritual and Remembrance in Minnesota Folk Celebrations," in *Humanities Education* 3, no. 3 (1986). Likewise, I have learned from Marcia Gaudet's presentations on Christmas Eve bonfires in Louisiana. Good articles on Latin-American and Carribbean urban carnivals by Katherine Williams and D. Elliott Parris can be found in the *1980 Festival of American Folklife Program Book*, edited by Jack Santino (Washington, D.C.: Smithsonian Institution). In the same issue are articles by Thomas Vennum, Jr., and Carol Babiracki, both on the Laskiainen winter carnival. Gerald E. Parsons has written about the origins and development of the yellow ribbon as a symbol in his "Yellow Ribbons: Ties with Tradition" in the *Folklife Center News* 4 (Apr. 1981). Thelma Lynn Lamkin's account of Spring Hill Decoration Day appeared in *Midwest Folklore* 3 (1953).

Other noteworthy books include Theodore C. Humphrey and Lyn T. Humphrey, eds. *"We Gather Together": Food and Festival in American Life* (Ann Arbor: UMI Research Press, 1988); Venetia Newall, *An Egg at Easter: A Folklore Study* (Bloomington: Indiana University Press, 1971); Maire MacNeill, *The Festival of Lughnasa: A Study of the Survival of the Celtic Festival of the Beginning of Harvest* (Oxford: Oxford University Press, 1969); E. Estyn Evans, *Irish Folk Ways* (New York: The Devin-Adair Company, 1957); Trefor M. Owen, *Welsh Folk Customs* (Cardiff: National Museum of Wales, 1968); Jennifer M. Russ, *German Festivals and Customs* (London: Oswald Wolff, 1982); Christel Lane, *The Rites of Rulers* (Cambridge: Cambridge University Press, 1981); Tristram P. Coffin, *The Book of Christmas Folklore* (New York: Seabury Press, 1973); Tristram P. Coffin and Hennig Cohen, eds., *The Folklore of American Holidays* (Detroit: Gale Research Company, 1987); Alan Brody, *The English Mummers and Their Plays* (Philadelphia: University of Pennsylvania Press, 1969); Roger Welch, *Oh! Dem Golden Slippers* (Camden: Thomas J. Nelson, 1970); Mildred Arthur, *Holidays of Legend* (New York: Harvey House, 1971); Earl W. Count, *4000 Years of Christmas* (New York: Ridert and Company, 1953); and Charles W. Jones, *St. Nicholas of Myra, Bari, and Manhattan* (Chicago: University of Chicago Press, 1978). Coffin and Cohen include the student "Spring riot" as a genre of celebration in their *Folklore from the Working Folk of America* (Garden City, N.Y.: Doubleday, 1973). For an excellent survey of literature related to Christmas traditions, see Sue Samuelson's *Christmas: An Annotated Bibliography of Analytical Scholarship* (New York: Garland Press, 1982). For American political rituals, see Conrad Cerry, "Two American Sacred Ceremonies: Their Implication for the Study of Religion in America," *American Quarterly* 21 (Winter 1969). See also James E. Combs, *Dimensions of Political Drama* (Santa Monica, Calif.: Goodyear Publishing Company, 1980).

Besides Victor Turner, many other anthropologists have written significantly about festive events. One of the finest volumes of analytical insight is Don Handelman's *Models and Mirrors: Towards an Anthropology of Public Events* (Cambridge: Cambridge University Press, 1990). Perhaps the single most important analytical article of this kind is "Deep Play: Notes on the Balinese Cockfight" by Clifford Geertz. The article is widely anthologized; it may be found in a volume edited by Geertz entitled *Myth, Symbol, and Culture* (New York: W. W. Norton, 1971). See also his *The Interpretation of Cultures* (New York:

Basic Books, 1973). Other relevant anthropological works include Gregory Bateson's *Naven* (1936; Stanford: Stanford University Press, 1958); Mary Douglas's *Purity and Danger* (London: Routledge and Kegan Paul, 1966); *The Reversible World*, edited by Barbara A. Babcock (Ithaca, N.Y.: Cornell University Press, 1978); Ruth Gruber Fredman's *The Passover Seder: Afrikoman in Exile* (Philadelphia: University of Pennsylvania Press, 1981); and Gillian Feeley-Harnik's *The Lord's Table: Eucharist and Passover in Early Chrisianity* (Philadelphia: University of Pennsylvania Press, 1981).

In 1949 Ralph and Adele Linton published a very good treatment of Thanksgiving for a general audience, called *We Gather Together: The Story of Thanksgiving* (New York: Henry Schuman), and a similar treatment of Halloween in 1950, called *Halloween Through Twenty Centuries* (New York: Henry Schuman). In 1955 Theodore Gaster published a small book called *New Year: Its History, Customs, and Superstitions* (New York: Abelard-Schuman). Clarence Seidenspinner's *Great Protestant Festivals* was published in 1952 (New York: Henry Schuman). For Kwanzaa, see Haki R. Madhubuti, *Kwanzaa: A Progressive and Uplifting African American Holiday* (Chicago: Third World Press, 1972); and Cedric McClester, *Kwanzaa: Everything You Always Wanted to Know But Didn't Know Where To Ask* (New York: Gumbs and Thomas, 1990).

Calendrical and life-cycle celebratory events have figured largely in the development of social history as a field of study. French historian Emmanual Le Roy Ladurie has led the way with his *Carnival in Romans*, translated by Mary Feeney (New York: George Braziller, 1979), in which the author combines the methodological tools of the historian, the anthropologist, and the folklorist in an attempt to conduct what I call retroactive ethnography. Ladurie attempts to understand the tensions and dynamics that led to a riot during a sixteenth-century European winter carnival. Generally speaking, social historians attempt to recapture the history of everyday life of the past that has been overlooked in historical studies that have focused on the ruling classes or the aristocratic levels of society. Often, these scholars, like Ladurie, find the most interesting data in the examination of ritual, festival, and celebration. Natalie Zemon Davis has studied the charivari custom, a kind of boisterous and aggressive mocking of couples whose relationship is somehow anomalous (for instance, a childless couple, a cuckolded husband, an older woman married to a younger man, and so forth) by members of the community who are often masked, or costumed. Her book *Society and Culture in Early Modern France* (Stanford: Stanford University Press, 1975) is a classic in the genre. J. M. Golby and A. W. Purdue have written an excellent treatment of a holiday, *The Making of the Modern Christmas* (Athens: University of Georgia Press, 1986). Folklorist Susan G. Davis has also produced an excellent social history related to calendrical studies, *Parades and Power: Street Theater in Nineteenth-Century Philadelphia* (Philadelphia: Temple University Press, 1986). H. H. Scullard's *Festivals and Ceremonies of the Roman Republic* (Ithaca, N.Y.: Cornell University Press, 1981) is a more standard but still excellent history of this important material which is at the base of so many modern calendrical holidays. For the days of the week, see F. H. Colson, *The*

*Week* (Cambridge: Cambridge Universiy Press, 1926); Udo Strutynski, "Germanic Divinities in Weekday Names," *Journal of Indo-European Studies* 3 (1975); and Eviatar Zerubavel, *The Seven-Day Circle* (Chicago: University of Chicago Press, 1985). A good study of Jewish traditions is Hayyim Schauss's *The Jewish Festivals: History and Observance* (1938; New York: Schocken Books, 1962). See also Arlene Rossen Cardazzo's personal testament, *Jewish Family Celebrations: The Sabbath, Festivals and Ceremonies* (New York: St. Martin's Press, 1982).

James H. Barnett's *American Christmas: A Study in the National Culture* (New York: Macmillan, 1954) has some history, a lot of interpretation, and a fairly good survey of Christmas popular culture. Another important study is *Ritual in Family Living* by James H. S. Bossard and Eleanor S. Boll (Philadelphia: University of Pennsylvania Press, 1950). Like these others, George R. Stewart's *American Ways of Life* (Garden City, N.Y.: Doubleday, 1954) is somewhat dated but still contains much useful and important information. W. Lloyd Warner's *The Living and the Dead: A Study of the Symbolic Life of Americans* (New Haven: Yale University Press, 1959) is an excellent study of holidays and celebrations in modern life. Robert Bellah's "Civil Religion in America" appeared in *Daedalus* 96 (1967).

There are countless books on Christmas and to a lesser extent the other holidays, ethnic festivals, and political celebrations of the United States and the rest of the world. These include children's books, travelogues, and recipe books, along with the more scholarly treatments. Many of them are important or at least of some interest, but it is impossible to list them all here. I have tried to indicate those works that most influenced me theoretically and methodologically, as well as those works I turned to for information. I hope that *All Around the Year* will inspire its readers not only to celebrate joyfully, but also to seek out some of these other works. The more one knows about the holidays, the more enjoyable they become.

Other materials in *All Around the Year* were gathered from interviews conducted by the author, and archival research conducted at the Northeast Archives, University of Maine at Orono; the Center for Archival Collections, Bowling Green State University; the Popular Culture Library, Bowling Green State University; the American Antiquarian Association, Worcester, Massachusetts; the Hayes Presidential Library, Fremont, Ohio; and the Bentley Library, University of Michigan, Ann Arbor.

# References Cited

Abrahams, Roger. 1982. "The Language of Festivals: Celebrating the Economy." *Celebration: Studies in Festivity and Ritual.* Edited by Victor Turner. Washington: Smithsonian Institution Press. 161–77.

———. 1987. "An American Vocabulary of Celebrations." *Time Out of Time: Essays on the Festival.* Edited by Alessandro Falassi. Albuquerque: University of New Mexico Press. 173–83.

Arthur, Mildred. 1971. *Holidays of Legend.* Irvington-on-Hudson, New York: Harvey House, Inc.

Baker, Holly Cutting, Amy Kotkin, and Steven Zeitlin. 1982. *A Celebration of American Family Folklore.* New York: Pantheon.

Bellah, Robert. 1967. "Civil Religion in America." *Daedalus* 96: 1–21.

Best, Joel, and Gerald T. Horiuchi. 1985. "The Razor Blade in the Apple: The Social Construction of Urban Legends." *Social Problems* 32: 488–99.

Brewer, Ebenezer Cobhan. 1970. *Dictionary of Phrase and Fable.* Centennial edition. Revised by Ivor H. Evans. London: Sasswell.

Briggs, Katherine. 1967. *The Fairies in Tradition and Literature.* London: Routledge and Kegan Paul.

Burke, Peter. 1978. *Popular Culture in Early Modern Europe.* London: Temple Smith.

Carmichael, Elizabeth, and Chloe Sayer. 1991. *The Skeleton at the Feast: The Day of the Dead in Mexico.* London: British Museum Press.

Cerry, Conrad. 1969. "Two American Sacred Ceremonies: Their Implication for the Study of Religion in America." *American Quarterly* 21: 739–54.

Chambers, Robert. 1906 (1860). *The Book of Days.* London: W. & R. Chambers Ltd.

Chase, Ernest Dudley. 1971 (1926). *The Romance of Greeting Cards.* Detroit: Tower Books.

Coffin, Tristram P. 1973. *The Book of Christmas Folklore.* New York: Seabury Press.

———, and Henig Cohen. 1975. *Folklore from the Working Folk of America.* Garden City, N.Y.: Doubleday.

Colson, F. H. 1926. *The Week.* Cambridge: Cambridge University Press.

Count, Earl W. 1953. *4000 Years of Christmas*. New York: Ridert and Company.

Cross, Tom Peete, and Clark Harris Slover. 1936. *Ancient Irish Tales*. New York: Henry Holt.

Danaher, Kevin. 1972. *The Year in Ireland*. Cork: Mercier Press.

Davis, Susan. 1986. *Parades and Power: Street Theater in Nineteenth-Century Philadelphia*. Philadelphia: Temple University Press.

Dawson, Chris. 1987. "Thanksgiving Dinner Is a Real Turkey." *Friday Magazine: The BG News* 4 Dec.: 10–11.

Douglas, Mary. 1975. "Deciphering a Meal." *Implicit Meanings: Essays in Anthropology*. Edited by Mary Douglas. London: Routledge and Kegan Paul. 249–75.

Ellis, Bill. 1989. "Death by Folklore: Ostention, Contemporary Legend, and Murder." *Western Folklore* 48: 201–220.

Eliade, Mircea. 1954. *The Sacred and the Profane*. New York: Harper Torchbooks.

Feeley-Harnik, Gillian. 1981. *The Lord's Table: Eucharist and Passover in Early Christianity*. Philadelphia: University of Pennsylvania Press.

Fredman, Ruth. 1981. *The Passover Seder: Afrikomen in Exile*. Philadelphia: University of Pennsylvania Press.

Gailey, Alan. 1977. "The Bonfire in North Irish Tradition." *Folklore* 88: 3–38.

Geertz, Clifford. 1971. "Deep Play: Notes on the Balinese Cockfight." *Myth, Symbol, and Culture*. Edited by Clifford Geertz. New York: W. W. Norton. 412–53.

Glassie, Henry. 1975. *All Silver and No Brass: An Irish Christmas Mumming*. Bloomington: Indiana University Press.

Grider, Sylvia. 1984. "The Razor Blades in the Apples Syndrome." *Perspectives on Contemporary Legend: Proceedings of the Conference on Contemporary Legend*. Edited by Paul Smith. Sheffield, U.K.: CECTAL. 129–40.

Hazlitt, W. Carew. 1965 (1870). *The Popular Antiquities of Great Britain*. New York: Benjamin Blom.

Hobsbawm, Erik, and Terrence Ranger. 1983. *The Invention of Tradition*. Cambridge: Cambridge University Press.

Jones, C. W. 1978. *St. Nicholas of Myra, Bari, and Manhattan*. Chicago: University of Chicago Press.

Kinser, Samuel. 1990. *Carnival American Style: Mardi Gras at New Orleans and Mobile*. Chicago: University of Chicago Press.

Krythe, Maymie R. 1962. *All About American Holidays*. New York: Harper and Row.

Ladurie, Emmanual Le Roy. 1979. *Carnival in Romans*. Translated by Mary Feeney. New York: George Braziller.

Lamb, Charles. 1924 (1823). "Valentine's Day." *Essays of Elia*. Edited by Thomas Hutchinson. London: Oxford University Press. 540–43.

Lamkin, Thelma Lynn. 1953. "Decoration Day in Spring Hill, Kentucky." *Midwest Folklore* 3: 157–60.

Lévi-Strauss, Claude. 1969. *The Raw and the Cooked*. New York: Harper and Row.

Linton, Ralph, and Adele Linton. 1949. *We Gather Together: The Story of Thanksgiving*. New York: Henry Schuman.

Lockwood, Yvonne Hiipaacka. 1987. "Immigrant to Ethnic: Symbols of Identity Among Finnish-Americans." *Folklife Annual.* Edited by James Hardin. Washington, D.C.: American Folklife Center. 92–107.

McAloon, John. 1984. *Rite, Drama, Festival, and Spectacle: Rehearsals Toward a Theory of Cultural Performance.* Philadelphia: Institute for the Study of Human Issues.

Moore, Willard. 1986. "Ritual and Remembrance in Minnesota Folk Celebrations." *Humanities Education* 3: 43–52.

Myerhoff, Barbara. 1978. *Number Our Days.* New York: Simon and Schuster.

———. 1982. "Rites of Passage: Process and Paradox." *Celebration: Studies in Festivity and Ritual.* Edited by Victor Turner. Washington: Smithsonian Institution Press. 109–35.

Newall, Venetia. 1971. *An Egg at Easter: A Folklore Study.* London: Routledge and Kegan Paul.

Parris, D. Elliott. 1980. "Caribbean Contributions to the U.S.A. Community." *1980 Festival of American Folklife Program Book.* Edited by Jack Santino. Washington, D.C.: Smithsonian Institution. 12–13.

Parsons, Gerard E. 1981. "Yellow Ribbons: Ties with Tradition." *Folklife Center News* 4, no. 2: 1, 9–12.

———. 1991. "How the Yellow Ribbon Became a National Folk Symbol." *Folklife Center News* 13, no. 3: 9–11.

Real, Michael. 1977. *Mass-Mediated Culture.* Englewood Cliffs, N.J.: Prentice-Hall.

Reidy, Chris. 1992. "A Celebration of Heritage." *Boston Globe* 26 Dec.: 27.

Russ, Jennifer. 1982. *German Festivals and Customs.* London: Oswald Wolff.

Russell, Jeffrey Burton. 1972. *Witchcraft in the Middle Ages.* Ithaca: Cornell University Press.

Sala, George Augustus. 1984 (1892). "A New Orleans Perspective: Mardi Gras as it Was." *Travel-Holiday* 161 (Feb.): 70–72.

Santino, Jack. 1986. "The Folk *Assemblage* of Autumn: Tradition and Creativity in Halloween Folk Art." *Folk Art and Art Worlds.* Edited by John Michael Vlach and Simon J. Bronner. Ann Arbor: UMI Research Press. 151–69.

———. 1989. *Miles of Smiles, Years of Struggle: Stories of Black Pullman Porters.* Urbana: University of Illinois Press.

———. 1992. "Yellow Ribbons and Seasonal Flags: The Folk *Assemblage* of War." *Journal of American Folklore* 105, no. 415: 19–33.

Seidenspinner, Clarence. 1952. *The Great Protestant Festivals.* New York: Henry Schuman.

Snyder, Philip V. 1983. *The Christmas Tree Book.* New York: Penguin.

Staff, Frank. 1969. *The Valentine and its Origins.* New York: Praeger.

Stewart, George R. 1954. *American Ways of Life.* Garden City, N.Y.: Doubleday.

Strutynski, Udo. 1975. "Germanic Divinities in Weekday Names." *Journal of Indo-European Studies* 3:363–84.

Stubbes, Philip. 1882 (1583). *Anatomie of Abuses.* London: Trubner.

Taeuber, Conrad. 1933. "Fastnacht in the Black Forest." *Journal of American Folklore* 46: 69–76.

Tooker, Elisabeth. 1979. *Native North American Spirituality of the Eastern Wood-lands.* New York: Paulist Press.

Turner, Kay. 1982. "Mexican American Home Altars: Towards Their Interpretation." *Aztlan: International Journal of Chicano Studies Research* 13: 309–26.

Turner, Victor. 1967. *The Forest of Symbols: Aspects of Ndembu Ritual.* Ithaca, N.Y.: Cornell University Press.

Van Gennep, Arnold. 1960 (1906). *The Rites of Passage.* Chicago: University of Chicago Press.

Walens, Stanley. 1982. "My Name Is Like a Mountain of Blankets." *Celebrations: Studies in Festivity and Ritual.* Edited by Victor Turner. Washington, D.C.: Smithsonian Institution Press. 178–89.

Warner, W. Lloyd. 1959. *The Living and the Dead: A Study of the Symbolic Life of Americans.* New Haven: Yale University Press.

Weisner, Francis X. 1952. *The Christmas Book.* New York: Harcourt, Brace and Company.

Wentz, Evan. 1973 (1911). *The Fairy Faith in Celtic Countries.* New York: Lemma.

Wiggins, William. 1982. "They Closed the Town Up, Man! Reflections of the Civic and Political Dimensions of Juneteenth." *Celebrations: Studies in Festivity and Ritual.* Edited by Victor Turner. Washington, D.C.: Smithsonian Institution Press. 284–95.

———. 1987. *O Freedom! Afro-American Emancipation Celebrations.* Knoxville: Univeristy of Tennessee Press.

Williams, Katherine. 1980. "Costuming: Latin American and Caribbean Urban Carnivals." *1980 Festival of American Folklife Program Book.* Edited by Jack Santino. Washington, D.C.: Smithsonian Institution. 9–11.

Yoder, Don. 1990 (1958). "The Harvest Home." *Discovering American Folklife.* Edited by Don Yoder. Ann Arbor: UMI Research Press. 227–45.

Zerubavel, Eviatar. 1985. *The Seven-Day Circle.* Chicago: University of Chicago Press.

# Index

JACK SANTINO is a professor of folklore and popular culture in the Department of Popular Culture at Bowling Green State University in Ohio. He holds the Ph.D. in folklore and folklife from the University of Pennsylvania and has been a folklife specialist at the Smithsonian Institution. He has published articles in scholarly journals and magazines on many aspects of occupational folklore, and on ritual, festival, and celebration, especially Halloween. His book *Miles of Smiles, Years of Struggle: Stories of Black Pullman Porters* was published by the University of Illinois Press. He is co-director of an ethnographic documentary film of the same name, which won four Emmy awards among other prizes. He has edited a collection of essays entitled *Halloween and Other Festivals of Death and Life* for the University of Tennessee Press. He was a Fulbright Research Fellow in Northern Ireland in 1991–92, and he was also awarded a British Council Research Attachment to the Ulster Folk and Transport Museum, where he researched Halloween traditions and the public uses of symbols.

UNIVERSITY OF ILLINOIS PRESS
1325 SOUTH OAK STREET
CHAMPAIGN, ILLINOIS 61820-6903
WWW.PRESS.UILLINOIS.EDU